Racing Research, Researching Race

Racing Research, Researching Race

Methodological Dilemmas in Critical Race Studies

EDITED BY

France Winddance Twine

AND

Jonathan W. Warren

New York University Press

NEW YORK AND LONDON

NEW YORK UNIVERSITY PRESS
New York and London

Library of Congress Cataloging-in-Publication Data
Racing research, researching race : methodological dilemmas in
critical race studies / edited by France Winddance Twine and
Jonathan W. Warren.
        p.   cm.
Includes bibliographical references and index.
ISBN 0-8147-8242-6 (pbk. : acid-free paper) —
ISBN 0-8147-8241-8 (cloth : acid-free paper)
1. Race—Research—Methodology. 2. Sociology—Research—
Methodology. 3. Race awareness. 4. Racism. 5. United States—
Race relations.   I. Twine, France Winddance, 1960–
II. Warren, Jonathan W.
HT1506 .R33 2000
305.8'007'2073—dc21   00-008317

For Kristin Luker

and

*In Memory of Joe Wood, Jr., who
disappeared on Mount Rainier on July 8, 1999*

Contents

Acknowledgments

We thank the contributors to this volume for patiently working with us during the past years. We are very grateful to our editor, Niko Pfund, whose enthusiasm, encouragement, and belief in this project brought it to completion. During the editorial process, Despina Papazoglou Gimbel handled this manuscript with skill and grace. We have been sustained intellectually, politically, and emotionally by friends and colleagues, old and new: Richard Appelbaum, Ingrid Banks, Tani Barlow, Vilna Bashi, Howard S. Becker, Carla Simone Barbosa de Brito, KumKum Bhavnani, William T. Bielby, Denise Bielby, Kathleen Blee, Philippe Bourgois, Karen Brodkin, Jacqueline Nassy Brown, Dave Carlson, Héctor Carrilla, Donald Martin Carter, Nelista Cuffy, William Darity, Jr., Angela Y. Davis, Mitchell Duneier, Troy Duster, Steve Epstein, Richard Flacks, John Foran, Ruth Frankenberg, Maria Franklin, Charles Gallagher, Pam Goldman, Lauren E. Goodlad, Avery Gordon, Antonio Sérgio Alfredo Guimarães, Phil Gorsky, Gail Hanlon, Michael Hanchard, Hella Heydorn, Arnell Hinkle, Judith Howard, Naheed Islam, Lucy Jarosz, Alan Jenkins, Lorraine Delia Kenny, Ellen Lewin, Donald Lowe, Kristin Luker, Jelani Mahiri, Irma McClaurin, Deirdre McDonald, Heather Merrill-Carter, Kenneth Mostern, Ruth Mostern, Pedro Antonio Noguera, Jodi O'Brien, Constance Penley, Sabrina Ramet, Darrel Robinson, Beth Schneider, Carolyn Martin Shaw, Nikhil Pal Singh, Stephen Small, Matthew Sparke, Becky Thompson, Mamie Lois Twine, Vron Ware, Alys Weinbaum, Brackette F. Williams, Ara Wilson, Howard Winant, John Wolfe, Joe Wood, Raihan Zamil, and Abebe Zegeye.

We are deeply appreciative of two extraordinary institutions—the University of Washington, Seattle, and the University of California, Santa Barbara—both of which provided numerous forms of institutional support that enabled this project to be brought to completion.

The Jackson School of International Studies at the University of Washington, Seattle, and the Department of Sociology at the University of California, Santa Barbara, allowed one of us (Twine) to rearrange her teaching schedule so as to facilitate the completion of this book. Our colleagues at these institutions provided inspiration, encouragement, and other forms of support. In Seattle we are especially grateful for the support of Jere Bacharach, Joel Migdal, Resat Kasaba, Victoria Lawson, and Cynthia Steele. In Santa Barbara we received emotional, administrative, and moral support from Chris Allen, Richard Appelbaum, William T. Bielby, Ed Donnerstein, Avery Gordon, Claudine Michel, John Mohr, Harvey Molotch, Constance Penley, Cedric Robinson, Elizabeth Robinson, Beth Schneider, and Nancy Willstatter.

Grateful acknowledgment is made to Cambridge University Press for permission to reprint a revised version of Philippe Bourgois, "Violating Apartheid in the United States," from *In Search of Respect: Selling Crack in El Barrio*. Copyright 1995 © by Cambridge University Press. It appears as chapter 8 of this book.

France Winddance Twine
and Jonathan W. Warren
Seattle, Washington
June 1999

Foreword

Troy Duster

On the campus of the University of California, Santa Barbara, a predominantly white campus, a student raised his hand in class and asked: "Why is it that when eight white students are having lunch at the cafeteria, we see this as just eight students having lunch—but when eight black students have lunch, it is called a balkanized racial enclave?" Part of the answer lies in the context, in the numbers and the demography. At a predominantly white campus, blacks "stand out." But that is only part of the answer.

"Why are black students having lunch together" has now become a research question. Beverly Tatum's (1997) *Why Are All the Black Kids Sitting Together in the Cafeteria?*[1] addresses "a concern" that does not even surface for serious inquiry for whites. The reason cannot be answered by reference to demography alone. Issues of stratification and political power intersect with demography and shape the very domain of inquiry that social scientists "normally" engage—or don't engage—inside their disciplinary borders. Indeed, in addition to the question of how do we study race, this collection of essays also addresses a more fundamental question: Who has race? The study of race relations has historically been the study of people of color. As several contributors to this volume note, for research purposes, whites do not "have race."

For many years, several of my white colleagues in sociology have complained to me about what they have seen as the unfortunate tendency for Black, Latino, Asian-American and Native American students to do what is characterized as "mere autobiographical sociology." They are referring to the fact that many students of Asian ancestry want to study problems of Asian-Americans, or that African-American students tend to study

African-American issues, or that Latino students wanted to study Latino American concerns. One of these colleagues pronounced with some passion that he would never want to study "his own group" because he was afraid of the implicit bias. What is remarkable is that his white students were routinely studying the lives of white Americans with no consciousness, no reflexivity, and little awareness that race was a feature of their studies as well.[2]

This collection is all about bringing to the surface, for examination and review and analysis, what it means to be conscious of "race" when one is doing research. There are those who argue that just to acknowledge race is to perpetuate the biological myth of race. But this is to confuse the biological with the social.

Analytically, there are two quite distinct issues in the study of race. One is a methodological matter: who has *access* to what scene, and with what outcome? But in addition to the question of access, there is the less frequently examined question of the very building blocks of knowledge construction, namely, *whose questions get raised* for investigation?

Let us examine this matter more closely, for it will lead us to an insight about the study of race. The basic point that my colleague was making was about "objectivity" and distance and comparative perspective. He said that he would "never study his own group" because he would be too committed to the outcome. But, what is his own group? He certainly studied the behavior of whites in America. But, like the Santa Barbara lunch group, he and his students "are just having lunch." He is not studying what he and others would call their "whiteness" precisely because whiteness is typically an unmarked category. Thus, he could circumnavigate the epistemological question of "how do we know he was not studying 'white behavior'" by the methodological legerdemain of not raising that question in the first place.

Issues of access are sometimes arbitrarily distinguished from matters of content. In the empirical world of social research, that distinction can fade. Some things they just don't tell you in that graduate methods course. One of them is the synergistic feature of race in the single interview versus the group interview. For several years, I was the principal investigator of a research project investigating how people in families with genetic diseases deal with those problems in their daily lives. The two most common inherited, potentially lethal, single-gene disorders in the United States are sickle-cell disease and cystic fibrosis. Cystic fibrosis occurs primarily among Americans of (North)

European descent, and sickle-cell disease occurs primarily among Americans of (West) African descent. This provided a somewhat unique opportunity to compare the variable penetration and meaning of genetic medicine in two populations differentiated by socially designated categories of race. The study combined fieldwork and observations in clinical settings, in support groups and in advocacy organizations serving individuals and families with sickle-cell disease and cystic fibrosis.

In the course of the research, we discovered that when our African-American interviewers made contact and interviewed African-Americans with sickle-cell disease or with family members who were carriers of the sickle-cell gene, we routinely were better able to penetrate into the various layers of both the immediate and extended families. This in turn provided increased access to a wider range of discussions about social and political issues than occurred with white interviewers. That is not a particularly surprising finding. However, we also conducted group interviews, mainly of members of different families. These group members had in common the diagnosis of the genetic disorder somewhere in their families. It was in these settings that we came across a truth about "research on matters racial" that is not taught in graduate methods courses.

It was in these group settings that we discovered the powerful salience of race, and the synergistic feature of discussions about a race-related topic. Some of the most important "concerns and issues" never surfaced for exploration with white interviewers, because the group being interviewed never headed down the road to frame the question in such a manner in the first place. I refer here to what whites would more likely see as "paranoid tendencies" on the part of African-Americans regarding the medical profession and the government interest in the health of blacks. In each of the four groups in which there was an all-black membership, these "paranoid tendencies" surfaced and then escalated into a steep spiral as the "call and response" features of commentary and exchange occurred. For example, it was not uncommon for blacks to cite the fact that Puerto Rican woman were first "practiced on" with the birth control pill for several years before the pill was distributed in this country to white women. Notions of governmental conspiracy to do research on black people and for biotechnology firms to try to make money by "practicing" on blacks not only surfaced in the black groups, but spiraled upwards into a cascade of larger and larger sets of imagery about "the government" and its role in health research relevant to blacks in America.

The thing that is most striking about this research is that this pattern occurred in all the all-black groups but never occurred when there was a white interviewer. Moreover, the phenomenon only barely surfaced when there was a black interviewer in a one-on-one interview. It did occur in the group setting. And while focus group research acknowledges the special role of "the group process" in mining certain truths that do not come out in individual interviews, race as a concept is not taught as having this special synergistic feature in getting at a collective version of reality.

The contributors to this volume are engaged in a process of collective redress of the imbalance of research on race—counterbalancing by increasing our consciousness of "ordinary" research in which race is embedded because it is unexamined, and unexamined because it is embedded. We are reminded that the goal is not to achieve symmetry—research on white lunch tables is hardly the point—but how and why we come to see certain social and political concerns as racialized.

NOTES

1. Published by Basic Books, New York.

2. The clearest example of this came when a student whose ancestry could be traced to the Indian subcontinent came up with a research project to study a community in India. My colleague expressed dismay and concern, and dismissed this as just one more example of "autobiographical sociology." But India has more than 930 million people—more than triple the size of the United States.

Chapter 1

Racial Ideologies and Racial Methodologies

France Winddance Twine

> Methodology is too important to be left to methodolo-
> gists.
>
> —Howard Becker

> Race was always salient and part of the dynamic in my
> interviews, because of and in spite of the subject mat-
> ter of the study.
>
> —Sylvia Tamale

> My success as an ethnographer necessitated a contin-
> ual negotiation of role expectations based on my light
> pigmentation, my femaleness, my middle-class status,
> and my American citizenship.
>
> —Faye Harrison

In January 1992 I went to a small town in the interior of the state of Rio de Janeiro to conduct field research on race and racism. In planning for this trip, I had consulted with graduate student colleagues and scholars who specialized in Brazilian Studies. In giving advice, no one had suggested that racism might be a factor in field research.[1] In fact, some had even suggested that race, or at least my phenotype, would be an advantage. In my field research, I still vividly remember one graduate student's encouraging words: "They will love you in Brazil because you'll be a *mulatta* there."

Despite these silences and "assurances" I did not go to Brazil expecting to find a racial paradise. Having informed myself of the experiences of other U.S. black anthropologists working in Latin America and the Caribbean I thought I was prepared for the multiple ways that my body might be coded as a light-skinned black American (Bolles 1985; Whitehead 1986; Harrison 1991; Gilliam 1970). However, what I had not anticipated was the suspicion, distrust, and racism to which I would be subjected by Brazilians of African ancestry. I had assumed that white Brazilians would exhibit some antiblack racism, but I was not prepared for the degree to which Brazilians of color would share their worldview. For instance, the following sentiments expressed by Henrique, a forty-three-year-old self-identified *negro,* were typical of those of other dark-skinned Brazilians interviewed. "Blacks marry whites because whites have good hair. [Whites] have good hair, their nose is not ugly [like ours]. Blacks normally have very large lips, like an animal's and people think this is ugly. I am trying to say that black people know that [their features] are ugly and white people also know that blacks are ugly" (Twine 1998: 91).

Negotiating a symbolic terrain in which my body was so disagreeable was difficult and emotionally challenging. And even more disquieting was confronting the fact that some of the Afro-Brazilians I knew assumed that I shared their valorization of whiteness simply because my partner, Jonathan Warren, who accompanied me to the field, was white. Without expressing any concern about the appearance of children I might have in the future, I was repeatedly told by Brazilian friends of color: "Don't worry, your children won't look like you. They will be whiter and have straighter hair and *olhos azuis* (blue eyes)."[2] Thus they projected on to me their desires of *embranquecimento* (whitening).

In retrospect I realize that even though I did not go to Brazil expecting to be a racial "insider" with Brazilians of salient African ancestry, I did assume that we would share some political and ideological affinities, given a similar history of slavery and white supremacy. In particular I erroneously took it for granted that we would have some shared critiques of antiblack racism. Consequently I did not anticipate their denial of their familial connections to African slavery. I was further surprised by the erasure slave ancestors of African descent in the family memories of people only two or three generations removed from slavery.[3] I was shocked when Brazilians of color accused me of being a racist simply for asking questions about racial disparities. I had expected to be treated as a professional researcher and was not prepared for the assumption by Brazilians of color that I was a maid, the illegitimate sister of my white partner, or his whore.

In the midst of negotiating this very unfamiliar and disorienting racial terrain, I decided to consult the *South American Handbook* (1991) in preparation for a trip to northeastern Brazil. Given the routine racism I had already encountered in Brazil, I wondered if this issue would be addressed. It wasn't. While the guidebook provided special suggestions for women and dealt with some of the problems of gender inequality and possible sexual harassment, neither race nor racism were mentioned as issues that could affect travelers of color. This was surprising, given the handbook's claim to being the "complete guide to South America." In view of the intensity of the everyday racism I had been negotiating I wrote a letter to the editor suggesting that they attempt to deal with this issue since they had demonstrated some sensitivity to the way gender could affect the travel experience. In my letter I expressed my concerns as a brown-skinned traveler of color:

> Your handbook lacks any specific hints for the brown traveler who may encounter racism and color prejudice in Brazil. This gap in your introduction results in an implicit assumption that foreign travelers are European or of European descent and thus physically distinct from much of the native South American population in countries such as Brazil. Although I found some benefits to being able to "blend" in with the native population [such as not being robbed since it was assumed that nonwhites don't have as much money as white tourists], I also found that I was subjected to qualitatively different treatment and to racism as compared to my white American partner. I believe that your section entitled "Introduction and Hints" could be expanded and thus made even more useful to the nonwhite traveler, if you included a section on racism and color prejudice. As a cultural anthropologist and traveler, I strongly encourage you to consider adding this section since there are tourists and business people from North America, Asia, and Africa who may be unexpectedly confronted with racism and prejudice if they leave the beaten track.

On January 11, 1994, Mr. Box responded to my letter. His letter reflected a general reluctance to include racism as a subsection in the

"Helpful Hints" section. He claimed that he had no knowledge about racism in South America since he had received no previous letters documenting this phenomenon. He asked for the names of individuals and organizations who could provide him with information about it. Finally, he informed me that they had no intention of renaming the handbook a "guide for white travelers," as I had suggested.

In thinking about the handbook's assumptions of a white traveler and its failure to even briefly acknowledge that race could be an issue, I began to reflect on my training in research methods as a graduate student. The anthropology department at the Berkeley campus of the University of California offered no graduate courses in qualitative research methods,[4] which is evidently typical of anthropology departments in the United States. As Akhil Gupta and James Ferguson have commented,

> It is astonishing but true, that most leading departments of anthropology in the United States provide no formal (and very little informal) training in fieldwork methods—as few as 20 percent of departments, according to one survey. It is also true that most anthropological training programs provide little guidance in, and almost no critical reflection on, the selection of fieldwork sites and the considerations that deem some places but not others as suitable for the role of "the field." (1997: 2)

Thus I turned to the sociology department, which fortunately offered some qualitative methods courses. Though I learned a number of invaluable lessons in these courses, race—let alone the particular racialized dilemmas that I encountered in Brazil—was not addressed.

Eventually I began to recognize that the absence of reflection on race in graduate seminars parallels much of the conventional qualitative methods literature. That is, my graduate course work was neither an aberration nor reflective of the idiosyncrasies of my professor. Rather, it mirrored the general state of thinking about the intersections of race and ethnographic research in U.S. universities. For example, after editing one of the four major journals devoted to qualitative methods, *Journal of Contemporary Ethnography,* for eight years, Patricia Adler and Peter Adler analyzed every submission to the journal. Their stated aim was to provide "a picture of the people who are doing ethnographic work, the kind of work they are doing and what this portends for the next generation of ethnographers and beyond" (1995: 4). In their "demography of ethnography" the Adlers found that between September 1986 and February 1994 only 5 percent of the submissions addressed race and ethnicity. Of those that were accepted for publication, none dealt with how racial ideologies and positions affected research methods. And of the meta-methodological texts published during this period, I was unable to locate any that addressed racial dilemmas.

Contemporary Ethnography is unfortunately not alone in its relative lack of attention to race matters. In Denzin and Lincoln's *Handbook of Qualitative Methods,* a very useful and comprehensive guide to theoretical debates in qualitative research, only two of the thirty-six articles address race or racism explicitly (Denzin and Lincoln 1994). And despite the occasional edited volume devoted to the dimensions of race and ethnicity (Harrison 1991; Stanfield and Dennis 1993), the current volume is the first to focus specifically on the dilemmas generated for antiracist researchers working in a range of disciplines conducting field research and participant observation. After decades of self-reflexivity among ethnographers analyzing the practices of writing and conducting field research, the lack of sustained attention to racialized dilemmas is particularly noteworthy, considering the degree to which other axes of power have been theorized.[5]

In summary, then, the *South American Handbook*'s failure to acknowledge the complex ways in which racial and color hierarchies mediate social interactions (and economic transactions) parallels much of the conventional research methods literature on field research. My research experiences, combined with the relative absence of empirically grounded theoretical discussions of the particular dilemmas I encountered as a U.S. black ethnographer, motivated me to commission this volume on race and research methods.[6] In conceptualizing *Racing Research* I hope that field researchers and ethnographers, even those whose research is not specifically concerned with racial disparities, will consider the significance of race as a methodological issue. My primary objective in conceiving *Racing Research* is to initiate a serious discussion of the potential ethical, emotional, analytical, and methodological dilemmas generated by racial subjectivities, racial ideologies, and racial disparities.

Racial Insiders and Racial Matching

In sociology it has long been recognized that the race of the interviewer may affect the respondents in survey research. For example, in a 1942 study of a thousand blacks in Memphis, Tennessee, Herbert Hyman (1954) reported that the race of the interviewer had dramatic affects on the responses of the interviewees.

> Twenty-one of the twenty-four questions had reliable differences by race of interviewer; the differences were often large, in five cases more than 20 percentage points. Even more impressive than their magnitudes was the innocuous character of several questions show-ing such effects. For example, differences occurred in the self-report-ing of education and of car ownership—both underreported to white interviewers. The direction of *all* the results was such as to present a relatively passive view of Negro aspirations and discontents to the eyes of white interviewers. (Hyman, quoted in Schuman and Con-verse 1971: 47)

It was not, however, until the charged political context of the 1960s, generated in large measure by post–World War II decolonization and antiracist movements, that findings like those of Hyman crystallized into the methodological rule of thumb of "racial matching." Inspired by the civil rights and black liberation movements, both the racism and overwhelming whiteness of the social scientific community came under intense scrutiny by antiracists inside and outside the academy. In de-scribing their experiences as white researchers during the mid-1960s, Robert Blauner and David Wellman offer a glimpse into the charged political climate that social scientists suddenly had to negotiate in racial and ethnic minority communities:

> As our study progressed, we exhausted our original contacts, and it became more difficult to get interviews. Potential respondents would systematically stand us up. People raised questions about our mo-tives. Some refused to have anything to do with us. Others demanded that we offer something besides money in exchange for their time. We became painfully aware that social researchers were not welcome in Black and brown communities. Many people resented the fact that the University of California had only recently begun active recruit-

ment of Third World students. They complained that they, like every-one else, were paying taxes for the university, yet were virtually de-nied access to its facilities.

Many Blacks saw themselves in a life-and-death struggle with white America. They believed sociologists had taken sides with the enemy and were therefore to be avoided at all costs. There was strong resentment toward the labels which social scientists have at-tached to racial minorities. People resented being tagged "culturally deprived," "disadvantage," with "matrifocal families." And our re-spondents knew that this has been primarily the work of sociologists. One thing "Black Power" seemed to mean was freedom to define oneself without interference by sociologists or any other outside group. (Blauner and Wellman 1998 [1973]: 321–22)

Individuals committed to decolonizing and democratizing higher ed-ucation pointed to these organic criticisms of the academy and devel-oped them into a general critique of cross-racial interviewing and field-work. The position of these scholars, most of them black, was that "1) whites are basically incapable of grasping black realities, 2) because of the very nature of their experiences, blacks and whites will approach the subject of race with very different foci of interest" (Wilson 1974: 324). Furthermore, in the words of Penny Rhodes, a white researcher, "black people's mistrust of white people in general will . . . be extended to the white researcher or interviewer, preventing access or, if access is obtained, distorting the quality of communication which ensues" (Rhodes 1994: 548). The overall message, then, was that "minority group scholars" were the best qualified to conduct research in minority communities (Zinn 1979: 210). Or in the words of Blauner and Well-man, "the white sociologist might well eschew focusing on Black and other Third World communities" (1998: 329).

As a methodological ideal "racial matching" was formulated in part in recognition of the everyday realities of black Americans in the United States who had a "distrust of the research enterprise," especially when carried out by racial outsiders (Zinn 1979: 211). But its emergence needs to be appreciated as more than simply a recognition of an empirical real-ity in which "outsider status can prohibit some sociologists from con-ducting field research in some minority communities" (1979: 211). It was also invoked as part of a racial justice movement to racially diversify the academy. In other words, "racial matching" was seized upon by those less concerned with whether white people could study nonwhites than with democratizing the social scientific community by opening it up to scholars of color. Thus, for instance, Blauner and Wellman's primary agenda is not with "improving research methodologies" but with generating a "legitimate methodological need" for justifying the integration of racial and ethnic minorities into the social scientific community:

> Social scientists realize the need for a series of deep and solid ethnographies of Black and Third World communities, and for more penetrating analyses of the cultural dynamics, political movements and other contemporary realities of the oppressed racial groups. Today the best contribution that white scholars could make toward this end is not firsthand research but the facilitation of such studies by people of color. We must open up the graduate schools in every discipline to Black, Chicano, Puerto Rican and other minority people, particularly those with strong ties and loyalties to their ethnic communities. (1998: 329)

Given this political context, the original skeptics of racial matching—such as Robert Merton (1972) who called for both insider and outsider research in communities of color—were construed by some as political reactionaries. The fear appears to have been motivated by a concern that these critiques might undermine the momentum of efforts to racially diversify the academy by removing some of the justification for these efforts. Ironically, in the current political climate of anti-affirmative action in which American Indians, blacks, Chicanos, and Latinos remain underrepresented in proportion to their numbers among social scientists and thus face the challenge of reproducing the next generation of scholars of color, it is antiracist scholars who have begun to reevaluate the wisdom of racial matching, which continues to inform much of the methodological common sense within sociology. As the British sociologist Penny J. Rhodes notes, "closeness of identity and, in particular, shared racial identity is generally presumed to promote effective communication between researcher and subject and, conversely, disparate identity to inhibit it" (1994: 550). In addition to being considered a better foundation for establishing rapport, racial matching is also widely believed to produce a more adept interviewer because, it is argued, "there are dimensions to black experience invisible to the white interviewer/investigator who possesses neither the language nor the cultural equipment either to elicit or understand the experience" (1994: 549).

One of the limitations of the racial matching model is that race is not the only relevant "social signifier." In the words of Rhodes, "The assumption that 'race' will dominate and will necessarily override other dimensions of differentiation or of affinity is not always warranted" (1994: 552). In the United States, where racial affiliation is such a salient basis for sociopolitical identity, "insiderness" is still constituted by other factors which may render race of secondary consequence. Thus, the meanings and impact of racial difference are complicated by age, class, accent, education, national origins, region, as well as sexuality. In a paper on insider research, John Aguilar analyzes the arguments on both sides of the issue. He argues that that "all sociocultural systems are complex. Many societies are fragmented by class, regional, urban-rural, and ideology related affiliative differences and all cultures are characterized by internal variation. . . . Despite this, the extreme arguments both for and against insider research rest on an implicit model that characterizes all researchers as either absolutely inside or outside homogeneous sociocultural style" (1981: 25).

Like urban anthropologists, sociologists have also critically examined the foundational assumptions of the "insider" perspective. For example, William Julius Wilson, a U.S. black sociologist, critiqued the arguments made by black sociologists for a "black" insider perspective (1974). Wilson argued that although "an individual scientist's unique experiences and orientations cannot be substituted for knowledge in the context of validation, they may play an important role in inventing and postulating hypotheses in the context of discovery."

> But there is no factual evidence to suggest that a sociologist has to be black to adequately describe and explain the experience of blacks. . . . Moreover, although the contrary is sometimes assumed, the black experience is not uniform. Despite the fact that all blacks may have been victimized by racist behavior, at one time or another, the black experience may nevertheless vary by social class, region of the country and age. Indeed some middle-class black sociologists may have experiences closer to that of middle-class white sociologists than to those of lower class blacks. (1974: 326)

Another criticism of racial insiderness is that researchers who belong to the same ethnic or racial groups as their interviewees evaluate respondents on the basis of conventional social criteria including prestige, white skin, high incomes, and education. Aída Hurtado, a Latina researcher, draws upon the interviewer evaluations of working-class Americans of Mexican descent who are bilingual in Spanish and English to challenge racial and color matching common sense. Hurtado reminds us that:

> Language alone is not what distinguishes the Mexican-descent population in this country. The population is a product of the racial commingling of native Mexican Indians, blacks and various European groups. This mixture has produced a range of phenotypes—fairskinned, European-looking individuals as well as dark-skinned, Indian-looking people. This study examined two aspects of the respondents' phenotype—skin color and facial features.
>
> The potential relationship between language and phenotype is especially important for national surveys in the United States. Even bilingual, ethnically matched interviewers may hold different performance expectations for respondents who speak a language other than English and do not look European. (1994: 80)

Thus, Hurtado observes that "whether the respondents speak English or Spanish and how Anglicized their facial features are "affect how the *interviewer* evaluates the respondent." That is, Latino interviewers evaluate Latino respondents on the basis of phenotype and status expectations (Hurtado 1994. Emphasis in original).

In this volume, Charles Gallagher discusses how he had initially assumed that his insider racial status as a "white" was sufficient to establish rapport with other whites. He had not considered how his social characteristics, such as being a university researcher, and his presumed ethnicity and class would affect his rapport with white respondents. In "White Like Me? Methods, Manipulation, and the Meaning of Whiteness," Charles Gallagher cautions white scholars to carefully examine the assumptions they bring to their research with other whites. Gallagher reminds us that "'Being white,' like being a member in any social group, has a host of contradictory, symbolic, and situationally specific meanings." He writes, "I saw myself, at least in retrospect, as unburdened by my color because whiteness was the focus of my study, because I am white, and because I would be interviewing other whites about the meaning they attach to their race." By providing an analysis of his racialized assumptions, Gallagher responds to earlier critiques of the "insider" perspective. Like Ruth Frankenberg (1993) and several contributors to this volume (see chapters by Blee, Kenny, and Warren in this volume) he nuances the practice of white-on-white qualitative research.

Josephine Beoku-Betts, a West African[7] conducting research in the United States, analyzes the contradictions for racial insiders conducting cross-national research. Beoku-Betts's research focused on U.S. black women in the Sea Islands of South Carolina and Georgia. While she claimed "insider status" on the basis of her African heritage, she notes that "my relationship as an insider was based on a process of negotiation rather than granted immediately on the basis of ascribed status" (1994: 417). Her social characteristics—such as a British accent, African origins, single marital status, and professional status as a university researcher—generated particular forms of social distance that she had to mediate despite her "racial insiderness."

> In my research I found that while I shared "insider status" with my research participants in ways similar to other black scholars conducting research in communities with which they had shared racial membership, that status was not enough to preclude other challenges I faced based on my nationality, gender, profession, and status as an unmarried woman. I also found my African identity both an advantage and a disadvantage in that it held a different meaning in different communities, on the basis of the extent of their knowledge and interest in Africa. (1994: 414)

Betty Lou Valentine, a U.S. black anthropologist, conducted research with her white partner, Charles Valentine, also an anthropologist, in a poor and predominantly black community in the northeastern United States three decades ago. As a university-educated black woman working as part of a married interracial research team, Betty Lou Valentine did not have automatic access to and rapport with other blacks in the community. However, she ultimately "succeeded well in spite of these barriers." In fact, eventually both of them became "insiders" by living under the same material conditions of poverty as their informants and participating in community activities, thus demonstrating their ethical allegiance to the community. Their analysis of how they mediated and negotiated the shift from "outsider" to "insider" status in a predominantly black urban community further complicates ideas of insiderness implicit in the racial matching model. For Betty Lou Valentine, her race did not grant her automatic insider status, nor did Charles Valentine's whiteness prove an insurmountable barrier to insiderness. While his race was obviously a disadvantage in terms of making inroads among residents who embraced black nationalist and separatist aims, his ethical position and vulnerabilities as a poor resident of this community enabled him to reposition himself as an insider despite his ascribed racial status.

Other critics of racial matching have noted that insiderness generates its own particular barriers. For example, insiders are expected to conform to cultural norms that can restrict them as researchers. Elisa Facio conducted research among Mexican-American/Chicana elderly women in northern California as a graduate student in sociology. In her analysis of the dilemmas she encountered, she describes how the traditional gender norms in the Mexican-American community restricted her access to men. As an insider in the Chicano community, Facio's "interactions were limited to the women . . . the age dynamic allowed for my greeting of men, but gender limited the types of conversations between us. On several occasions when I did attempt to 'challenge tradition,' the women expressed their disapproval" (1993: 85). In addition, she was expected to conform to a gendered division of labor and to engage in gender-prescribed activities.

Drawing from her research experiences while interviewing black foster care providers in London, Penny J. Rhodes, a white British researcher, identifies several advantages to being a racial outsider. Inspired by the code of racial pairing, Rhodes employed two Afro-Caribbean research associates from working-class backgrounds to help her conduct her interviews:

> But, even when discussing such sensitive subjects as racism, being white was not always the handicap expected. Many people were prepared to talk openly at length about their experiences and opinions and several confided that they would not have a similar discussion with another black person. People treated me to information which they would have assumed was the taken-for-granted knowledge of an insider. As one woman in her twenties explained: "I wouldn't have

had a talk like this with another black person. I can discuss these sorts of things more easily with you. With a black person, you would just take it for granted." In these discussions, I adopted the equivalent of a pupil role with the informant a teacher. People spoke to me as a representative of white people. . . . In these encounters [they] were speaking as a black person to a white person: the significance of skin color became paramount, but as a stimulant rather than a block to communication. . . . The following comment, for example, was from a woman in her sixties: "A white person wouldn't know a black person's ways or understand a black family properly because *you* have been brought up differently." (1994: 552. Emphasis in original)

Realizing that racial outsiderness may have its own advantages and that insiderness may simply create a different set of pluses and minuses, many have argued—echoing Robert Merton from the early seventies[8]— that it is optimal to have both racial insiders and outsiders conducting research because they reveal different—not better—kinds of knowledge. In his evaluation of the differences between being a racial insider or outsider in two different field sites—the Lahu Hill tribes of Northern Thailand, and his native community of blacks in Denver, Colorado—Delmos Jones, a U.S. black anthropologist, concludes that "the whole value of the insider researcher is not that his data or insights into the actual social situation are better—but that they are *different*. Most of the few black anthropologists operating in this country are looking for something new, questioning old assumptions about social processes, developing new ones, and exploding old myths, and in the process developing new ones" (1982: 478. Emphasis in original).

Ann Phoenix, a black British feminist researcher, has also critiqued commonsense notions of "colour" matching. She argues that "'race' and gender positions, and hence the power positions they entail, enter into the interview situation, but they do not do so in any unitary or essential way. As a result the impact of 'race' and gender within particular pieces of research cannot be easily predicted. Prescriptions for matching the 'race' and/or gender of interviewers and respondents are too simplistic" (1994: 49).

The argument that black interviewers are best used for black interviewees is sometimes rooted in a realist epistemology, the central tenet of which is that there is a unitary truth about respondents and their lives which interviewers need to obtain. Black interviewers are considered to "blend in" better with black interviewees and thus to be more likely than white interviewers to get data which is "good" because it captures the "truth." Some studies have found that the colour of the interviewer does have an impact on the data collected. . . . The complexity of this impact, however, makes it difficult to be clear whether the matching of interviewees with interviewers on particular characteristics will produce "better" or "richer" data than not matching. If different types of accounts about "race" and racism are produced with black and with white interviewers this is in itself important data and may be good reason for using interviewers of both colours whenever possible since it illustrates the ways in which knowledges are "situated." It is, therefore, not methodologically "better" always to have black interviewers interviewing black interviewees. Politically, this strategy may also lead to marginalization of research on black researchers since it is easy for white researchers to consider that black interviewers can only contribute to research on black informants. In addition, it renders invisible any contributions they make to research which is not only on black samples or on "race." (1994: 66)

These last sentences point to a potential pitfall of racial matching as a practical measure for furthering antiracism. Phoenix suggests that racial matching may contribute to the marginalization of black scholars relegated by the logic of racial matching to studying only those of the same race. Or, as Penny Rhodes, another British researcher, puts it, "as a long term strategy for gaining access to the research establishment, [racial matching] risks promoting the very marginalization and devaluation of black people and their concerns which it seeks to redress" (1994: 557).

Racial Standpoints?

One of the central premises of the racial matching model is that racial subordinates have a particular worldview. It is presumed, for instance, that racial subalterns better understand racial prejudice and discrimination, are less racist, and identify more closely with members of their presumed racial group. This is precisely why proponents of color matching have hypothesized "that a) a black interviewer would be more likely to share the experience of racial prejudice and discrimination with a black informant who would, therefore, feel more comfortable discussing these issues than with a white person; b) black people's mistrust of white people in general would be extended to a white interviewer and inhibit effective communication; c) a white interviewer would be [more] likely to conduct an interview and interpret the data in a prejudiced manner" (Rhodes 1994: 550).

However, racial subalterns do not automatically better understand racism nor do they necessarily identify more closely with members of their racial group because, as Philomena Essed has argued, people have "multiple identifications" (Essed 1994). Racial subordination does not mechanistically generate a critical stance vis-à-vis racism any more than colonialism created anticolonial subjectivities (Fanon 1967; Memmi 1991). This explains in part why Sylvia Tamale, a black Ugandan feminist with a degree from Harvard, did not understand how everyday racism operated even though she had lived in the United States for several years. And so when she began her study of racism in the United States, she compared herself to the white American journalist John Howard Griffin who had conducted research on racism in 1959.

> Although my skin pigmentation was naturally black, in many ways, I shared Griffin's anxieties, naiveté and discoveries in the course of my field research. Like him, I was consciously "living" racism first hand for the first time. Prior to the study, my outside status had "protected" me from a lot of pain and degradation that comes with a heightened sensitivity to racism. (1996: 479)

Her racial position as a black African living in the United States had not led her to acquire a particular understanding of the processes of racism naturally. Rather, she obtained these insights only through a careful study of the matter—insights which may appear commonsensical on the surface, but which in reality are lessons that most United States blacks are carefully taught in the U.S. black community (Essed 1991; Feagin and Sikes 1994).

In a different national context Brazil also illustrates epistemologies that do not necessarily correspond to a different location in the nexus of power. Although Brazilians are materially and symbolically marginalized on account of their ancestry phenotype, Brazilians of salient African descent do not typically possess a different political standpoint from whites when questioned about definitions of racism, and racial disparities (Twine 1998). Thus, rather than mistrusting a white researcher, racial subalterns in Brazil may be more likely to identify with them. My experiences suggest that some Brazilians of color do not necessarily feel more comfortable discussing the topic of race and racism with those who resemble them racially. Rather, this particular topic generates discomfort regardless of the racial origins or phenotype of the interviewer. Moreover, prestige hierarchies and the valorization of whiteness resulted in some Brazilians of color preferring to be interviewed by my white research partner.

We see, then, that the utility of racial matching is contingent on the subordinate person having acquired a particular subjectivity. It is premised on racial subalterns considering their skin folk their kin folk and being more distrustful of members of the racially dominant group. In my experience, U.S. scholars typically interpret this as an inevitable by-product of racism. That is, they presume that different ideological positions are attached to one's location in racial hierarchies. It should be evident, however, that when racial subalterns do not possess a developed critique of racism or idealize the racially privileged group, race matching may not be an efficacious methodological strategy.

Researching Racial Fields

In the 1960s Choong Soon Kim, who was born and raised in Korea, went to rural Tennessee and Mississippi to conduct field research among blacks, American Indians, and whites. One of Kim's principal predicaments as an Asian researcher involved the social scripts attached to his phenotype:

> In the field, I experienced a constant pressure to conform to the role expected of an Asian. Almost all of the southerners I studied during my fieldwork expected me to behave as a foreigner. I do not think they had consciously constructed a model of what an Asian should be, but they had enough explicit notions to constitute a stereotype. For example, an Asian should have yellowish skin and straight black

hair, be short and stocky, and wear eye glasses. He must say "thank you" more than three times for every simple thing or event, even if it is not deserving of so much appreciation. He ought to be polite and humble in his manner. But more than anything else, he should not speak English fluently. (1977: 12–14)

Kim's experiences illustrate how researchers must often navigate racialized fields in particular local and national contexts. They frequently have to negotiate the way their bodies are racialized and the meanings attached to these racializations. The racializations Kim encountered seemed to affect whether he was perceived as "foreign" (i.e., his national identity) and the behavioral etiquette to which he was expected to conform, which in turn affected his access or degree of immersion in his research community.

Like Kim, my body was racialized within a particular national field. In Brazil I was rarely considered an "authentic" North American from the United States but rather a "naturalized" American or a Brazilian attempting to pass as a North American. My experiences were not unlike those described by Faye Harrison, a light-skinned black American who conducted research in Jamaica in the 1970s. She observes:

My social status as a light colored Afro-American intellectual was imbued with a great deal of ambiguity. . . . Initially, Oceanview folk perceived me to be almost anything other than my own self-conception, i.e. a Black social scientist with a strong identification with oppressed Black people. While the majority of Oceanview people saw in me a middle-class "brown" woman, some presumed and insisted that the "American doctor doing research" was socially—if not genealogically—"white." For Jamaicans who have never been to the U.S. and who have exposure to the stereotypes through the media and through Jamaican emigrants' self-tailored tales of success as "foreign," the symbol "American" often means affluent White U.S. citizens. Black Americans encountered in Jamaica are frequently assumed to be West Indian immigrants with American accents. . . . In a society where color variations are keenly perceived and endowed with social meaning, light skin is often construed to be a salient mark of class privilege and social distance from the Black masses. The stereotypic brown woman would not be expected to undertake research that would reflect the interests of ghetto people. It would be more plausible for her to seek information which could be used for purposes of social control, containment and manipulation. (1991: 98–99)

Faye Harrison's description of Jamaica in the late 1970s mirrors some aspects of my research experiences in Brazil in the 1990s as a U.S. black. In the community in which I worked local residents (particularly working-class people who lacked the resources to travel to the United States) racialized the United States as a white nation and were reluctant to accept my claims that I was a U.S. native. They assumed I was of Brazilian parentage and thus simply "passing" as a North American. This often gave me access to a particular type of Brazilian experience reserved for "local" *brasileiras,* which facilitated some aspects of my research. However, since I was assumed to be a Brazilian native, or "insider," particularly among working-class people in rural areas, I was rarely perceived to be a credible researcher.

Harrison's observations also underscore the fact that racialized fields are neither stable nor uniform. Researchers who work in non-native settings must often manage differences in the constitution of ethnic and racial boundaries, color hierarchies, categories, and meanings. For example, just as a U.S. white may not be regarded as white in New Zealand (see Warren and Twine 1997), Harrison, a U.S. black, was not considered black in Jamaica. Instead, some labeled her "'white' or 'brown'—or sometimes 'red'— . . . representative of 'Babylon,' the Rastafarian designation for Black Jamaicans' domestic and foreign oppressors." Others, "having internalized the 'colonial mentality,'" considered her a "nice brown woman" (Harrison 1991: 99).

The effects of not being taken seriously as a researcher became more apparent to me when I began conducting research in central England in 1995. Here my Americanness was not only accepted without suspicion, but as a U.S. black I was often perceived to be quintessentially American. I was rarely quizzed about my origins and my accent was taken as proof of my Americanness. Furthermore, a certain authority and chicness attached itself to me as a representative of the U.S. black middle class. The local calculus of color and race may thus determine which segments of the community the researcher can easily access, and the normative social roles and social scripts to which s/he is expected to conform.

Moreover, despite the salient cultural differences between me and the Caribbean immigrants (such as my inability to speak patois, understand local humor, or cook West Indian food), in British professional circles and community events the local people typically treated me as a transatlantic cousin who had returned home. They considered me as part of a larger pan-African community linked to them through a common history of slavery and struggle against antiblack racism. In a sense, then, I found in England among the Caribbean immigrants the transnational black community that I had anticipated encountering in Brazil. One can easily imagine how being positioned as a "cousin who is concerned with black liberation" rather than as a "*mulatta* struggling to become white" might have very different implications for the type of data one ultimately collects. Thus, conducting research in Britain illuminated how much the national context can alter one's ascribed racial or ethnic position.

Eroticism and Racism

The erotic dimensions of field research are shaped by geopolitical forces (Michalowski 1996). While lesbian, gay, and queer scholars have advanced analyses of erotic subjectivity in the field (Kulick and Willson 1995; Lewin and Leap 1996), there has been little discussion of how racism affects eroticization. Jonathan Warren and Michael Hanchard analyze this issue with reference to Brazil. As a U.S. black political scientist, Michael Hanchard explores in "Racism, Eroticism, and the Paradoxes of a U.S. Black Researcher in Brazil," how U.S.-Brazil political relations affected the ways he was eroticized as a man of salient African descent. His status as a professional researcher did not make him "immune to such categorization." In fact, it was clear at one party he attended, hosted by a white anthropologist, that he was positioned as an erotic object much as women tend to be reduced to their sexuality in patriarchal societies. Describing his visual experiences at this party, he writes, "Virtually all the artwork on the walls—an assortment of postcards, paintings, and advertisements of romantic and sexual couplings of white women with black men—depicted black men with white women. When linked to the party thrower and the overwhelmingly dark, overwhelmingly male presence at the party and the sight of the hostess dancing among several of these men. . . . I had the distinct feeling of déjà vu."

Jonathan Warren, a white sociologist, examines another dimension of racialized erotic fields in Brazil. In "Masters in the Field," Warren argues that for white researchers the eroticization of racial categories may be experienced as pleasurable and indeed nonracist. In a context in which whiteness is valorized, white researchers may be exotified and eroticized but in contrast to blacks they are not typically reduced to merely hypersexed objects. Since whiteness is associated with intelligence, prestigious pedigrees, and middle-class positions of authority, this particular form of eroticization may create a symbolically affirming context—unlike the disempowering and negative climate for black men. However, even this radically different erotic and emotional climate can generate its own peculiar methodological pitfalls. Warren contends that because eroticization can affirm white researchers, they may be motivated to misread and thus misrepresent the ways in which racism operates in Brazil.

Racial Discourses

Another dimension of racialized fields which has serious methodological and ethical implications, is racial discourse. Here I am referring to the way people talk about race, their racial vocabularies, racial narratives, and their definitions of racism. In "Doing My Homework: The Autoethnography of a White Teenage Girl," in this volume, Lorraine Delia Kenny discusses the difficulties of doing research in "color-blind" fields such as the white middle-class community on Long Island that she studied. As an ethnographer, who is building upon the work of Ruth Frankenberg, who argues that in such contexts white women aspire to "'not see' race difference despite its continued salience in society and in their own lives" (Frankenberg 1993: 149), she devised "methods for naming the unnamable, marking the unmarked, seeing the invisible, or, more importantly, articulating the meaningfulness of its carefully constructed meaninglessness." Furthermore, Kenny notes that when studying a race-evasive culture such as her childhood home of Long Island one encounters the ethical dilemma of inevitably violating that culture because one is making visible that which people struggle and desire to keep invisible. "In inflammatory terms, the very groundwork of my study sets me up as a race traitor: if whiteness, or at least middle-class whiteness, maintains its social hegemony through a kind of measured silence and anonymity, . . . an ethnographer of whiteness necessarily seeks to break this code and hence give the lie to white privilege. . . . to articulate that which cannot and should not be said."

In "Masters in the Field," Jonathan Warren suggests that white North American researchers have racialized the discourses of race which Kenny studied. Scholars tend to associate a color- and power-evasive language of race with whites and in particular with middle-class whites. Subsequently, when they encounter this "culture of avoidance" amongst people of color, they may erroneously interpret this as evidence that racism is absent. In a sense, then, they assume a standpoint epistemology, in which different locations within racial hierarchies will result in different perspectives. Thus they do not expect whites, as members of the dominant racial group, to be knowledgeable about race and racism. In contrast, racial subalterns are assumed to possess a sophisticated understanding of racism. When they do not, this is misinterpreted as an absence of racism. Thus it is presumed that if racial inequalities existed, racial subalterns would have a critique of their subordination; they would not have "the privilege" to be able to avoid the issue of race.

In their chapter on conducting transnational research in prisons Kum-Kum Bhavnani and Angela Davis raise the issue of researching racism in national contexts, including Cuba and the Netherlands, in which racism is either avoided (not named) or has very different meanings. In the United States, they write, "racism is often understood to refer to institutional and individual discrimination against black, Latino, Native American, and Asian-American people. In Europe, *racism* is viewed as synonymous with *xenophobia*. Thus in the Netherlands . . . responses to our questions about racism tended to focus on attitudes toward foreigners, rather than on racism by white Dutch people against non white Dutch citizens."

In 1992, I encountered the problem that Bhavnani and Davis refer to when I had difficulties generating discussions about racial disparities in Brazil for a number of reasons: it was a taboo subject, since "seeing racism meant being racist" (Frankenberg 1993: 147); local definitions of racism were narrow compared to those in the United States (Twine 1996, 1998); and most residents imagined their community as non-racist. The advantage of researching race in such a context is that there is much less censorship because it is assumed that racism is not really an issue. However, it can also become virtually impossible to engage in sustained discussions of racism because people either do not possess the vocabulary for talking about white supremacy or have not given racism their attention because they do not consider it to be a serious problem.

Aesthetics and Ethics

Another aspect of conducting research in racialized terrains involves the issue of representations, or "writing culture." In the 1980s several groundbreaking books were published, including James Clifford and George Marcus's *Writing Culture: The Poetics and Politics of Ethnography*, which initiated a postmodern discussion of ethnographic authority and representations (Clifford and Marcus 1986; Marcus and Fischer 1986; Abu-Lughod 1991). However, as Deborah D'Amico-Samuels correctly points out, one of the noted weaknesses of these studies is their failure to address race:

> Absences in the reflexive and critical ethnography discourse . . . are [difficult] to explain. One wonders, for example, why Gwaltney's *Drylongso* (1980: 81) is not considered among the new forms of ethnography discussed in *Writing Culture*. It includes many of the elements of the ethnographies which are discussed—experimental form and method, reflexivity on the part of the ethnographer, multiple authorship, and the flavor of fieldwork dialogue and experience. Did Clifford and Marcus not know of this book, and if not, why? The exclusion of Gwaltney's book would seem to signal either the peripheralization of African-American scholarship and the issues of race in the discourse of reflexive anthropology/critical ethnography, or a judgment that consideration of the issues Gwaltney raises would not contribute to the discussion of writing culture, or both. What underscores each of these possibilities, I believe, is a reluctance to deal with the effects of race on fieldwork and the production of ethnographic texts. (1991: 78)

Race, of course, greatly affects one's authority to make certain knowledge claims. There is little question that one can make certain arguments with more credibility depending on the race of the researchers and their subjects. For example, Mitchell Duneier's nonracist portrayal of homeless men (Duneier 1999) probably carries more credibility and legitimacy—at least in certain circles—because he is a white man. In "Racism, Eroticism, and the Paradoxes of a U.S. Black Researcher in Brazil," in this volume, Michael Hanchard raises a related issue of racial authority and scientific objectivity. Describing the initial responses to his research topic of some of his white colleagues and mentors at Princeton University, he notes that when white researchers study white-controlled institutions and movements, their research is not perceived as "biased." However, when he chose to study a black movement in another national context, concerns were raised about his topic being too "narrow" and possibly biased.

In addition to the question of authority, the issue of representation seems to be a particularly agonizing and complicated one for those researching communities vulnerable due to racial and ethnic inequalities. A dilemma that often emerges is, how does one "realistically" represent racially subordinate communities without conforming to idealized racial tropes of the sort Alastair Bonnett (1996) documented in his analysis of antiracist discussions of race in Britain and the United States?

Anti-racists have often placed a myth of whiteness at the center of their discourse. This myth views "being white" as an immutable condition with clear and distinct moral attributes. These attributes often include being racist; not experiencing racism; being an oppressor; not experiencing oppression; silencing; not being silenced. People of colour are defined via their relation to this myth. They are defined, then, as "non-whites"; as people whose identity is formed through their resistance to others' oppressive agency." (1996: 105)

In fact, in Bonnett's opinion it would seem that "the romantic stereotype of the eternally resisting, victimised 'black community' is required to be further strengthened in order to create a suitable location for escapees from 'whiteness'" (1996: 105).

In my own work in Brazil I have encountered some criticism, I believe, because I have not reproduced idealized representations of the African-descent community (includes people who self-identify as black, brown, and white) in Brazil. In the Brazilian community I studied, most racial subalterns were not actively challenging racism. In fact many were quite complicit with white supremacy. But such a message, of course, violates romanticized imaginings of resistance.

José Limón describes well the dilemmas and challenges faced by scholars who portray racial subordinates as blemished. In "Notes of a Native Anthropologist," Limón discusses the possible consequences of his departure from the more romantic representations of "the lower-class mexicano world of popular dancing" that were composed by his predecessor Américo Paredes:

> Yet this move in the direction of the unheroic immediately plunges me into a serious contradiction: as I stake out this ground, I am obligated to speak fully about the *mexicano* world, to articulate not only its concerns with dancing but also its violence, its exaggerated masculinity, and its toll on women—all of which representations potentially place me in an uncomfortable relationship with a history of denigrative "Mexican" stereotypes often used to validate the mistreatment of these, my people. Beyond the purely personal level, this potential relationship is also discomforting in political-intellectual terms, and it poses a contradiction within my work. First, I myself have written critically about such stereotyping (1973), and second, such a position runs counter to a deeper indebtedness to my precursor. That is, while I do not think it possible now, in the seventies and eighties, to render "heroic" worlds, nonetheless I wish to speak of the critical politics possible in the world of El Cielo Azul, just as Parades did for the world of Gregorio Cortez. (1991: 129)

While speaking from different racialized positions, Philippe Bourgois, a white ethnographer of a community marginalized along the axes of race and class, wrestled with the same issue. In "Violating Apartheid in the United States," in this volume, he notes that he "worried . . . that the life stories and events presented in [his] book would be misread as negative stereotypes of Puerto Ricans, or as a hostile portrait of the poor." He observes that this "fear of succumbing to a pornography of violence that reinforces popular racist stereotypes" had created an "imperative to sanitize the vulnerable [that] is particularly strong in the United States because of the survival-of-the-fittest, blame-the-victim theories of individual action that dominate popular 'common sense.'"

Bourgois struggled over these issues for years but ultimately decided that "countering traditional, moralistic biases and middle-class hostility toward the poor should not come at the cost of sanitizing the suffering and destruction that exists on inner-city streets. Out of righteous or a 'politically sensitive' fear of giving the poor a bad image, I refuse to ignore or minimize the social misery I witnessed, because that would make me complicit with oppression." One of his strategies to mitigate a neoconservative reading of his ethnography was to develop "the historical and political economy context first and [portray] them as victims of social structural oppression and interpersonal abuse before subsequently confronting the reader in later chapters with the fuller horrors of these very characters as perpetrators of violence and abuse against their own loved ones and against their immediate community."

As an ethnic insider, Naheed Islam also grappled with issues similar to those of Bourgois. As she describes it in "Research as an Act of Betrayal," in this volume, she struggled with whether to document the intense antiblack hostilities she found in the Bangladeshi immigrant community in Los Angeles. Her concern, however, was less that it would not conform to a heroic, idealized image of the Bangladeshi community but rather that it would undermine their credibility as "victims" of racism as well as her place in that community. Interestingly, for Islam the pressure to produce this image sprang not from the academic community—as seemed to be the case with Bourgois, whose Puerto Rican informants agreed with his portrayal—but from the Bangladeshi interviewees:

> Some wished to present an idealized model minority image of the community that necessitated severing any relationship to blacks and Latinos. As a researcher parts of the community expected me to censor and skew my presentation to meet these interests. One interviewee who was making racist jokes at a social event found me unresponsive and gathered that I did not share his views. He then turned to me and said, "I know, I know, you are gathering data. You are going to say we are racist. But you don't need to write about what we think of them [blacks]. Focus on what we are going through. That is what your focus should be on. Focus on us." He insisted that I focus on his experiences of racism and omit his own racism toward other groups.

Islam ultimately decided, like Bourgois, that it was best not only as a social scientist but also as one committed to racial justice to expose the racism she had encountered. But, unlike Bourgois, the risks were different. Bourgois was forced to deal with being positioned as a "racist." Islam, on the other hand, chanced "being viewed as a traitor to my ethnic community." Thus her dilemma paralleled that of many of the contributors to this volume who focus on whiteness, in that their decision to privilege their commitment to antiracism and their refusal to be silent about racist discourses led them to be positioned as "race traitors."

Islam's dilemmas illuminate another dimension that racism brings to the social scientific research process for researchers concerned with racial justice. In their essays several white contributors address the issue of complicity with the political agendas of the research communities in which they worked. Kathleen Blee, Philippe Bourgois, and Mitch Duneier, for example, raise the issue of how one's research may be employed by the communities one is studying.

In "Race and Peeing on Sixth Avenue," in this volume, Mitch Duneier discusses his research on black unhoused street vendors in New York City. He suggests that some of the men with whom he worked tolerated his presence because it allowed them to participate in a project that could potentially present a more humane representation of them. Their investment in Duneier's research can be understood in the context of racist and class-biased portrayals of the working poor and unhoused black men in particular. Duneier decided to publish their real names in his book *Sidewalk* (1999) because he wanted other social scientists to be able to verify what he had found. In contrast to Duneier, Kathleen Blee had to find a way to counter the strategic deployment of her published research by white racist activists who wanted to use her work to propagate and publicize themselves and their political organizations. As she describes it in "White on White," she ultimately decided not to publish the names of the people she interviewed, to undermine the efforts of racist activists to publicize themselves through her research.

Conclusion

I commissioned the chapters in this volume in order to advance theoretical debates in qualitative research methods scholarship about the particular dilemmas racial ideologies and racialized fields generate for researchers. These dilemmas have theoretical implications for the way knowledge about racial and social inequality is produced. Furthermore, I wanted to integrate the concerns of research methodologists and critical race theorists in a single book. The chapters in this volume provide empirical examples of some of the issues that field researchers confront as antiracists. Nonetheless, *Racing Research* is not an exhaustive analysis of the methodological issues in field research. Rather, my aim is to inspire and initiate renewed interdisciplinary dialogue among researchers, to explore how the fields in which they operate are "raced" in ways that are neither unitary nor predictable.

All the contributors to this volume address the process of conducting research in racialized fields of power specifically as antiracists. A recurring theme in this volume is the dilemmas generated when conducting qualitative research in the context of racial disparity and racial oppression. The instability and unnaturalness of "race" and the uneven meanings of racism can have methodological consequences for qualitative researchers even when their research is not primarily focused on the issues of race or racism. Researchers committed to an antiracist agenda may find they are being positioned as "traitors" to their communities on account of their research.

The contributors to this volume work in the fields of African-American Studies/Black Studies, Asian American Studies, Cultural Studies, Latin American Studies, Womens' Studies, Philosophy, Political Science, and Sociology. It is my hope that by providing a template of some of the methodological dilemmas faced by antiracist researchers, this volume will inspire other researchers to consider the local matrices of racial ideologies, racial discourses, and racialized exclusions that ground their particular research projects. I would like to thank Jonathan Warren for his theoretical insights and careful, engaged critique of this chapter. His engagement with my work has left its mark on this analysis.

NOTES

1. Unfortunately David Hellwig's edited volume (*African-American Reflections on Brazil's Racial Paradise* [Philadelphia: Temple University Press, 1992]) was published after I completed my first period of field research.

2. Unpublished field notes, March 1992.

3. See my chapter, "White Inflation and Willful Forgetting," in *Racism in a Racial Democracy: The Maintenance of White Supremacy in Brazil* (Twine 1998).

4. In 1991 I was a member of the first class to enroll in a Visual Anthropology course taught by Jack Potter which was the only qualitative research methods course offered to nonarchaeologists.

5. Thanks to the theoretical innovations by feminist, gay/lesbian, and queer theorists, there is a developed body of literature on gender, sexuality, and erotic subjectivity. For examples, see Golde 1970; Warren 1988; Whitehead and Conaway 1986; Maynard and Purvis 1994; Kulick and Willson 1995; Wolf 1996; Lewin and Leap 1996.

6. In conceptualizing and carrying through this project I benefited greatly from my conversations with Stephen Small and Jonathan Warren.

7. She does not provide any information about her specific national origins but does indicate that she was educated in England.

8. Merton concluded that it is optimal to have the perspectives of both racial insiders and outsiders. In his words: "Insiders and outsiders in the domain of knowledge, unite. You have nothing to lose but your claims. You have a world of understanding to win" (1972: 44).

REFERENCES

Abu-Lughod, Lila. 1991. "Writing against Culture." In *Recapturing Anthropology: Working in the Present,* edited by Richard Fox, pp. 137–62. Santa Fe, N.M.: School of American Research Press.

Adler, Patricia, and Peter Adler. 1995. "The Demography of Ethnography." *Qualitative Sociology* 24 (1): 3–29.

Agar, Michael. 1980. *The Professional Stranger.* New York: Academic Press.

Aguilar, John L. 1981. "Insider Research: An Ethnography of a Debate." In *Anthropologists at Home in North America: Methods and Issues in the Study of One's Own Society,* edited by Donald A. Messerschmidt. Cambridge: Cambridge University Press.

Altorki, Soraya. 1988. "At Home in the Field." In *Arab Women in the Field: Studying Your Own,* edited by Soraya Altorki and Camillia Fauzi El-Solh, pp. 49–68. Syracuse: Syracuse University Press.

Anderson, Margaret L. 1993. "Studying across Difference: Race, Class, and Gender in Qualitative Research." In *Race and Ethnicity in Research Methods,* edited by John Stanfield II and Rutledge Dennis. Newbury Park, Calif.: Sage.

Becker, Howard S. 1970. *Sociological Work: Method and Substance.* New Brunswick, N.J.: Transaction Books.

Bell, Diane, Pat Caplan, and Wazir Jahan Karim. 1993. *Gendered Fields: Women, Men, and Ethnography.* New York: Routledge.

Beoku-Betts, Josephine. 1994. "When Black Is Not Enough: Doing Field Research among Gullah Women." *NWSA Journal* 6 (3): 413–33.

Blauner, Robert, and David Wellman. 1998. "Toward the Decolonization of Social Research." In *The Death of White Sociology: Essays on Race and Culture,* edited by Joyce Ladner. Baltimore: Black Classic Press. Originally published in 1973.

Blee, Kathleen M. 1998. "White-Knuckle Research: Emotional Dynamics in Fieldwork with Racist Activists." *Qualitative Sociology* 21 (4): 381–99.

Bolles, A. Lynn. 1985. "Of Mules and Yankee Gals: Struggling with Stereotypes in the Field." *Anthropology and Humanism Quarterly* 10 (4): 114–19.

Bonnett, Alastair. 1996. "Anti-Racism and the Critique of 'White' Identities." *New Community: The Journal of the European Research Centre on Migration and Ethnic Relations* 22 (10): 97–110.

Bourgois, Philippe. 1995. *In Search of Respect: Selling Crack in El Barrio.* Cambridge: Cambridge University Press.

Brown, Jacqueline. 1998. "Black Liverpool, Black America, and the Gendering of Diasporic Space." *Cultural Anthropology* 13 (3): 291–325.

Carter, Donald Martin. 1997. *States of Grace: Senegalese in Italy and the New European Immigration.* Minneapolis: University of Minnesota Press.

Clifford, James, and George Marcus, eds. 1986. *Writing Culture: The Poetics and Politics of Ethnography.* Berkeley and Los Angeles: University of California Press.

Collins, Patricia Hill. 1991. "Learning from the Outsider Within: The Sociological Significance of Black Feminist Thought." In *Beyond Methodology: Feminist Scholarship as Lived Research,* edited by Mary Margaret Fonow and Judith A. Cook, pp. 35–59. Bloomington: Indiana University Press.

D'Amico-Samuels, Deborah. 1991. "Undoing Fieldwork: Personal, Political, Theoretical, and Methodological Implications." In *Decolonizing Anthropology,* edited by Faye Harrison. Washington, D.C.: American Anthropological Association.

Denzin, Norman, and Yvonna S. Lincoln, eds. 1994. Handbook of Qualitative Research. Thousand Oaks, Calif.: Sage.

Duneier, Mitchell. 1999. *Sidewalk.* New York: Farrar, Straus, and Giroux.

Ellis, Carolyn. 1995. "Emotional and Ethical Quagmires in Returning to the Field." *Journal of Contemporary Ethnography* 24 (1): 68–98.

Essed, Philomena. 1991. *Understanding Everyday Racism: An Interdisciplinary Theory* (Sage Series on Race and Ethnic Relations, vol. 2). Newbury Park, Calif.: Sage.

———. 1994. "Contradictory Positions, Ambivalent Perceptions: A Case

Study of a Black Woman Entrepreneur." *Feminism and Psychology* (special issue entitled *Shifting Identities, Shifting Racisms*): 99–118.

Facio, Elisa. 1993. "Ethnography as Personal Experience." In *Race and Ethnicity in Research Methods,* edited by John H. Stanfield II and Rutledge Denis. Newbury Park, Calif.: Sage.

Fanon, Frantz. 1967. *The Wretched of the Earth.* Harmondsworth, England: Penguin.

Feagin, Joe R., and Melvin Sikes. 1994. *Living with Racism: The Black Middle-Class Experience.* Boston: Beacon Press.

Fine, Gary Alan. 1993. "Ten Lies of Ethnography: Moral Dilemmas of Field Research." *Journal of Contemporary Ethnography* 22, no. 3 (October): 267–94.

Fox, Richard. 1991. *Recapturing Anthropology: Working in the Present.* Santa Fe, N.M.: School of American Research Press.

Frankenberg, Ruth. 1993. *White Women, Race Matters: The Social Construction of Whiteness.* Minneapolis: University of Minnesota Press.

———. 1997. *Dis-Placing Whiteness: Essays in Social and Cultural Criticism.* Durham: Duke University Press.

Gallagher, Charles. 1995. "White Reconstruction in the University." *Socialist Review* 94 (1/2): 165–88.

Gilliam, Angela. 1970. "From Roxbury to Rio and Back in a Hurry." *Journal of Black Poetry* 1: 8–12.

Ginsburg, Faye. 1989. *Contested Lives: The Abortion Debate in an American Community.* Berkeley: University of California Press.

Golde, Peggy, ed. 1970. *Women in the Field: Anthropological Experiences.* Berkeley: University of California Press.

Gupta, Akhil, and James Ferguson. 1997. "Discipline and Practice: The 'Field' as Site, Method, and Location in Anthropology." In *Anthropological Locations: Boundaries and Grounds of a Field of Science,* edited by Akhil Gupta and James Ferguson, pp. 1–46. Berkeley and Los Angeles: University of California Press.

Gwaltney, John L. 1976. "Going Home Again—Some Reflections of a Native Anthropologist." *Phylon* 30: 236–42.

———. 1980. *Drylongso: A Self-Portrait of Black America.* New York: Random House.

Harper, Dean. 1994. "What Problems Do You Confront? An Approach to Doing Qualitative Research." *Qualitative Sociology* 17 (10): 89–95.

Harris, Marvin. 1952. "Race Relations in Minas Velhas: A Community in the Mountain Region of Central Brazil." In *Race and Class in Rural Brazil,* edited by Charles Wagley, pp. 47–81. Paris: UNESCO.

———. 1956. *Town and Country in Brazil.* New York: Columbia University Press.

Harrison, Faye. 1991. "Ethnography as Politics." In *Decolonizing Anthropology: Moving towards an Anthropology for Liberation,* edited by Faye Harrison, pp. 88–109. Washington, D.C.: Association of Black Anthropologists/American Anthropological Association.

Hatchett, Shirley, and Howard Schuman. 1975–76. "White Respondents and Race-of-Interviewer Effects." *Public Opinion Quarterly* 39 (4): 523–28.

Hurtado, Aída. 1994. "Does Similarity Breed Respect? Interviewer Evaluations of Mexican-Descent Respondents in a Bilingual Survey." *Public Opinion Quarterly* 58: 77–95.

Hutchinson, Harry. 1957. *Village and Plantation Life in Northeastern Brazil.* Seattle: University of Washington Press.

Hyman, Herbert, with William J. Cobb and others. 1954. *Interviewing in Social Research.* Chicago: University of Chicago Press.

Jones, Delmos. 1982. "Towards a Native Anthropology." In *Anthropology for the Eighties: Introductory Readings,* edited by Johnetta B. Cole, pp. 471–82. New York: Free Press, originally published in 1970.

Kim, Choong Soon. 1977. *An Asian Anthropologist in the South: Field Experiences with Blacks, Indians, and Whites.* Knoxville: University of Tennessee Press.

Kondo, Dorinne K. 1990. *Crafting Selves: Power, Gender, and Discourses of Identity in a Japanese Workplace.* Chicago: University of Chicago Press.

Kulick, Don, and Margaret Willson. 1995. *Taboo: Sex, Identity, and Erotic Subjectivity in Anthropological Fieldwork.* London: Routledge.

Ladner, Joyce. 1998. *The Death of White Sociology: Essays in Race and Culture.* Baltimore: Black Classic Press. Originally published in 1973.

Lewin, Ellen, and William Leap. 1996. *Out in the Field: Reflections of Lesbian and Gay Anthropologists.* Urbana: University of Illinois Press.

Limón, José E. 1991. "Representation, Ethnicity, and the Precursory Ethnography: Notes of a Native Anthropologist." In *Recapturing Anthropology: Working in the Present,* edited by Richard Fox. Santa Fe, N.M.: School of American Research (Advanced Seminar Series).

Loewen, James W. 1971. *The Mississippi Chinese: Between Black and White.* Prospect Heights, Ill.: Waveland Press.

Marcus, George E. 1998. *Ethnography through Thick and Thin.* Princeton: Princeton University Press.

Marcus, George, and Michael M. Fischer, eds. 1986. *Anthropology as Cultural Critique: An Experimental Moment in the Human Sciences.* Chicago: University of Chicago Press.

Maykovich, Minado Kurokawa. 1977. "The Difficulties of a Minority Researcher in Minority Communities." *Journal of Social Issues* 33 (4): 108–19.

Maynard, Mary, and June Purvis, eds. 1994. *Researching Women's Lives from a Feminist Perspective.* London: Taylor and Francis.

Memmi, Albert. 1991. *The Colonizer and the Colonized*. Expanded edition. Introduction by Jean Paul Sartre. Boston: Beacon Press. Originally published by Orion Press in 1965.

Merton, Robert. 1972. "Insiders and Outsiders: A Chapter in the Sociology of Knowledge." *American Journal of Sociology* 78 (July): 9–47.

Messerschmidt, Donald. 1981. *Anthropologists at Home in North America: Methods and Issues in the Study of One's Own Society*. Cambridge: Cambridge University Press.

Michalowski, Raymond J. 1996. "Ethnography and Anxiety: Field Work and Reflexivity in the Vortex of U.S.-Cuban Relations." *Qualitative Sociology* 19 (1): 59–82.

Naples, Nancy. 1996. "A Feminist Revisiting of the Insider/Outsider Debate: The 'Outsider Phenomenon' in Rural Iowa." *Qualitative Sociology* 19 (1): 83–106.

Narayan, Kirin. 1993. "How Native Is a 'Native' Anthropologist?" *American Anthropologist* 95: 671–86.

Phoenix, Ann. 1994. "Practising Feminist Research: The Intersection of Gender and 'Race' in the Research Process." In *Researching Women's Lives from a Feminist Perspective*, edited by Mary Maynard and June Purvis. London: Taylor and Francis.

Powdermaker, Hortense. 1939. *After Freedom: A Cultural Study in the Deep South*. New York: Atheneum.

Rhodes, Penny J. 1994. "Race-of-Interviewer Effects: A Brief Comment." *Sociology: The Journal of the British Sociological Association* 28 (2): 547–58.

Roediger, David. 1991. *The Wages of Whiteness: Race and the Making of the American Working Class*. New York: Verso Press.

Schuman, Howard, and Jean M. Converse. 1971. "The Effects of Black and White Interviewers on Black Responses in 1968." *Public Opinion Quarterly* 35 (1): 44–68.

Schutte, Gerhard. 1991. "Racial Oppression and Social Research: Field Work under Racial Conflict in South Africa," *Qualitative Sociology* 14 (2): 127–46.

Segrest, Mab. 1994. *Memoir of a Race Traitor*. Boston: South End Press.

Shaw, Carolyn Martin. 1995. *Colonial Inscriptions: Race, Sex, and Class in Kenya*. Minneapolis: University of Minnesota Press.

Simpson, Jennifer. 1996. "Easy Talk, White Talk, Back Talk: Some Reflections on the Meanings of Our Words." *Journal of Contemporary Ethnography* 25 (3): 372–89.

Skeggs, Beverly. 1994. "Situating the Production of Feminist Ethnography." In *Researching Women's Lives from a Feminist Perspective*, edited by Mary Maynard and June Purvis. London: Taylor and Francis.

Smith, Dorothy. 1987. "Women's Perspective as a Radical Critique of Sociology." In *Feminism and Methodology: Social Science Issues,* edited by Sandra Harding. Bloomington: Indiana University Press.

South American Handbook. 1991. 67th ed. Chicago: Passport Books.

Stanfield, John H., and Dennis Rutledge, eds. 1993. *Race and Ethnicity in Research Methods.* Newbury Park, Calif.: Sage.

Tamale, Sylvia R. 1996. "The Outsider Looks In: Constructing Knowledge about American Collegiate Racism." *Qualitative Sociology* 19 (4): 471–95.

Telles, Eduardo, and E. Murguia. 1990. "Phenotypic Discrimination and Income Differences among Mexican Americans." *Social Science Quarterly* 71 (4): 682–93.

Twine, France Winddance. 1996. "O hiato de gênero nas percepçoes de racismo: O caso dos afro-brasilieros socialmente ascendentes." *Estudos Afro-Asiáticos* 29 (March): 37–54.

———. 1998. *Racism in a Racial Democracy: The Maintenance of White Supremacy in Brazil.* New Brunswick, N.J.: Rutgers University Press.

———. 1999a. "Bearing Blackness in Britain: The Meaning of Racial Difference for White Birth Mothers of African-Descent Children." *Social Identities: Journal of Race, Nation, and Culture* 5 (2): 185–210.

———. 1999b. "Transracial Mothering and Anti-Racism: The Case of White Mothers of 'Black' Children in Britain." *Feminist Studies* 25 (3): 729–46.

Valentine, Charles A., and Betty Lou Valentine. 1970. "Making the Scene, Digging the Action, and Telling It Like It Is: Anthropologists at Work in a Dark Ghetto." In *Afro-American Anthropology: Contemporary Perspectives,* edited by Norman E. Whitten, Jr. and John F. Szwed. New York: Free Press.

Ware, Vron. 1992. *Beyond the Pale: White Women, Racism, and History.* London: Verso Press.

Warren, Carol A. 1988. *Gender Issues in Field Research.* (Qualitative Research Methods Series, vol. 9). Newbury Park, Calif.: Sage.

Warren, Jonathan W., and France Winddance Twine. 1997. "White Americans, The New Minority? Non-Blacks and the Ever-Expanding Boundaries of Whiteness." *Journal of Black Studies* 28, no. 2 (November): 200–218.

Wellman, David T. 1977. *Portraits of White Racism.* Cambridge: Cambridge University Press.

Whitehead, Tony Larry. 1986. "Breakdown, Resolution, and Coherence: The Fieldwork Experiences of a Big, Brown, Pretty-Talking Man in a West Indian Community." In *Self, Sex, and Gender in Cross-Cultural Fieldwork,* edited by Tony Larry Whitehead and Mary Ellen Conaway. Urbana: University of Illinois Press.

Whitehead, Tony Larry, and Mary Ellen Conaway, eds. 1986. *Self, Sex, and Gender in Cross-Cultural Fieldwork.* Urbana: University of Illinois Press.

Whitten, Norman E., Jr. 1974. *Black Frontiersmen: Afro-Hispanic Culture of Ecuador and Columbia.* Prospect Heights, Ill.: Waveland Press.

Williams, Brackette F. 1996. "Skinfolk, Not Kinfolk: Comparative Reflections on the Identity of Participant-Observation in Two Field Situations." In *Feminist Dilemmas in Field Research,* edited by Diane Wolf. Boulder, Colo.: Westview Press.

Wilson, William Julius. 1974. "The New Black Sociology: Reflections on the 'Insiders' and the 'Outsiders' Controversy." In *Black Sociologists: Historical and Contemporary Perspectives,* edited by James E. Blackwell and Morris Janowitz. Chicago: University of Chicago Press.

Wolf, Diane L., ed. 1996. *Feminist Dilemmas in Fieldwork.* Boulder, Col.: Westview Press.

Zinn, Maxine Baca. 1979. "Field Research in Minority Communities: Ethical, Methodological, and Political Observations by an Insider." *Social Problems* 27 (2): 209–19.

Chapter 2

Research as an Act of Betrayal
Researching Race in an Asian Community in Los Angeles

Naheed Islam

As a Bangladeshi-American antiracist researcher working in the Bangladeshi immigrant community in Los Angeles, I had to negotiate two contradictory locations. Because of my Bangladeshi origins—my ethnicity/nationality—the academic community viewed me as an insider within my research community. However, the community questioned my insider status. Critical to this dynamic was my research topic. In this chapter I employ a *transnational* frame to explore how, when, and where "race" and "racism" entered the discourses of the Bangladeshi immigrants I interviewed in Los Angeles. I also examine how the discursive practices I detected (located within their ideological and material contexts) sustained antiblack and Latino racism while resisting racial hierarchies that positioned Bangladeshi-Americans as "not white" in the U.S. national context.

During interviews and informal conversations people told me what my research should be about, whom it should include, and what aspects I should omit. At the research site they staged a gendered, racialized, and class-based struggle to define the boundaries of their community and represent its content because "outsiders" would view this representation. I would be the informant and translator, and therefore possibly the ambassador and traitor to the community. In this chapter I wish to present the ethical and methodological dilemmas I faced when my research interests as a Bangledeshi-American woman with political and social ties to communities (including U.S. blacks and Latinos) beyond the boundaries of the South Asian immigrants conflicted with the interests of the research community.[1]

In their critique of positivist research methods feminists have demonstrated that researchers interpret, define, and therefore construct reality (Collins 1991; Reinharz 1992). But this constructivist perspective has been slow to change research on race and immigrant communities. Social scientists are only just beginning to acknowledge that research methodologies within the sociology subfields of race and ethnicity have been shaped by dominant discourses on race that have excluded more recent ethnic groups like South Asian immigrants.

> The personal experience focus in qualitative research is particularly problematic in racial and ethnic research. In a race-centered society it is not surprising to find that, historically, Euro-Americans have constructed the rules of procedure and evidence. Thus, even though there are classical cases of, say, Afro-Americans doing participant observation studies, the ethos guiding how they collect experiential data and interpret those data is rooted in Eurocentric hegemony. (Stanfield and Rutledge 1993: 8)

Although John Stanfield and Dennis Rutledge acknowledge that the scholarship in their respective disciplines is dominated by a European-American framework, and that race is socially constructed within specific national contexts, they provide little insight as to how scholars who are members of racial and ethnic minorities have negotiated these disciplinary biases.

In the sociological literature, immigrant communities are discussed in the context of three distinct concerns, namely, immigration, ethnicity, and race. The literature on immigration (Portes and Rumbaut 1990) uses an assimilationist model, examining how immigrants adjust to life in the United States. Ethnicity is seen as a resilient identity that shapes the immigrant experience. The ethnicity literature focuses on the culture of immigrants to explain differences between groups. Robert Parks's model of race relations—competition, conflict, accommodation, and assimilation—informs these discussions of race and ethnicity (Park 1950). Immigrant groups entering the United States have been described as encountering a range of different social, political, and economic conditions (Glazer and Moynihan 1963; Jibou 1988; Waters 1990).

Recent discussions on immigrant groups have been informed by a re-shaped ethnicity framework. The continued primacy of ethnic identity, community (Chang and Leong 1994; Park 1997), and entrepreneurship (Light and Bonacich 1988) are used to analyze a group's location within the economy. Economic processes, the labor market, and class are considered more fundamental than race (Bonacich 1980; Wilson 1978). However, while ethnicity constructs group identity, group boundary, and social relationships, an analysis limited to ethnicity masks how race operates in the United States. This framework avoids an analysis of the structural and ideological underpinnings of racial inequality.

A reformulation of race theory has been slow in light of the rapid demographic shifts that have accompanied the new socioeconomic and political relationships in the United States (Waldinger 1996). Asians are among the fastest growing new actors entering the stage (Espiritu 1997). These new actors are racialized within the structural, discursive, and ideological spheres. The state plays a role in controlling their labor by delineating the boundaries of race and the citizenship/immigration processes. While a growing body of literature has examined the social and legal construction of whiteness (Roediger 1991; Frankenberg 1993; Allen 1994; Ignatiev 1995; López 1996) and the material context of such ideological and discursive shifts, the new actors in the urban landscape have been largely ignored. In general, racialized group relations have been analyzed in relation to studies of blacks and whites (Gordon 1964; Jordon 1977; Essed 1991). A few scholars have explored the position of Latinos (Rodriguez 1991; Almaguer 1994; Gutierrez 1995). With the exception of Loewen (1971), scholarship about and by Asian and South Asian Americans have mostly focused on the areas of literary studies (Chin et al. 1974; Kim 1982) and history (Melendy 1981; Takaki 1987, 1989; Jensen 1988; Okihiro 1994).

This project attempts to address these gaps by examining the impact of South Asian immigration on racial formation in Los Angeles. Furthermore, it analyzes how relations are racialized between ethnic minority groups and ultimately how racist ideology is reproduced, maintained, and transformed. I argue that the experiences of Bangladeshis are linked to their racialization and to their racialized relationships with blacks, Latinos, other Asians, and whites in Los Angeles. It is also related to their understanding of "Americanness" and the U.S. racial categories imposed on them and the grounds on which they contest them. By focusing on their agency as social actors to transform as well as reproduce racial ideologies, I hope to provide an insight into how new actors in the landscape negotiate (within) structures and ideology. In this chapter, I present the particular issues that I as a Bangledeshi American woman researcher faced as an "insider" working within transnational frameworks of reference.

Outer Boundaries: Research Design

This research project contributes to the literature on South Asian Americans and on racism and racial formation in Los Angeles. My research examines a relatively new and growing immigrant community, that of the Bangladeshis in Los Angeles. I employed a three-pronged approach consisting of interviews, participant observation, and review of documents regarding the history of racial claims made by South Asians in the legal arena.

During the summer of 1993, I interviewed fourteen Bangladeshi women and four men. I had a Bangladeshi acquaintance who owned a store in the Los Angeles area. Her husband worked as a community organizer. Both introduced me to members of their community. I asked them to refer me to women engaged in a variety of occupations, living in different neighborhoods. I used a snowball method, asking each interviewee to introduce me to a few other Bangladeshis, to select the initial sample. Through these interviews I identified different segments of the community and initiated contact for the next stage of research.

Between 1993 and 1995, I spent eight months in Los Angeles. My initial survey located two distinct class-segregated communities. The first was a working-class community[2] in downtown Los Angeles, while the second was composed of professionals, including middle- to upper-middle-class immigrants. They had distinct organizations, the Bangladesh Association of Los Angeles (BALA) and the Bangladesh Association of California (BAC), respectively. In both organizations a small group of people were actively involved in organizing large community events.[3] I made many of my contacts through these organizations, though only four of my interviewees were active members. As I mentioned, I extended the interview sample by means of a snowball technique. I used meetings with Bangladeshis who worked at gas stations, at fast food and grocery stores, or as parking attendants, as well as chance encounters on street corners and in the hallways of apartment buildings, to generate more contacts. I talked to at least a hundred people informally in various social and community gatherings and at their workplaces whenever possible.

I conducted sixty taped interviews, each lasting between two to four hours. I interviewed most people at least twice. The interviews had two sections. The first was a series of general questions regarding a person's date of migration, socioeconomic background, immigration status, and the box[4] he or she filled when asked his or her race. Then I used open-ended, semi-structured interviews to analyze the everyday discourse of race, racism, self, and other in different spheres of immigrant life (Essed 1991; Twine, Warren, and Fernandiz 1991; Twine 1998). I asked how people defined racism, and whether they had ever faced any incidents of racism. Open-ended questions allowed me to analyze how they structured discourses on race and how they defined *race* and *racism,* to identify disruptions and continuity in their narratives, and to see what kinds of situations brought out racialized narratives. This process maximized "discovery and description."[5]

However, the scope of my participant observation study of the Bangladeshi community was limited by the complexities of my position in the community and therefore by the kind of access I had to informal social gatherings. This complexity will become apparent as I discuss the boundaries of the community and my place inside and outside it. This method complemented the interviews and explored racial discourse within multiple settings. I also reviewed the popular Bengali-American newspaper *Thikana* over a two-year period, to examine discussions of racialized experiences in the United States. A review of the history of legal racial classifications of Indians, Bangladeshis, and South Asians[6] in the United States was also made to examine the contestation and transformation of racial categories by Bangladeshis and South Asians at the state level. Multiple methods were thus used to achieve a triangulation method in order to link the micro and macro processes of racialized identity construction and to examine racialized experiences.

Language and Transnational Constraints

There is no word for race in Bengali. My interviews were conducted primarily in Bengali, the official language of Bangladesh. I read, write, and speak both Bengali and English fluently. Most of the people I interviewed had limited knowledge of English. This linguistic gap is indicative of the differences in the concepts of race and its contents in Bangladesh, the United States, and transnational communities.[7] Middle- to working-class interviewees did not typically respond to direct questions regarding the racial group they thought they belonged to, that is, what their "racial" identity was. Yet when asked about their experiences in the United States, racialized discourse became critical to their narratives. In conversation, *American* was equated with "white" Anglo-Americans and blacks, white being the norm. They translated some English terms into Bengali. Thus, European-Americans or whites were called *shada* (white) and black Americans were called *kallu* (black). They also used the English terms *negro, black, red Indian,* and *Native American*. People of Spanish-speaking backgrounds were referred to as Mexican or Spanish rather than Latino, Chicano, or Hispanic.

Interviewees had several responses to questions about racism and racial discrimination. A few had had no experience of racism or anti-immigrant sentiment. This may have been because they did not experience it, did not conceptualize it as such, or did not wish to share it with me. But most men and women provided many examples of what I viewed as a form of racial discrimination or racism. They offered three types of narratives. First, in some narratives they described being discriminated against because they were "foreign"; second, some narratives had an implicit element of racism, as when someone pointed to their "nonwhite" status; and third, some were explicitly racist.

"Foreign and American" is a racialized oppositional construction (Espiritu 1997) used to exclude racial minorities. As Lisa Lowe points out, "In the last century and a half, the American citizen has been defined over and against the Asian immigrant, legally, economically and culturally" (1996: 4). Therefore, I view the claims to antiforeign and nonwhite status as interrelated forms of racialized exclusion. But these are also distinct narratives in which the interviewees do not *name* their experience as racism. Respondents usually shared these narratives with me during discussions about their everyday lives and problems rather than in response to direct questions about racism. Therefore, it is critical that researchers explore descriptive life histories. Such a method uncovers the conceptual framework of respondents, which is different from the one the researcher employs.

For a researcher working in immigrant communities, questions about race can be particularly tricky. The categories of race are not stable or static in any context (Omi and Winant 1986; Root 1992; Davis 1993; Twine 1996; Warren and Twine 1997).[8] But this is especially true when we deal with *transnational* notions of race, for racial concepts do not travel easily across national contexts or translate across languages and conceptual frameworks (Rodriguez 1991; Marable 1993). First, the very notion of "race" needs to be problematized and explored for its content. Second, narratives need to be examined for the immigrants' unique and multiple notions of race and racism, and to identify where and how these notions reside in the narrative. Third, one must recognize the critical problems posed when one analyzes the experiences of immigrant communities solely within a nationality/ethnicity framework. Immigrant groups are racialized in specific ways in the post–civil rights United States. As they develop and/or acquire a racialized identity in relation to other racial groups, their location within the United States can transform their notions of "race" and Americanness. A researcher therefore needs to develop strategies to highlight and contextualize indigenous, postcolonial, *and* U.S. systems of racialization in immigrant narratives.

Me and My Community: Confronting Outsider within Status

I concur with Patricia Hill Collins (1991) and extend her analysis to include a Bangladeshi-American researcher. As an outsider in the U.S. academic community I can provide a unique perspective about the experience of Bangladeshi immigrants. But I also question the construction of community boundaries, asking who and what constitute belonging to a community. There are many axes of difference and commonality between me and "my community." Growing up in Bangladesh and interacting with Bangladeshi-American communities gave me an insight into some of the differences across gender, class, ethnic, religious, linguistic, cultural, and national lines that I would have to negotiate. Thus I anticipated some issues but also discovered others during my research. These negotiations interacted with my research interest to produce particular dilemmas. Maxine Baca Zinn, a Chicana sociologist, describes her research with Chicano families. She argues that minority scholars can generate questions that are different and that they face less distrust, hostility, and exclusion from minority communities (Andersen 1993: 41). I did face less hostility in some areas and could ask many questions about race and racism that "outside" scholars cannot do. But as an insider I also faced specific sites of hostility and dilemmas because of my class, gender position, the questions I asked, and the research product I have presented to the "outside" world.

I am a sociologist of upper-middle-class[9] Bangladeshi Muslim origin. I have lived in Bangladesh and the United States for almost equal lengths of time. My parents live in Bangladesh, while I have established a home in Oakland, California. This transnational experience shapes my communities and sense of belonging. I have always defined my community in the United States as multiethnic and multiracial—primarily men and women of color who are gay, lesbian, and straight. This is a community built out of political alliances, class, and academic settings. But since my marriage to a second-generation Bangladeshi-American in 1992, I have become a part of the Bay Area Bangladeshi community as well. This multiplicity of belongings raises the question, am I conducting research in my "own" community when I do research in the Bangladeshi community in Los Angeles? What are the contours of this belonging or exclusion?

Contours of Belonging/Exclusion

Most of my colleagues in the U.S. academy view me as an "insider" in my research community. However, the essentialized categories of nationality and ethnicity mask the complexities of "community" and its transnational boundaries. We are not automatically considered insiders in our respective ethnic communities. And both insider and outsider status hold specific meaning and consequences. Whenever I entered an interview session, I was interviewed first. I was always asked a series of questions about my background. These questions probed my class background, marital status, and my attitudes regarding a woman's role in the house and family. The most common questions were about my father's occupation, my parents' region of origin, my marital status, my role as a cook and homemaker, and my plans for motherhood. These questions were a means of evaluating my relationship to the individual members of the community and specific gendered constructions of community boundaries.

As South Asian feminist scholars have documented, in the early twentieth century, a nationalist discourse about "woman" became critical to the struggle against British imperialism in the region (Liddle and Joshi 1986; Banerjee 1989). The interaction between imperialism and nationalism created a binary opposition between world and home, Western(ized) and Eastern(deshi or national) (Chatterjee 1989).[10] Women were defined as belonging within the home and as symbols of tradition and upholders of the moral order (Liddle and Joshi 1986; Chatterjee 1989).[11] Nationalism reified middle-class women as the norm and reinscribed their role in the domestic sphere. Their sexuality and labor were controlled through marriage (Hartman 1981; Liddle and Joshi 1986). But middle- and upper-class women could avoid housework by purchasing the labor of working-class men and women. The ideal South Asian woman was also partially constructed against the notion of "Western" women. Western was defined as white and viewed in terms of the good woman-bad woman dichotomy (Jayawardena 1995). Good women are those who maintain gender hierarchy, while bad women are sexually immoral and licentious. South Asian women were/are scrutinized for signs of Westernness which was/is symbolized by their clothing and other markers.[12] In light of this nationalist discourse, the questions asked of me by members of the Los Angeles Bangladeshi community can be understood as an evaluation of my place within the class, gender, and race-specific notions of Bangladeshness and Westernness.[13]

An acquaintance invited me to a social gathering which was described as a young bicultural group. I dressed in jeans and a jacket. When I arrived, I found that all the women were wearing saris. For a large part of the evening I spoke to the only non-Bangladeshi woman in the room. She was a white high school teacher. I became embroiled in a conversation regarding Bangladeshi youth in the area's high schools. After the party one of the women informed me that I was being talked about. I was seen to have been acting white and wanting to be white. Another woman at the party casually told me, "No matter what people say, I don't care what people tell me, that they have white friends, they will never be white. And whites will always treat us as something inferior." A person's mannerisms, clothing, and frequent use of Americanized English are coded as symbols of Westernness/whiteness and outsider status. By speaking to a white woman, I was seen to have chosen whites over Bangladeshis and to have distanced myself from the Bangladeshi community. I was seen to have betrayed the community instead of showing my gendered ethnic solidarity with it.

My short hair, and the way I walked and talked, all inscribed me as outside the dominant nationalist definition of Bangladeshness. While I always tried to answer questions truthfully, I also policed how I presented myself. For example, I modified my clothing to appear "respectable." I never wore anything that revealed any skin or was tight. I developed a uniform for all my interviews. I chose two loose jumpsuits that were almost identical. I also wore a couple of long dresses that reached my ankles and had long sleeves. I found them to be convenient; once I had them on, I did not have to think about which parts of my body were covered, and how.[14]

I had arrived at the home of a lower-middle-class Bangladeshi woman to conduct an interview. I sat next to her on the couch. She examined my body silently and carefully, noting my (short) hair and clothes. After asking me about my marital status, parents, background, and the like, she asked me to give her my hand. She slowly rubbed her hand over the palm of my hand and examined it. She noted approvingly, "uh, you have a worker's hand." Then she asked me if I cooked at home and what we ate on a regular basis. I described some of the food I cooked. She picked the most common everyday item, *bhorta*,[15] and asked me how I would cook it. I told her. She nodded briefly and moved on to questions about my spouse, marriage, and reasons for not having had children so far.

After she had completed her evaluation, she allowed me to ask her about her life. I interpreted her questions as an attempt to evaluate my class status and to decide whether I had avoided domestic work. Through this exchange she was assessing and challenging my class status and *deshiness*[16] or my belonging to a gendered national community.[17] She was also actively controlling the parameters of the conversation. I managed my presentation of self (Goffman 1959) by highlighting my gendered knowledge base and containing my Western outsider status.

My *marital* status and housework skills helped me establish relationships with married women and gain respectability. Since my husband had not accompanied me to Los Angeles, I brought up his name occasionally to remind people that I was married. It provided me with a "legitimate" relationship with male members of the community. Men would call me *bhabi* or sister-in-law. Though most of them had never met my husband he became the fictive brother through whom we could establish a relationship.[18] This helped me establish some close and cordial relationships with men.

Nevertheless, I had a very difficult time setting up interviews with men, particularly when they were single.[19] Sociologist Shulamit Reinharz cautions that "the researcher who is young and female may be defined as a sex object to be seduced by heterosexual males" (Reinharz 1992: 58). I was repeatedly warned by members of the community that if I went to a man's house alone my reputation would be tarnished and my safety would be at stake. I tried to meet some men in cafés. But most men were uncomfortable sharing a meal or tea with a woman in a public space. Such encounters were also charged with sexual innuendo. I found that the most comfortable site when interviewing single men was at their workplace, or at a friend's workplace or home. Despite these efforts, toward the end of my research I started to receive anonymous and harassing phone calls from men telling me that my number was being circulated as "a woman who was available" to talk to. I dealt with these calls by explaining that I was a researcher documenting the experiences of Bangladeshi immigrants. I used my professional researcher status to distance and shield myself from the sexual advances of men.

While being a female interviewer created particular challenges, my gendered class background gave me privileges that were also problematic. A male interviewee explained why he preferred living in the United States. He had a master's degree. But he had been unable to find a good job in Bangladesh because he was not related to any wealthy people. He was very happy in the United States since he had a well-paying job and never faced any form of discrimination. It was in Bangladesh that the upper class had treated him poorly. While he shared this story with me he also reminded me that I was a part of the group that had treated him with disrespect.

> They advertise for jobs. But they have already decided who they are going to take. Either the guy [job seeker] has him [employer] in his back pocket [has bribed him] or he knows someone who knows this guy. You run from office to office, you wait in the waiting room for hours and sometimes they never call you, then they tell you come

tomorrow, sometimes they call you in and they are not even interested in you. And you have been running from door to door. But no one wants to hear about your qualifications. It's all set. In our country people treat you like dogs. They don't think we are human. We are just dogs, running around with your head cut off, all running after a job. Here there is dignity of labor. I make my money, come home in peace and I don't have to bow my head to anyone. If you are in Bangladesh even if you make your own little money any rich man in front of you sees you as his servant. He may not know you but he will feel free to order you around. Here I don't have to answer to anyone. In Bangladesh we are nothing more than animals to the rich men. I cannot tell you how many offices I ran to. . . . Didn't you say your father was an officer? Well then you know what I mean.

His comments focused on the class differences that had shaped our experiences and positions of privilege and disadvantage in Bangladesh. I responded by acknowledging that the upper class treated those of a lower social class condescendingly. Throughout our discussion he maintained an idealized image of the United States. Later, when I his interviewed his wife this narrative was disrupted. She explained that they had moved from Texas because they had gotten tired of the harassment they faced and wanted a new start. When her husband walked home from work a group of white men would routinely throw beer cans at him and shout profanities.[20] She said he always kept walking and never reported these incidents to anyone. They moved when he found a job in Los Angeles. Her husband had merely told me that he had moved to a better job. Perhaps my class and gender position had foreclosed discussions of experiences he considered humiliating. He also wished to portray an idealized place in which he could maintain his pride and dignity. I wondered whether men (and women), particularly those of a lower class than myself, were less likely to share experiences that were humiliating.

My class, gender, and bicultural identity all shaped my relationship to members of the community. I had to survey my own presentation constantly to remain inscribed within community boundaries. In this section I have traced the axis of differences which were negotiated in order to produce this research. The examples I have given show how interviewees questioned and challenged my position as a researcher and shaped the research process and product. While this interaction demonstrates the schisms of power and difference, it should not mask my power to shape the final research product. Therefore, keeping in mind that some life stories are always inaccessible, I focus on locating the spaces within which respondents shared their experiences. While my insider status provided me with unique insights and access, it also created particular dilemmas.

Assumed, Shared Racism

Most of the time I was considered a racial insider. During interviews people felt very comfortable making vehemently racist statements against blacks and Latinos because it was assumed that I would share these views. Most people freely made statements, in public and private, which were particularly virulent against black Americans. Blacks are commonly called *kallus* (blackies) in Bengali. During a cultural event attended by eight hundred people the MC opened the program with a joke about *kallus*.[21] Such routine racialized hatred was usually expressed in Bengali rather than English. The comments ranged from claims that blacks ruined property values, that they were thieves, were lazy and deserved an occasional reminder of their place in society through a beating, that they were stupid, and that black women were licentious, to the general assumption that they were an inferior group of people. Blacks were considered naturally savage and delinquent. This inferiority was seen to be proven by their enslavement. Patricia Hill Collins has called these "controlling images" (Collins 1990). Such images are used by the political and economic elite to naturalize racism, sexism, and poverty. Immigrant groups who face specific controlling images can also reproduce controlling images of their own about groups such as blacks, thus participating in the maintenance of a racial hierarchy.

Racist discourse about black Americans was common in conversations about life in the United States. One day I struck up a conversation with a Bangladeshi man, Shahed, who was working in a parking lot. Within the first ten minutes he identified the main source of his problems as black Americans. He said vehemently, "I hate blacks. Black people are my worst enemy. Even if someone slapped me I would forgive them, but I would never forgive a black. I will always hate blacks, they are my worst enemy in this country." He said he constantly distanced himself from blacks to gain dignity in the United States (see Warren and Twine 1997). People shared such views freely with me in public and private spaces. Shahed had made the above comment while standing outside his booth, on a street corner. As I glanced over my shoulder I saw three older black men sitting on a bus stop bench, a Latino family of four walking past us, and a white man driving past the parking booth, all within earshot. Shahed was insulated from all these people because he was speaking in Bengali. Our "foreign" language had created a private space even in a public arena. This shared language created an insular and permissive space for such conversation.

On another occasion, I had finished talking to three middle-class Bangladeshi men and was getting ready to leave. As I packed my things they started discussing local events. I had faded into the background. Jafar was talking about a shooting incident in the area during which one black man had shot and killed another. The altercation was said to have been over a can of beer.

> Jafar said, "This *kallu* just killed this other *kallu* [laugh] over this small thing, just killed him! Just kill each other off, why do you need the white man, you can do the job, you people are gone case."
>
> I froze in my chair. I tried to think of the right comment or question. After a few seconds I asked, "Um, I am not sure what you mean. Why is it a good thing for a black man to have died or . . . for black men to kill each other?"
>
> Jafar turned to look at me and seemed surprised that I still considered myself a part of the conversation. He laughed, glanced over me, and responded by looking at the two other men. "[Laugh]! What are *shadas* [whites] going to do with them [blacks]? They have fed, bred, and looked after[22] them for all these years, still they have not been able to do anything for themselves. They have not been able to stand on their own feet. They say it's all the whites' fault. What is the point in always blaming the whites? The white man didn't pull the trigger, it was a black man. They are doing this. Living just like animals, not like humans. So, what can you do, just let them kill each other off."

The other two men sat silently as Jafar laughed at his own comments. While it was not clear whether the others agreed with his sentiments, they did not challenge him. Neither did I. The men continued with their conversation as though I had already left. I sat in silence for a few moments.

When I got up to leave they stood up, smiled, and asked if they could walk me to my car. I declined the offer and left the building. I had repeatedly been made visible and invisible during the conversation. As I indicated earlier, my age and gender position contributed to such interactions. At times these power dynamics made it difficult to have a dialogue. Yet my assumed insider status and language skills gave me access to many formal and informal exchanges about black Americans that would probably have been inaccessible to an outsider.

When I first met people in the community they would ask me where I was from in the United States. When I said I lived in Oakland, California, many of them would earnestly advise me to immediately move out of this "black" area. This imagery clearly evoked fear and concern in them. During a chance encounter with a Bangladeshi woman I did not interview, I was told to move out of the "Black City." I laughed and replied, "That is why I live there—because I am black too." The stunned, confused woman was speechless. She simply walked away from me without saying another word. This incident occurred within the first week of my stay in Los Angeles. After this short interaction I began to ponder my response and its place in my research. Should I challenge these views? To what extent and in what form would I respond to such comments within and outside the interviews?

Interviewee Responses

Striking Back

I was interviewing Arif and was asking him about the categories he was usually mistaken for in the United States. He told me that most people mistook him for an Indian or Spanish person (referring to a Latino/Mexican category). I asked him if he had ever been mistaken for black man. He immediately recoiled physically in his seat. He vehemently denied that he had ever been mistaken for a black. He was obviously offended. As an "insider" I recognized that skin color is a very sensitive issue in the Bangladeshi community. White and fair skin signify beauty and power. There is an intricate color hierarchy, in which darker-skinned people are called dirty and fairer ones are called clean.

Being very dark automatically means one is ugly. It is considered rude to point to the darkness of one's skin color unless the person being referred to is absent. When people want to speak about someone who has dark skin they always say, "*even though* s/he is black . . . (they have a sweet face or . . .)." The man sitting in front of me was very dark. Having such insider information, I did not want to appear insulting. I commented on my own experience. The following is an excerpt from my field notes: "So I quickly added that in Ohio I had been mistaken for black. He shot back, 'I can see that.' And then in a more calm voice he said, 'I hope you don't mind but there are a lot of light skinned, mixed blacks and you don't really look like a Bangladeshi.'"

In this interaction and in other situations I have found that while people would deny that they had ever been mistaken for a black person, they would turn around and say that I could easily pass for black. These interactions carried two kinds of meaning. The first response was what I call *striking back*. They were insulted by what they considered my insinuation about their skin color and that they may pass for the "idea" of black in America. They were retaliating by calling me black. Noting skin color and/or associating it with blacks was a way of telling me that I was not fair skinned (superior) myself. I was the one who could pass for black, not the other way around. After the interview I realized that I should have followed up with questions regarding the markers he was using to evaluate me as "black" versus himself as "not black." Instead I had tried to redirect the focus away from the insinuation that he could be "black." Therefore, as a researcher I had to negotiate my own insider knowledge about the connotations and sensitivity around skin color and decide how and when to call attention to it. Just as my insider status gave me access to particular discourses, it also made others difficult to explore.

From my exposure to different Bangladeshi communities, I was familiar with racist attitudes toward U.S. blacks. But I was not prepared for the extent to which it was a part of everyday life and conversation. This "discovery" forced me to recognize all the times when I had listened to similar comments and ignored them or had been silent in its presence. I had focused on the experiences I shared with other Bangladeshis such as food, language, and memories of places and ways of life. It provided me with a slice of home and belonging which I could not get from friends from other backgrounds. This commonality gave me access and entry into the Bangladeshi community in Los Angeles.

But as I entered the community as a researcher, I contemplated the price for my inclusion in "my community." If I challenged antiblack comments I could be silenced by being ignored and made invisible. The hostility generated by my questions could easily shut me out of critical parts of the community and my research interest. But if I were to remain silent I would be participating in perpetuating racist discourse. Since I had been reminded that I could be symbolically expelled from the community if I associated members of the community or myself with the category "black," the price for my entry and inclusion was my silence.

Marking Ethnicity

The second response to my question regarding racial identity was to *mark ethnicity.* Bangladeshis tacitly recognize that they can easily be coded as black and Latino in the United States. They point to their ethnic markers as a way of distancing their own bodies from blacks. They create a racialized discourse about the ways in which they are culturally and physically distinct from blacks and Latinos. These distinctions are class- and gender-specific. Blacks and Latinos, particularly of the working class, are seen to be promiscuous and immoral. In the U.S. context, the gendered anticolonial definitions of Western as white are expanded to include working-class white, black, and Latina women. "Their" women's immorality is marked by their choice of clothing, body language, associations with men outside the family, and consumption of alcohol. Therefore, an idealized Bangladeshi woman cannot and does not do any of these things. As described earlier, faced with such gendered definitions of ethnicity, I policed the way I presented myself. This process of marking ethnicity also demonstrated how the boundaries of ethnicity are constructed against specific racialized images. Therefore, ethnicized and racialized discourses are intertwined.

Presenting the Community: Containing Boundaries

An immigrant community redefines the boundaries of "community" when there is a sudden and dramatic shift in geography and socioeconomic and political context. This shift can lead to intense struggles over representation and contestation by groups to control the boundaries of community in the new social order. The following are excerpts from some interviews that highlight the slippery terrain of these boundaries and the way race, class, and gender shapes them in the U.S. context. These contestations occurred in three arenas, through attempts to exclude the stories of earlier immigrants because of their racial affiliations and social location, which marked some members of the same national group as racial outsiders, and marked me as a racial other. These stories illustrate how immigrant communities redraw community boundaries in a system where bodies are racially marked and where racial signification is linked to power and status in the larger society (Islam in press).

Those Racially Other Bangladeshis

The markers of nationality and ethnicity are considered primary in researching immigrant communities in the United States. Yet no national and/or ethnic community is homogeneous. And in the context of the U.S. racial order, not all groups in such communities occupy the same racial location. For example, in Bangladesh the Hill Peoples of the south are marked by their clothing and language and by the Animist, Buddhist, and Hindu religions. Although seen as Bangladeshi citizens, they are second class (Tripura 1992). They are socially and politically repressed through the military and by an ideology of ethnic and religious inferiority. When Bangladeshi immigrants construct a new community in the United States, they try to create it on the basis of old boundaries and new contexts. While Hill People and lowland Bengali Muslim immigrants do have some connections, they are limited to individual contacts. The relationships and markers of exclusion and inclusion between the two groups are further complicated by the racialized terrain of American society.

I met two Hill People immigrants in Los Angeles by a mixture of luck and my own insider identity. There are very few Hill immigrants in the United States. One of the ways they have left Bangladesh is through the support of Buddhist temples in South and Southeast Asia. Therefore, those who live in the Los Angeles area associate with Cambodian Buddhist communities and have married Cambodian women. While I was interviewing a store owner in a predominantly Southeast Asian segment of the city, I ran into one such immigrant. I was introduced to him because I grew up in southern Bangladesh, though I am not a member of a Hill community. Through him I was able to speak to two other immigrants. They informed me that in the United States they are viewed as East Asian. Their associations through temple, family, and friendship in combination with physical markers had shaped this racialization:

> Went to . . . street. Predominantly South East Asian Neighborhood. A few Blacks. Two patrol cars on the way down 10th and two parked almost in front of the house I was going to. The apartment was in an old dilapidated building, a few people standing outside and talking. Bars on doors and windows, peeling paint. Walked to the door and knocked. . . . They are not involved in/with the Bengali/Bangladeshi community. Just getting to know a few Bengalis now since one has opened a store down the street. . . . Both Opu and Shefal said they were viewed as Asians/East Asians, by most people. Never mistaken for Indian or Bangladeshi. They say even Bangladeshis exclaim when they ever run into each other. They think they are Chinese or South East Asian. (Fieldnotes)

Hill People and tribes and other ethnic and religious minorities in Bangladesh are excluded from the boundaries of Bengali/Bangladeshi identity. These ethnic identities have carried over to the immigrant landscape. But the immigrant space also helps pry open assumed categories and transposes new lenses—a racialized lens. After the interviews with Opu and Shefal I asked Non-Hill Peoples from Bangladesh how Hill Peoples were viewed in the community. A few people said that while they "admitted" that Hill Peoples were Bangladeshi, they did not see them as part of the Bangladeshi community. They asked me rhetorical questions about how Hill Peoples were all "obviously" different from "us." One woman said, "They are more comfortable with people like them. That is why I think they mix with [East] Asians." Bengali interviewees shared with me the "fact" that Hill Peoples had "chinky chinky" eyes (a derogatory reference to Chinese people and the shape of their eyes) and, "when you look at them you can just understand immediately that they are not like us." When I asked this interviewee if he would have noticed the same physical distinctions in Bangladesh, he replied, "Yes. But that may not have caught my eye because maybe I would think they are from the Chittagong Hill tribe. But usually when you saw them in Dhaka they could speak Bengali, so you knew they were only the tribals."

Racial categories are not stable and may be transformed upon migration. Groups whose exclusion from the dominant Bangladeshi communities may have been based on religious and ethnic differences can take on a racial meaning in the United States. While dominant groups in the Bangladeshi community wish to represent the Hill Peoples as "outsiders," the particular experiences illustrate the way Bangladeshi experiences are racialized in the United States. When community boundaries are reconstructed in a new national context, a homogenized, contained and deliberately exclusive version of a community will be produced. Scholars must therefore be conscious of the contestation and transformation of racial categories by immigrant communities in the United States.

Mixed Marriages and Early Immigrant History

During my research I uncovered evidence of early Bangladeshi immigration (1900–1945)[23] most of it by poor male merchant marines who overstayed their shore leaves. They faced segregation, antimiscegenation laws, and were employed at low-wage agricultural and service jobs. They married black and Mexican-American women and became integrated into multiracial communities. The men who married black women faced some social distancing from those who married Mexican women. All these immigrants have died. The next group of immigrants (1945–1975) consisted of students and middle-class male professionals who brought back wives from Bangladesh. I tried to trace the lives of the early immigrants to document their racialized location and track how and if it changed for later immigrants who possessed more resources.

Mr. Mir, a middle-class immigrant, immigrated to the U.S. in the 1950s. While he distinguished his class background from the merchant marines, his current socioeconomic position in the United States did not differ significantly. He knew the earlier merchant marine immigrants and attempted to restrict the representations of community history by excluding the stories of the widows of these immigrants and their children. He did not see these families, or for that matter himself, as part of a history worth remembering. He did not want what he termed "the humiliation of initial immigrants facing racism" to be made public. He wished to erase his hardships from history. So he directed and tried to control the boundaries of my research. While he was willing to talk to me he refused a formal interview and tried to block my efforts to contact the black and Mexican-American spouses. He also spread the word to other older immigrants and asked them to deny me interviews.

I had talked to Mr. Sheikh who came in the 1950s and knew the earlier immigrants. He had initially promised an interview. But when I called back to set up a time I faced questions and barriers and eventually a refusal to be interviewed because of my interest in earlier immigrants. He claimed that this was not a legitimate arena of inquiry. He went on to ask why I was looking for the Mexican-American wives of their old friends, and told me that there was no point in my interviewing older immigrants. They were too few in number, he said. Then he decided to tell me how to conduct my research. He said, why do you need to talk to people, why don't you just send off a survey questionnaire? That would be a lot better. When I tried to answer his questions, he reminded me that he spoke from a position of authority as he was an older male and had studied "pure science." I had run into that before. He was not listening, but was comfortable thwarting my questions and explanations by the sheer authority of his "knowing" (as a science major) and his own agenda. It was not a tone of inquiry—rather he would cut me off before I could even answer his questions. This time he was not being the supportive older male happy to give an interview. He was now not interested in my research but was probing to find out who I would talk to and why. He indicated he had spoken to Mr. Mir about this. Mr. Mir had suggested, he said, that he should not talk to me. He said I should be talking to the newer immigrants. And what would I do with the older generation story?

These older immigrant men kept in touch with the families of their deceased friends. Yet they guarded these stories and families, keeping them out of the community's history. Mr. Sheikh used his "authority" as an older male to discipline and silence me.[24] This group of immigrants had decided that Mexican-American and black spouses were not legitimate purveyors of community history, though they had created the space in their homes for the community to meet and build itself up. The children of mixed black, Mexican, and Bangladeshi heritage were not seen as being "inside" the community. Although patriarchy inscribes children as the father's "property," in this instance the children were associated with their mothers "race." They were not considered a part of the Bangladeshi community.[25]

The reason why the older immigrants were trying to "shelter" this part of the community's history had to do with the racial and class positions of the early immigrants. Most of the initial immigrants came from poor backgrounds and wanted to escape their lower status. Some came from middle-class backgrounds and found themselves unable to maintain their class status in the United States. And they faced a racially divided world in which they saw themselves as being at the bottom. They were excluded from citizenship, delegated to the worst agricultural jobs, not allowed to buy land or to work in most jobs (Jensen 1988), and were forced to live in segregated neighborhoods as did blacks, Asians, Latinos (and other racial minorities), based on their "race." In the eyes of later generations, this generation of immigrants had not realized the "American Dream" but had led an American nightmare in many ways. As bell hooks points out, "To experience the pain of race hatred or to witness that pain is not to understand its origin, evolution, or impact on world history. . . . We were given romantic notions of the 'new world,' the 'American dream,' America as the great melting pot where all races come together as one . . ." (1981: 119–20). Many immigrants took their inability to realize this dream as a bitter personal failure and wished to silence stories that brought their failure to light.

Most of the early immigrants told me what I should write about the later immigrants who are professionals, have been economically successful, and have had more "dignified" histories. Show the good face of the community, they instructed. Men who were poor and/or had married black and Mexican women were not the good face and neither were their families. Efforts were also under way to systematically eliminate or contain the stories of women and the working class. Only middle- and upper-class, legal immigrants deemed economically successful were worthy of representing Bangladeshis. Therefore, the legitimate storytellers were assigned by class, gender, and racial position, association, and history.

This attempt to contain a community's representation is reflected in the desire of segments of that community to maintain a model minority image (Espiritu 1997; Okihiro 1994). This image is constructed against the image of blacks who are seen to have failed due to their inability to take advantage of the American Dream. This dream serves as a "controlling image" repressing both Asian Americans and blacks (Espiritu 1997), while justifying the racial hierarchy. France Winddance Twine theorizes, in the context of her research in Brazil, that silences that do not challenge racism maintain white supremacy. Many professional Bangladeshis (and other Asians) reproduce and maintain this racial hierarchy by accepting and perpetuating the model minority myth. By challenging the border patrols of representation and unpacking the racialized narratives in the framework of domination and resistance, Bangladeshi and Asian American scholars can attempt to break this silence and challenge racial hierarchies.

The Researcher as Translator and Betrayer

I spent many hours with interviewees who recounted stories of their own degradation as nonwhites and foreigners in U.S. society. They described facing intense forms of racism and exclusion. Bangladeshis viewed themselves as under attack from the U.S. state which restricted their immigration and rights, and from "Americans"[26] (defined as whites and blacks) and East Asians (at times defined as white) in their everyday lives. They described incidents that were daily reminders of their low social status. They claimed that both blacks and whites reminded them that even if they gained official citizenship they would not be included in the cultural representations of an "American." They would always be seen as "foreigners" and asked where they were really from. Middle-class Bangladeshis reported that they confronted the glass ceiling in the workplace and other forms of exclusion. Working-class Bangladeshis reported frequent incidents of physical violence and threat of violence or verbal abuse from Americans. They described verbal racialized violence and humiliation from whites, blacks, and East Asians. They did not mention Latinos in this context.[27] Thus, faced with the idea of permanent exclusion from the U.S. national community and multiple forms of discrimination, they felt besieged as well.

People in the community saw my research project as an opportunity to document their community history for the next generation, to present themselves to the larger (white) American community, to voice their grievances, and to fulfill my personal and academic interests. They documented their life stories and own racialized oppression while reproducing a racist ideology about "other" racial minorities. Some wished to present an idealized model minority image of the community that necessitated severing any relationship to blacks and Latinos. As a researcher parts of the community expected me to censor and skew my presentation to meet these interests. One interviewee who was making racist jokes at a social event found me unresponsive and gathered that I did not share his views. He then turned to me and said, "I know, I know, you are gathering data. You are going to say we are racist. But you don't need to write about what we think of them [blacks]. Focus on what we are going through. That is what your focus should be on. Focus on us." He insisted that I focus on his experiences of racism and omit his own racism toward other groups.

Given this context, a Bangladeshi scholar documenting the experiences of her "own" community faces a critical responsibility. By outlining the contours of the racial ideology of Bangladeshi immigrants I risk being viewed as a traitor within my ethnic community. My very insider status allowed me to participate in and overhear conversations that routinely included racist views. The price of my inclusion in the community was to leave racist discourses uncontested. Should I reveal this "dirty laundry" once I have completed my research? By doing so, will I be distancing myself from and claiming to be better than the rest of "my community"? The history and experiences of the Bangladeshi community in the United States are yet undocumented. Should its introduction be "overshadowed" by the racist discourse the community reproduces? How should I represent a marginalized community within and through my work?

A Bangladeshi community is a part of my community. But I challenge the notion of an essentialized national and/or ethnic community. The Bangladeshi immigrant communities themselves reconstruct community boundaries within the racialized context of the United States. Those who do not fit the dominant interests of the community and its idealized image are excluded. If a part of that exclusion is based on one's antiracist politics then I claim my own belonging within a different political community.

As bell hooks reminds us, third world nationals (within and outside the U.S.) can illuminate their own oppression yet be silent about the position of those of African descent:

> We often forget that many third world nationals bring to this country the same kind of contempt and disrespect for blackness that is most frequently associated with white western imperialism. While it is true that many third world nationals who live in Britain and the United States develop through theoretical and concrete experience knowl-

edge of how they are diminished by white western racism, that does not always lead them to interrogate the way in which they enter a racialized hierarchy where in the eyes of whites they automatically have a greater status and privilege than individuals of African descent. (1990: 93–94)

Conclusion

My research reemphasized my own need to interrogate everyday narratives since racism is deeply embedded in everyday language, and in ways of knowing and living. If I sanitize and silence parts of my research that challenge the Bangladeshi community's image of itself and its role in perpetuating racism, I betray my commitment to struggle against racism. Describing the process by which Bangladeshis reproduce racism and racist ideologies need not negate a presentation of the oppression Bangladeshis themselves face, and vice versa. Silencing either may be viewed as an act of betrayal. Scholars facing such dilemmas may choose to remain silent about how minority communities can participate in and reproduce racist ideologies. Ultimately such silences subvert an analysis and understanding of how racism operates and how racialized systems of domination and inequality are maintained. Therefore, such silences are a betrayal of antiracist politics.

NOTES

I would like to thank France Winddance Twine for her editorial comments and support in writing this chapter. Sucheta Mazumdar inspired this work through her pioneering article documenting the antiblack attitudes of South Asians.

1. My political and social ties were with U.S. blacks, Latinos, Filipinos, and other Asian Americans of diverse national origins and diverse political and cultural histories.

2. Bangladeshis who live in the downtown neighborhoods range from unskilled laborers to those who are college educated. But due to the undocumented (illegal) status of some, the job market, and other factors they were all involved in blue-collar, service sector jobs. I define them as working class because of their current class position in the United States, not because of their middle-class or upper-middle-class origins in Bangladesh.

3. Typical events were large picnics where an admission fee included food, a visiting Bangladeshi singer, dancer, or theater group, or local cultural events where area residents presented their own talents.

4. France Winddance Twine asked interviewees how they self-identified racially when forced to choose from among the identity boxes on federal and other official forms. This enabled her to analyze the construction of racial identity and racial consciousness among young adults who had one black and one nonblack (Asian, white, Latino) parent in the post–civil rights United States. See Twine, Warren, and Fernandiz 1991; and Twine 1996.

5. From Janice Raymond, *The Transsexual Empire: The Making of the She-Male* (Boston: Beacon Press, 1976), quoted in Reinharz 1992.

6. Bangladesh was a part of India until 1947 and of Pakistan until 1971. Therefore, Bangladeshis appear in historical documents as Indian and Pakistani citizens. Recent scholarship in the United States has placed Bangladeshis within a South Asian category (Islam 1993). Therefore all these categories are applicable to Bangladeshi immigrants.

7. Some did not speak English at all. This difference in language skills usually reflected class background. People from upper-class or middle-class backgrounds were much more likely to speak English fluently. Depending on people's language skills, I also used Bengali and English interchangeably in some interviews. I later translated and transcribed all the interviews into English.

8. Scholarship on the construction of the U.S. categories referred to as black and white has illuminated the social construction of race. People of ambiguous racial ancestry who self-identify as "mixed race" or multiracial have always posed a challenge to the naturalness of these racial categories and boundaries.

9. My life history encompasses a few shifts in class position. I have moved from middle-class to upper-middle-class status through my parents' upward mobility and my own marriage.

10. *Deshi* is a Bengali and Urdu/Hindi word meaning "of one's own country."

11. Chatterjee notes that Indians could utilize science and technology in the outside world but at home their "true identity" was to be maintained. Within the home the man was also the ruler, a role denied him in the public world by the colonizer. "In the world, imitation of and adaptation to western norms was a necessity; at home they were tantamount to annihilation of one's very identity" (1989: 239).

12. Class and Westernness are often intertwined. Upper-class women are more likely to be viewed as Western.

13. I will be using the terms Bangladeshiness and Westernness to signify dominant discourses of nationality and inclusion developed within a South Asian anticolonial context.

14. Most Bangladeshi women have adapted their clothing to the U.S. context. They have begun to wear long dresses and loose "Western" clothing. Therefore, I tried to wear clothing appropriate to the context. Pants and a shirt were usually not considered acceptable female attire.

15. *Bhorta* is a Bengali word for a type of cooking used to cook vegetables with little or no oil. Since vegetables are relatively cheap and oil is expensive, this type of cooking is associated with a lack of wealth.

16. Deshiness refers to an evaluation of one's relationship to a *deshi* (national) community. Within the context of this chapter it refers to a specific hegemonic discourse of Bangladeshi identity.

17. While a nationalist discourse constrains and controls women's roles, women also challenge it. This interviewee told me that she approved of the way I had managed my home, independence, and educational goals. She too had broken gender barriers in her life.

18. My spouse was living in Hawaii and Oakland while I was conducting my research in Los Angeles. We only had occasional weekend visits in Oakland or Los Angeles. Thus he was an almost invisible figure in the community.

19. Many immigrant men are forced to live without their families. Men come as primary migrants and are unable to bring their families to the United States due to immigration restrictions and financial instability. There are also many unmarried men between the ages of twenty and thirty.

20. She did not tell me exactly what these men had said. She said she could not bring herself to speak such words. But she described them as being against foreigners.

21. "Inside there was a male and female MC each coming alternately. The woman was speaking in English and the man mostly in Bengali. He was making all kinds of football jokes and then in one of the World Cup jokes he says, 'A Blackie (*kallu*) asked me . . . if' . . . imitates a 'Black' accent, a kind of nondescript accent" (field notes).

22. Jafar was using a Bengali phrase, *pele pushe,* which is commonly used to describe the relationship between a benevolent superior and dependent subordinates or pets.

23. There has been mention of a few early Bangladeshi immigrants in documents on South Asian-American history (Jensen 1988; Melendy 1981). But my research is the first to document the life stories of Bangladeshis arriving between 1910 and 1960.

24. Anthropologist Dorinne Kondo addresses similar problems, describing how she was viewed as a subordinated daughter/woman, rather than a competent researcher, by older men in the Japanese community (Kondo 1986).

25. During my visits to Bangladesh since this research I have noticed children of mixed race and how they are perceived there. Children born to

Bangladeshi mothers or fathers are treated as Bangladeshi. Families do often joke that these children are "foreign." But second-generation Bangladeshi-Americans both of whose parents are Bangladeshi are also referred to as foreign, referring to their culture rather than their race.

26. Though inscribing blacks within the "American" category is fraught with silences about their exclusion and oppression, Bangladeshi immigrants view blacks as the "other" Americans. While whites are the "norm," blacks are seen to have successfully claimed their status as "Americans" in a way that Asian and Latino groups have not been able to.

27. Bangladeshis may view upper-class Latinos as whites since they partly define *white* by skin color. Working-class and brown-skinned Latinos are viewed as "illegal," "alien," and inscribed outside the construction of the category "American."

REFERENCES

Almaguer, Tomas. 1994. *Racial Fault Lines: The Historical Origins of White Supremacy in California*. Berkeley: University of California Press.

Allen, Theodore. 1994. *The Invention of the White Race*. New York: Verso.

Andersen, Margaret L. 1993. "Studying across Difference: Race, Class, and Gender in Qualitative Research." In *Race and Ethnicity in Research Methods,* edited by John Stanfield and Dennis M. Rutledge. Newbury Park, Calif.: Sage.

Banerjee, Sumanta. 1989. "Marginalization of Women's Popular Culture in Nineteenth Century Bengal." In *Recasting Women: Essays in Colonial History,* edited by Kumkum Sangari and Sudesh Vaid. New Delhi: Kali for Women.

Blauner, Robert. 1972. *Racial Oppression in America*. Berkeley: University of California Press.

Bonacich, Edna. 1972. "A Theory of Ethnic Antagonism: The Split Labor Market." *American Sociological Review* 37: 547–59.

———. 1973. "A Theory of Middleman Minorities." *American Sociological Review* 38: 583–94.

———. 1980. "Class Approaches to Ethnicity and Race." *Insurgent Sociologist* 10 (2): 9–23.

Chan, Sucheng. 1991a. *Asian Americans: An Interpretive History*. Boston: Twayne Publishers.

———. 1991b. *Asian Californians*. San Francisco: MTL/Boyd and Fraser.

Chang, Edward T., and Russell Leong, eds. 1994. *Los Angeles—Struggles toward Multiethnic Community*. Seattle: University of Washington Press.

Chatterjee, Partha. 1989. "The Nationalist Resolution of the Women's Question." In *Recasting Women: Essays in Colonial History,* edited by Kumkum Sangari and Sudesh Vaid. New Delhi: Kali for Women.

Chin, Frank, Jeffery Chan, Lawson F. Inada, and Shawn Hsu Wong, eds. 1974. *An Anthology of Asian American Writers.* Washington, D.C.: Howard University Press.

Collins, Patricia Hill. 1990. *Black Feminist Thought: Knowledge, Consciousness, and the Politics of Empowerment.* New York: Routledge.

———. 1991. "Learning from the Outsider Within: The Sociological Significance of Black Feminist Thought." In *Beyond Methodology: Feminist Scholarship as Lived Research,* edited by Mary Margaret Fonow and Judith A. Cook, pp. 35–59. Bloomington: Indiana University Press.

Davis, James. F. 1993. *Who Is Black? One Nation's Definition.* University Park: Pennsylvania State University Press.

Espiritu, Yen Le. 1997. *Asian American Women and Men.* Thousand Oaks, Calif.: Sage.

Essed, Philomena. 1991. *Understanding Everyday Racism: An Interdisciplinary Theory* (Sage Series on Race and Ethnic Relations, vol. 2). Newbury Park, Calif.: Sage.

Fisher, Maxine P. 1980. *The Indians of New York City: A Study of Immigrants from India.* New Delhi: Heritage Publishers.

Frankenberg, Ruth. 1993. *White Women, Race Matters: The Social Construction of Whiteness.* Minneapolis: University of Minnesota Press.

Glazer, Nathan, and Daniel P. Moynihan. 1963. *Beyond the Melting Pot.* Cambridge: M.I.T. Press.

Goffman, Erving. 1959. *The Presentation of Self in Everyday Life.* New York: Anchor Books.

Gordon, Milton. 1964. *Assimilation in American Life: The Role of Race, Religion, and National Origins.* New York: Oxford University Press.

Gutierrez, David G. 1995. *Walls and Mirrors: Mexican Americans, Mexican Immigrants, and the Politics of Ethnicity.* Berkeley: University of California Press.

Hartman, Heidi. 1981. "The Unhappy Marriage of Marxism and Feminism: Towards a More Progressive Union." In *Women and Revolution,* edited by Lydia Sargent. London: Pluto.

hooks, bell. 1981. *Ain't I a Woman: Black Women and Feminism.* Boston: South End Press.

———. 1990. *Yearning: Race, Gender, and Cultural Politics.* Boston: South End Press.

Ignatiev, Noel. 1995. *How the Irish Became White.* New York: Routledge.

Islam, Naheed. 1993. "In the Belly of the Multicultural Beast I Am Named South

Asian." In *Our Feet Walk the Sky: Women of the South Asian Diaspora*, edited by the Women of South Asian Descent Collective. San Francisco: Aunt Lute.

——. In press. "Race Markers Transgressors: Mapping a Racial Kaleidoscope within an (Im)migrant Landscape." In *American Encounters*, edited by Rajini Srikanth, Roshni Rustomji-Kerns, and Leny Strobel. Boston: Rowan and Littlefield.

Jayawardena, Kumari. 1995. *The White Woman's Other Burden: Western Women and South Asia during British Rule*. New York: Routledge.

Jensen, Joan M. 1988. *Passage from India: Asian Indian Immigrants in North America*. New Haven: Yale University Press.

Jibou, Robert M. 1988. *Ethnicity and Assimilation: Blacks, Chinese, Filipinos, Japanese, Koreans, Mexicans, Vietnamese, and Whites*. Albany: State University of New York Press.

Jordon, Winthrop D. 1977. *White over Black: American Attitudes towards the Negro, 1550–1812*. New York: Norton.

Kim, Elaine H. 1982. *Asian American Literature: An Introduction to the Writings and Their Social Context*. Philadelphia: Temple University Press.

Kondo, Dorinne K. 1986. "Dissolution and Reconstruction of Self: Implications for Anthropological Epistemology." In *Cultural Anthropology* 1 (1): 74–88.

Liddle, Joanna, and Rama Joshi. 1986. *Daughters of Independence: Gender, Caste and Class in India*. New Brunswick, N.J.: Rutgers University Press.

Light, Ivan, and Edna Bonacich. 1988. *Immigrant Entrepreneurs: Koreans in Los Angeles*. Berkeley: University of California Press.

Loewen, James W. 1971. *The Mississippi Chinese: Between Black and White*. Prospect Heights, Ill.: Waveland Press.

López, Ian F. Haney. 1996. *White by Law: The Legal Construction of Race*. New York: New York University Press.

Lowe, Lisa. 1996. *Immigrant Acts: Asian American Cultural Politics*. Durham: Duke University Press.

Marable, Manning. 1993. "Beyond Racial Identity Politics: Towards a Liberation Theory for Multicultural Democracy." *Race and Class* 35 (1): 113–30.

Mazumdar, Sucheta. 1989. "Race and Racism: South Asians in the United States." In *Frontiers of Asian American Studies*. Pullman: Washington State University Press.

Melendy, H. Brett. 1981. *Asians in America: Fillipinos, Koreans, and East Indians*. New York: Hippocrene Press.

Min, Pyong Gap. 1996. *Caught in the Middle: Korean Merchants in America's Multiethnic Cities*. Berkeley: University of California Press.

Okihiro, Gary Y. 1994. *Margins and Mainstreams: Asians in American History and Culture*. Seattle: University of Washington Press.

Omi, Michael, and Howard Winant. 1986. *Racial Formation in the United States: From the 1960s to the 1990s*. New York: Routledge.

Ong, Paul, Edna Bonacich, and Lucie Cheng. 1994. *The New Asian Immigration in Los Angeles and Global Restructuring*. Philadelphia: Temple University Press.

Park, Kyeyoung. 1997. *The Korean American Dream: Immigrants and Small Business in New York City*. Ithaca: Cornell University Press.

Park, Robert E. 1950. *Race and Culture*. Glencoe, Ill.: Free Press.

Portes, Alejandro, and Ruben G. Rumbaut. 1990. *Immigrant America: A Portrait*. Berkeley: University of California Press.

Reinharz, Shulamit. 1992. *Feminist Methods in Social Research*. New York: Oxford University Press.

Rodriguez, Clara E. 1991. *Puerto Ricans: Born in the U.S.A.* Boulder, Colo.: Westview Press. Originally published in 1989.

Roediger, David. 1991. *The Wages of Whiteness: Race and the Making of the American Working Class*. New York: Verso.

Root, Maria P. 1992. *Racially Mixed People in America*. Newbury Park, Calif.: Sage.

Stanfield, John H., and M. Dennis Rutledge, eds. 1993. *Race and Ethnicity in Research Methods*. Newbury Park, Calif.: Sage.

Takaki, Ronald, ed. 1987. *From Different Shores: Perspectives on Race and Ethnicity in America*. New York: Oxford University Press.

———. 1989. *Strangers from a Different Shore: A History of Asian Americans*. Boston: Little Brown.

Tripura, Prashanta. 1992. "The Colonial Foundation of Pahari Ethnicity." *Journal of Social Studies* 58 (October): 1–16. Dhaka: Centre for Social Studies.

Twine, France Winddance. 1996. "Brown-Skinned White Girls: Class, Culture, and the Construction of White Identity in Suburban Communities." *Gender, Place, and Culture* 3 (2): 205–24.

———. 1998. *Racism in a Racial Democracy: The Maintenance of White Supremacy in Brazil*. New Brunswick, N.J.: Rutgers University Press.

Twine, France Winddance, Jonathan W. Warren, and Francisco Fernandiz. 1991. *Just Black? Multiracial Identity*. New York: Filmmakers Library.

Waldinger, Roger. 1996. "When the Melting Pot Boils Over: The Irish, Jews, Blacks, and Koreans of New York." In *The Bubbling Cauldron*, edited by Michael Peter Smith and Joe R. Feagin. Minneapolis: University of Minnesota Press.

Warren, Jonathan, and France Winddance Twine. 1997. "Whites, the New Minority? Non-Blacks and the Ever-Expanding Boundaries of Whiteness." *Journal of Black Studies* 28 (2): 200–218.

Waters, Mary C. 1990. *Ethnic Options: Choosing Identities in America.* Berkeley: University of California Press.

Wilson, William Julius. 1978. *The Declining Significance of Race.* Chicago: University of Chicago Press.

Wong, Sau-Ling Cynthia. 1993. *Reading Asian American Literature: From Necessity to Extravagance.* Princeton: Princeton University Press.

Chapter 3

White Like Me?

Methods, Meaning, and Manipulation in the Field of White Studies

Charles A. Gallagher

I came to my research project with the understanding that my racial background would be an asset. As a young white male from a working-class neighborhood I had been exposed to a raw, unadulterated, unapologetic kind of racism. The filtered and perfumed racism I encountered when I left my neighborhood and interacted with individuals from middle- and upper-middle-class backgrounds was made socially palatable by use of qualifiers, caveats, and appeals to meritocratic and individualistic principles. Being white and moving in different social circles has allowed me to sample (and at times be a part of) the way racism is expressed in different white communities. The "white stories" I heard growing up had, I was told, sensitized me to the ways of whites, which would inform and guide my research project. I thought I was uniquely positioned, a native son of white America, who could easily and readily chronicle the souls of white folks.

When I started my initial research on white identity construction by focusing on the way whites view themselves I did not need—or so I thought—to do much more than quickly gloss over how my social location might effect the interview process. I was trained to take into account the background characteristics of those we research and, to a lesser extent, the way the researcher's race, class, gender, and personal biography influence the research enterprise.

Reflecting on how personal biography influences the research process is a well-traveled road. But the development of the field of "white studies" has introduced new methodological terrain that has yet to be adequately mapped. If this line of research is to move from description to one concerned with rethinking and dismantling the way racial categories are constructed and made static, assumptions about access, rapport, and automatic insider status based on one's race need to be revisited and reconceptualized. In order for whiteness to be demystified and stripped to its political essence, our interviews must generate counternarratives of whiteness which give respondents the opportunity to rethink the white scripts, those "unquestioned assumptions" about race that are constantly being written, rewritten, and internalized.

I saw myself, at least in retrospect, as unburdened by my color because whiteness was the focus of my study, because I am white, and because I would be interviewing other whites about the meaning they attach to their race. In addition, the first phase of my research as an advanced graduate student involved interviewing white respondents from the metropolitan area in which I had been raised. I knew the stereotypes, economic profiles, and racial tensions which characterized my respondents' neighborhoods.[1]

There was a temptation to assume that I had access to respondents simply because of our skin color. Access to others because of one's race is often perceived as a methodological given. Describing how middle-class researchers use their own experiences as a template in which to bracket those they interview, Norman Denzin warns of the dangers of taking social location for granted in the interview: "They assume that all subjects will have a common perspective on such matters as annual income, patterns of sexual behavior, attitudes towards war, and so on: and they translate their stance on those issues into the interaction process, seldom questioning the legitimacy of their decision."[2]

It may be assumed that since the researcher and respondents are white and the interviews are about what whiteness means, the social biography and location of the researcher need not be scrutinized as critically as when, for example, a black researcher interviews Korean grocers in a black neighborhood or a self-identified Jewish researcher interviews members of Posse Comitatus. The legitimacy of one's role in the research process may be questioned, but because race and racial divisions are so central to the way we structure every aspect of our lives, the belief in a common perspective or narrative of whiteness may guide research assumptions and the interaction between respondent and researcher. One may be—as I initially was—lulled into the belief that the experiences of 200 million whites in the United States are linked by a common cultural thread because whites are the dominant racial group. However, while the majority of whites enjoy many privileges relative to other racial groups, one must nevertheless critically access where one's social location, political orientation, religious training, and attitudes on race fit into the research project.

Not only did I imagine myself having access to whites because I was white, but much of the literature on qualitative methods suggests that ascribed status should guide (at least in part) who one is able to study. John and Lyn Lofland, while cautioning researchers not to overemphasize the ascribed status of the interviewer, post this warning in their widely used qualitative methods textbook: "If you are black, studying Ku Klux Klan members and sympathizers will probably not be feasible. Nor are you likely to reach the desired 'intimate familiarity' if you are male and attempting to study a radical lesbian group."[3]

Providing an overview of how social location influences what researchers "see and do not see," John H. Stanfield II argues that "only those researchers emerging from the life worlds of their 'subjects' can be adequate interpreters of such experiences."[4] As a white researcher studying whites I saw myself situated squarely within the insider doctrine, which "holds that insiders have monopolistic or privileged access to knowledge of a group."[5] While inscribing myself within these interviews as a racial insider I was also able to maintain the role of the "objective" outsider. This methodological legerdemain could be maintained simply by embracing the neutral techniques of qualitative methods outlined in textbooks which define the field. I could embrace the role of detached dispassionate researcher-outsider with access to knowledge "accessible only to nonmembers of those groups" while simultaneously being an insider because of my color.[6]

However, being an insider because of one's race does not mute or erase other social locations which serve to deny access, create misunderstanding, or bias interviews with those from the same racial background. Nor does perceiving or defining oneself as an outsider allow one to claim that one's research is value-free. Skin color does not necessarily allow one to automatically pass into and have access to individuals or communities because of shared ascribed characteristics.

"Being white," like being a member of any social group, has a host of contradictory, symbolic, and situationally specific meanings. As a northerner raised in the working-class section of a big city who now lives in the South, being white will not provide me with automatic cultural access to the whites I will be interviewing in rural southeast Georgia. How will my whiteness smooth over differences based on my age, gender, or presumed ethnicity in my interviews? Will my Yankee dialect and status as professor with an urban university affiliation position me as a cultural outsider? Will the perception that I am Jewish, and the racial confusion many have concerning this category, make me a "racial" outsider? The argument could be made (and I have been told this already) that even though most people view me as white I will still be viewed as an outsider here in Georgia. In either scenario, as a cultural and/or racial outsider, I will have to consider how my perceived characteristics may shape the interview.

White Like Me: Who's Inside, Who's Outside?

After my partner and I had settled into a somewhat integrated working-class neighborhood in Philadelphia we went to our corner bar and began talking with the proprietor about our new surroundings. His father had owned the eponymous Tony's before him and his extended family had lived within one block of the bar for over sixty years. In an almost boastful manner I explained to Tony that until the late 1950s my Italian grandparents had lived four blocks away. As a boy my mother frequently and figuratively traveled back to her old neighborhood to shop and expose me to "authentic" Italian-American culture. I intimated to Tony that moving into this neighborhood was a third-generation return to a community that had always had larger-than-life status in my family's history. The exchange with Tony was pleasant, respectful, and even somewhat nostalgic. I then asked him how the neighborhood had changed since the 1950s. He looked at me for a moment and out poured a string of epithets and expletives about how blacks had destroyed what had once been a beautiful, cohesive community. The intensity and maliciousness of his comments caught me off-guard but did not surprise me. I have been privy to such language before. What was startling was his assumption that my partner and I would be responsive to such an ugly racist creed.

Upon further reflection, however, I realized that I had projected a kind of racial solidarity with this man. No doubt this connection was due in part to a shared ethnic affiliation, working-class roots, and family histories—but the common denominator that linked us was our whiteness. As this graying middle-aged bartender saw me, I was a white man who would be supportive of or at least sympathetic to the emotional grief blacks had caused him. Within fifteen minutes of chatting our race had linked us in a perceived union of mutual hate.

During our conversation a neighborhood black man dressed in a city transit worker's uniform entered the bar. Our conversation was suspended, Tony greeted this local warmly, and the man left with a six-pack. There was no animosity or disrespect toward him, nor was there any indication on Tony's part that this black man was part of the group that had "destroyed" his community. Tony smiled at this neighborhood resident and politely took his money.

On a different occasion, a young white male travel agent sitting next to me on a plane confided to me that when he could save enough money he was moving from New York City to Australia. Identity politics, multiculturalism, gay rights, feminism, affirmative action, political correctness, and the influx of nonwhite immigrants had made the United States a perverse, hostile, almost foreign environment for straight white "American" men like himself. Going to Australia, he explained, would be like going back to the United States in the 1950s. Although this man was too young to have experienced the white racial bliss of this imagined era nonetheless it represented for him a time when the cultural practices of straight white males had been the invisible and unchallenged norm.

More recently, a real estate agent in Atlanta, angry that she could not make a left turn because the oncoming black driver was going too slow, made the off-hand comment that "some groups of people just *do not* know how to drive." This college-educated, middle-class white woman was at ease using racial stereotypes in our company because our whiteness served as a common currency and language which presumably links all whites to an omnipresent antipathy toward blacks; it is a "white thing" that other whites understand.

White Stories: Linked by Race and Racism

What I found most surprising when recounting these experiences with other whites was that almost everyone had similar "white stories." A white colleague was told by a white barber that white men needed to keep a watchful eye on "our white women" or they would be sexually abused by nonwhites. A white taxi driver explained to a white friend why he did not pick up black passengers. A white neighbor told me about the "open-minded" white coworker who told a racist joke when the setting became all-white.[7]

All these white stories have this in common: many whites are comfortable expressing their racism to white strangers because they believe their skin color makes them kindred spirits in racism, or at least sympathetic to the "white experience." White researchers examining the meaning whites attach to their race are cognizant of this, either explicitly capitalizing on their whiteness to gain access and rapport to respondents, or, more dangerously, tacitly believing that their whiteness makes it unnecessary for them to examine their own racial biography. One's whiteness becomes a form of methodological capital researchers can use to question whites about the meaning they attach to their race.

Perceiving oneself as a white insider and interrogating whiteness from the outside as a researcher creates a number of methodological and ethical questions. For example, did the kinds of comments made above by whites I did not know give me immediate or easy access to any of these people as potential respondents simply because I am white and my questions were about their racial identity? Am I automatically an insider because of my skin color? Is the potential for tension, misunderstanding, or lack of rapport minimized because race is so central to the way we structure our lives that the whiteness shared by researcher and respondent transcends other social markers? Is it possible to be manipulated into reproducing the racist stereotypes of whites, particularly working-class whites, by asking questions about race and race relations that use the language and ideology of white victimology constructed, circulated, and endorsed by neoconservatives, the media, and survey research?

To what extent does the "objective interviewer" stance taken by many researchers allow white respondents to validate and justify the existing racial hierarchy that privileges whites, while simultaneously allowing these respondents to claim they are now at a social and economic disadvantage because of their skin color? The ethical and moral implications for those working in white studies is clear. Asking questions which decontextualize and treat whiteness as normative or existing outside the established racial hierarchy makes the researcher complicit in valorizing and creating a narrative of whiteness which absolves researcher and informant of the responsibility of challenging white racism and white privilege.

In this section I want to explore some of these concerns and examine how my status as a white middle-class male affects various aspects of the research enterprise. I have conducted fourteen focus groups and forty in-depth interviews with white adults and college students in the Northeast and Rocky Mountain regions of the United States. I am currently interviewing whites in two working-class and poor communities in rural Georgia. One county is 99.7 percent white, while the second is almost 80 percent black. Both counties mirror each other on a number of socioeconomic measures, namely, median household income, levels of education, and the percentage of whites at or below the poverty line. I will contrast how whiteness is understood by whites in an all-white community to those whites who live in a community where they are the racial minority.

A number of overlapping and interrelated concerns emerged in my research which led me to question the extent to which I was engaged in antiracist scholarship or whether my questions were reproducing a variation on what Stuart Hall calls "inferential racism." Hall argues that the way we represent or frame the idea of race, "whether 'factual' or 'fictional' which have racist premises and propositions inscribed in them as a set of unquestioned assumptions . . . enable racist statements to be formulated without ever bringing into awareness the racist predicates on which the statements are grounded."[8] Hall's "inferential racism" is a critique of the way the media normalizes racist ideology through various representations of race. Hall's examination of the pernicious ways in which the media maintains and reproduces racial hierarchy could just as easily serve as a warning to researchers, prompting them to question how their research normalizes whiteness by relying on "unquestioned assumptions" about racial identity construction, racism, or the dominant belief that whites do not think of their whiteness or their race in relation to other racial groups.

Many of my white respondents would often frame their own racial identity based on information about race that was factually incorrect. Respondents routinely double- and triple-counted the black and Asian population in the United States, dismissed contemporary racism as a thing of the past, and saw the workforce as significantly biased against whites. As an academic committed to antiracist research, it became unclear to me whether I was conducting the "normal science" of a racist paradigm or was engaging in "inferential racism" by allowing my respondents beliefs to go unchecked. Since I did not explain to my respondents that whites make up about 75 percent of the U.S. population, was I confirming and lending academic legitimacy to their anxious and fearful version of U.S. race relations and white victimology? Was it possible that those I interviewed thought that whiteness was under attack or unfairly maligned, and therefore in need of academic attention? This concern was made clear to me when an older secretary to whom I explained that I was examining the meaning whites attached to their race retorted sharply, "Good, it's about time somebody studied us." Was I condoning racism or encouraging white supremacy by validating a view of race and power relations that was largely fictive? By not challenging these reactionary versions of white identity construction the chance to engage in direct antiracist action was lost. Furthermore, responses that might have generated counternarratives or created a crisis of whiteness could not emerge or be explored.

I also want to suggest that there is an inherent danger in claiming insider status because researcher and respondent are both white. Henry Giroux reminds us that "racial categories exist and shape the lives of people differently within existing inequalities of power and wealth."[9] These inequalities exist both within racial categories as well as between them. The recent scholarship on the cultural meaning of "white trash" is yet another way whites have been sorted along a socioeconomic continuum by academics.[10] When I first started asking questions in my focus groups and interviews, I had partially leveled the "within" group differences that existed among my respondents. The internal variation which exists in the way 200 million whites in the United States understand, mark, and articulate their race creates formidable research challenges. The "unquestioned assumption" of white invisibility, that whites view themselves as colorless or, as Richard Dyer agues, "having no content," or, as Alastair Bonnett puts it, "existing outside of the political and economic forces that seem to shape other racialized identities" is a metanarrative which should be resisted.[11] In my interactions with whites throughout the country, there was enormous variation in the way individuals came to understand, ignore, or validate their whiteness depending on their spatial location in a city or suburb, as well as within a particular region of the United States. Class, geography, education, political ideology, sexuality, religion, age, gender, local culture—these qualify and shape the construction of whiteness for my respondents, just as they did for me as an interviewer.

The "social geography of race," to borrow Ruth Frankenberg's phrase, varies in real and idiosyncratic ways.[12] Researchers studying whiteness and the various meanings, expressions, and emotions whites attach to their racial position need to reexamine the insider/outsider dilemma which arises when studying something as slippery as racial identity construction. Being white may be a necessary condition to gain access and trust with *some* white respondents, but being white is not sufficient in and of itself. Access or rapport based on skin color may be negated by other aspects of one's social identity that pose a greater threat or suspicion among respondents.

I was reminded of my white-as-"outsider" status among whites when an elderly working-class Italian-American I had been building rapport with in Philadelphia was told by a neighbor that I was a graduate student. This seventy-year-old high school dropout and numbers runner no longer viewed me as just a "young white guy" from the neighborhood. Recently in Georgia I was talking with an older woman at a yard sale and she asked me, "What country are you from?" "Pennsylvania" did not appear to be a satisfactory answer. In the eyes of some southerners, my olive skin color, dark hair, and brown eyes had cast me as the generic, racially ambiguous, foreign "other." It was not clear if this woman thought I was white, but I was left pondering how her view of my racial identity might unfold, influence, and shape the outcome of an interview about her definition or understanding of her whiteness.

I also want to suggest that researchers examining whiteness can be unintentionally (or intentionally) manipulated into racism by embracing a set of "commonsense" assumptions about white racial attitudes which guide their research. Henry Giroux's work on how whiteness is reproduced and normalized is instructive. A counterhegemonic narrative which provides a cultural space for whiteness to be "renegotiated as a productive force in a politics of difference linked to a racial democratic project" should be as central to white studies as the inclination to demonstrate that white identity construction is based only on "what one isn't and on whom one can hold back," to quote David Roediger.[13]

Finally, I want to suggest that the whole enterprise of white studies and the rush to critique whiteness as a sociohistorical category results in an essentialized and ultimately racist discourse. While whiteness is understood as a socially constructed category, the internal variation within this category is often leveled. Without acknowledging how culture, politics, geography, ideology, and economics come together to produce numerous versions of whiteness, researchers will continue to frame and define whiteness monolithically. Just as we might cringe in a classroom when a student starts a conversation by stating that "all blacks do this . . ." or "gays always seem to . . ." we should be careful not to accept the political construction that whiteness is culturally or ideologically monolithic. Without critically examining how the questions we ask as researchers reshape the meaning of race, whiteness can be reconstituted and rearticulated, and the essentialist beliefs which undergird the idea of race go unchallenged.

Locating Researcher and Respondent

Was I perceived to be an insider by the nineteen-year-old white woman from a Montana trailer park, the white thirty-seven-year-old single mom ex-junkie who despised black women on welfare, the right-wing white retired military colonel, or the gay white college professor? Does my status as a white interviewer erase other cleavages that typically divide individuals? How does the interview itself, as a socially and politically situated endeavor, level, fail to capture, or mute the various ways white identity is understood and expressed? How can the highly nuanced and ever-shifting social locations which position and reposition whiteness as a salient social identity be captured by an interview?

As a researcher in my mid-thirties, to what extent did my age influence the discussion I had with young respondents about the *contemporary* meaning of whiteness? In one focus group exchange John, a twenty-year-old white college student, asked the other white respondents to consider the idea that being raised in the post–civil rights era had allowed them to transcend the old fashioned racism which many thought characterized the racial beliefs and discriminatory actions of the generations that preceded them. Speaking for the focus group John used age to sort those older folks who possibly engaged in the vile, overt racism of yesterday from the more enlightened, innocent color-blind post–civil rights cohort. At least in the eyes of many whites born in the generation after 1975, the "old fashioned racism" had gone the way of the buggy whip and phrenology:

We are past it [old fashioned racism]. You know we are not our ancestors. We didn't do that stuff. We don't do it now—none of us. I don't know how old you are but nobody in this room was alive in 1965. . . . I don't think any of us in this room have gone out and tarred and feathered someone or done anything like that. . . . I haven't been around black people enough to really do anything really bad. . . . I've never done any prejudiced act. I don't think anybody else in here has either but still, you guys are white and you're the enemy.

John may have included me in the "enemy" category because we were both white, but since I was born before 1965 had I been marked as an outsider because of my age? Did this generational divide "race" these young whites in a way that was different from the way I came to understand my own racial identity? Mary, a nineteen-year-old, also used the civil rights movement as a way to distinguish between older whites who were responsible for overt forms of racism and her generation, which she viewed as being unfairly linked to the racist behaviors and attitudes of the older generation:

They say they have been oppressed. They have not. The students here at this university right now have not been oppressed. They have not experienced the Watts riot, they didn't experience being hosed down by the police. Granted, the white population was responsible for that but we are not. We are not responsible. Therefore, we should not be put out because of that. We didn't do it. We're not doing it now, therefore they have no right to say, well, we've been oppressed.

It was unclear whether Mary viewed me as being part of the generation that was responsible for black oppression, and I was left wondering what role my age played in the dynamics of the focus group interactions. Would the responses have differed if I had been a twenty-two-year-old or a sixty-two-year-old interviewer?

Being born before 1965 may have indirectly linked me to traditional Bull Connor forms of racism with the early twenty-something crowd, but it was also a source of pity among those a generation or two older than myself. Sarah, a fifty-three-year-old executive secretary born and raised in Atlanta, described how white privilege had changed from one generation to the next:

I think probably that in generations before me, as in my parents and my grandparents, I think that they probably were given preferential treatment because they were Caucasian. I do not know [whether] that was the case with the beginning of my generation. And I am glad because we should remove all prejudice. . . . I think that if anything there is a bit of reverse discrimination because particularly blacks are put in positions when more qualified whites are there, so I think it has gone just the reverse.

Did Sarah view me as being part of the generation that was now subject to reverse discrimination in the labor market? Was I viewed as both a researcher and a white male victim as we talked about the meaning of whiteness in the United States? Is it possible that I was viewed as doubly disadvantaged by my race and gender?

In a number of my interviews my class background and that of my respondent framed how whiteness was discussed. As I ran focus groups and individual interviews throughout the country I realized I was more in tune with the social and cultural background of lower-middle and working-class respondents. My questions were relatively consistent throughout my interviews but my own class position, or at least the one in which I was raised, allowed me to more throughly probe respondents who were from a similar class background. The economic anxieties of the working class and of lower-middle-class whites and the way those fears become racially grounded was something I understood viscerally and intellectually. However, I was not able to draw on the same cultural markers and reference points when I interviewed respondents from very wealthy backgrounds. We may have been white but the stark contrast in our class backgrounds created diffrent understandings and narratives of whiteness. Dan, a twenty-year-old from a self-described "rich" neighborhood in Phoenix, Arizona, commented that he did not use race to place people in categories. Within his social circles it was class, not color, that mattered. In a focus group with other well-off students attending an elite, expensive private school, Dan outlined how class overrode color:

I don't ever think about being white or identifying with white. It's more of class. I came from a high school where everyone was like me, even if they were black, you know, people drive their own car, go to the club, and play golf. You know that kind of stuff, if I see someone who has a nice car and I see them hitting balls, I'll go and talk to them. It doesn't matter what race you are. But then I don't identify with people who don't have money to wear nice clothes and don't have the money to go to this school, or people on financial aid. I feel uncomfortable around them.

Based on his description I would not be one of those toward whom Dan would feel a sense of social solidarity. I grew up wearing my older brother's hand-me-downs and irregular clothing, and was on financial aid throughout college. Ironically, for three summers in elementary and early high school I had worked on a golf course selling hot dogs and Italian ices to the Philadelphia golfing clique, many of whom were from the social background Dan described. Perhaps divulging my class experiences to Dan might have provided him with the opportunity to reconsider the extent to which class triumphs over race as a social identity. Dan said he was not "trying to show off" or sound "conceited," but it was difficult for me to think otherwise. As Dan was describing his upper-middle-class country club white existence I thought to myself that while we were both male and white I had very little in common with the way he lived his life or constructed his worldview. However, upon further reflection perhaps my slightly condescending view of Dan's privileged bourgeois existence was driven in part by a deep-seated, working-class resentment and jealousy of the leisure class.

Throughout my interviews, it was quite obvious that whiteness was spatially as well as socially located. The researcher and respondent are as sociably situated as the site of the interview. As a number of interviews and focus groups slowly revealed to me, respondents became conscious of their race as they moved from one setting to the next. Many respondents could ignore whiteness or be preoccupied with it in different ways throughout the day. For instance, a respondent may be racially unconscious while shopping in the early morning with his white friends at a suburban mall. His late morning layup shots are a deliberate, much rehearsed combination of Michael Jordan's and Dennis Rodman's best moves. He grooves to a TuPac Shakur song on his car radio as he weaves his way from his white neighborhood to the city for his afternoon class. Driving through the black northern part of the city to Urban University, however, makes him nervous. He thinks about what might happen to him if his car breaks down five blocks from campus. He feels a bit anxious parking near the projects or staying late on campus. He is reminded of his race and his outsider racial status when he sees recruitment posters of the Daughters of Kush, the Black Pre-Law Society, and the Korean Cultural Club on campus kiosks. He walks quickly through the surrounding black neighborhood relieved his car is still there, gets in, and drives home through the black part of the city with locked doors, and slowly, as the racial terrain becomes familiar, his anxiety eases and his world becomes "normal" again. In the course of his day this respondent has thought about his whiteness in different ways in response to changing circumstances.

Taking into account the social location of a participant and the personal biography of the researcher, and approaching the interview knowing that the meaning whites attach to their race varies by region, class, gender, sexual orientation, and political philosophy allows for a more reflexive and nuanced understanding of the complex and contradictory ways whites understand their race and define who they are. Apart from benefits that accrue to whites because of their skin color no single metanarrative of whiteness exists. The "white stories" I defined earlier may link racist and nonracist, researcher and respondent together in a perceived or fleeting sense of racial understanding or solidarity. However, if whiteness is treated as a monolithic identity based on privilege or the assumption that all whites harbor certain negative (or positive) attitudes toward other racial groups, researchers will miss the opportunity to examine the social complexities and the social geography of how and where racial identities are constructed and the multiplicity of meanings that define whiteness. The difficulty mapping white racial identity construction is poignantly problematized by John Hartigan, Jr. in his research on race and whites in Detroit. He notes that it is *not* possible to "compile a more or less thorough aggregate of whites, abstract out from them a common condition or an intrinsic set of connections, and have neatly defined by these efforts a succinct, abiding identity—whiteness."[14]

Marking or Manipulating Whiteness: Resisting the Racial Template

The field of inquiry now defined as "white studies" has grown enormously in the last decade. A number of "white scholars" are examining the ways in which white identity intersects with the issues of class, gender, law, economics, and popular culture. Influenced by postmodern theories of deconstructionism, this nascent field of inquiry has taken it upon itself to strip away the subjectivity of whiteness and expose the relational and situational nature of white identity. This intellectual scrutiny has moved whiteness from being merely a backdrop in the discourse on racial identity formation to becoming the subject of study.

When I started my project in 1992 little empirical work had been done on how whites define whiteness, on the social and political situations which push whiteness to the forefront as a social identity for whites, and on the way the construction of whiteness is linked to structural elements which shape those meanings. This is no longer the case. However, the systematic, empirically grounded gathering and telling of white people's narratives about their understanding of their race, as opposed to the way whites define the racial "other," is still relatively unexplored.

When I initially formulated the questions that would inform my data collection I was not aware just how much my research project was being manipulated by my own assumptions about whiteness. In an attempt to provide different measures of the same social phenomena I employed focus groups, in-depth interviews, and a survey. But using surveys to tap something as complex as how someone constructs their racial identity raised a number of thorny issues. Could I examine whiteness so as to capture the social complexities and varied cultural nuances which define racial categories by using a questionnaire? Could racial identity be conceptualized as a temporally static and discreet category, like height, weight, or income? Could I, as I was instructed at one point, create a "white index" using factor analysis which would rank on a single scale the "whiteness" of one respondent relative to another? If I did not produce data that could stand up to at least a test of Chi-square would I be left, as I was told, with "only stories" about whiteness based on my focus groups and interviews which could not, by themselves, stand up to peer review?

After much deliberation and pretesting, my position was that by their very design, surveys could neither tap nor measure how, why, or to what extent whites come to understand the complex, contradictory, and subtle ways whiteness is articulated. A mixed methodological approach allowed me to use the cultural expressions of whiteness voiced by respondents in my interviews to frame and complement the survey questions. This allowed me to examine the underlying ideological and structural influences that mediate the process of white racial identity formation.

My struggle to create a methodological approach that included both rich textured accounts of the *meanings* whites attached to their racial positions and surveys that allowed for some generalizability beyond my population masked the more pressing ethical and political concerns that became apparent in subsequent interviews. As is the common practice in survey research, my questions were drawn from existing studies that purported to tap the attitudes of whites. The final survey questions and semistructured interview guide were drawn from "commonsense" notions about whites derived from surveys, popular opinion polls, social science research, the input of my committee members, and what I perceived to be the issues that shape white identity construction.

The resulting white template I designed, and which guides much of the research on race relations, is based on a priori assumptions about how social scientists understand and define white attitudes, white fears, and white culture. These survey-generated beliefs become the white attitudinal baseline which influences how researchers in other fields structure their interview guides and data matrices, or redesigned their survey questions. If white identity is conceptualized only in oppositional terms, alternative narratives of whiteness cannot emerge in the interview.

A portion of my survey and interview schedule have been included in Appendix 1 and 2. The overwhelming majority of questions in Appendix 1 reflect an early and (in retrospect) rather simplistic understanding of how and why whites attach meaning to their race. My survey questions tap a narrow version of whiteness that frames racial identity construction only in opposition to racial minorities. However, the open-ended questions in the survey did sensitize me to issues of identity construction which had not been adequately addressed in the literature. Not all whites construct their racial identity in opposition to blacks, Asians, or Latinos, nor did whiteness serve as a proxy to a reactionary worldview. These expressions, which challenged the "commonsense" literature on whiteness, became the basis for questions I would later ask in my focus groups and interviews. While relatively unstructured, my interview schedule reflects an approach to whiteness that attempts to capture whiteness as being constructed in oppositional and cultural terms. I believe the field of white studies is moving to a more nuanced yet critical understanding of white identity construction. The view that "Whites' "consciousness" of whiteness is predominately unconsciousness of whiteness"[15] or the that "Transparency, the tendency of Whites to remain blind to the racialized aspects of that identity, is omnipresent"[16] is no longer a sustainable narrative in the wake of racial identity politics. The view of whiteness as invisible will be supplanted by a theoretical approach to whiteness that will, as Henry Giroux argues, mark "whiteness as a form of identity and cultural practice" which "makes the distinction between 'whiteness' as a dominating ideology and white people who are positioned across multiple locations of privilege and subordination."[17] The idea of whiteness is being constructed, reinterpreted, and molded by whites for whites as a cultural product understood in ways other than being in opposition to nonwhites.[18]

Researching Whiteness as an Antiracist Project

In almost all my focus groups I asked or respondents offered their views on affirmative action. Respondents who had been reticent throughout the focus group discussion suddenly came to life, arguing forcefully about the need for, or more often the inherent unfairness of, affirmative action. In many interviews this topic was a turning point. Many whites took the opportunity to articulate a narrative of their whiteness that was based on victimization.[19] This conversation often led to a discussion about welfare, multicultuarlism, and downward economic mobility because the labor marked now preferred blacks and Asians to whites. The laments, outrage, and pent-up guilt about this topic were fascinating, sociologically rich, and deeply troubling.

But what if, after these issues had been exhausted, I had asked my focus groups to consider another scenario? What if they had been provided with a number of social facts about the relative social standing of whites compared to other racial groups in the United States? How might whites define themselves if it was demonstrated that racial discrimination in the labor market is unquestionably still a sorting mechanism that privileges whites, that whites are twice as likely to graduate from college as blacks, that the face of welfare in the United States is white, that almost every socioeconomic measure—from infant mortality, to home ownership rates, to the accumulation of wealth—favors whites over blacks, Latinos, or many Asian groups?

If the belief that whites are losing out to blacks or Asians was refuted in the interview and whites had a chance to articulate an identity that could not be based on victimology, what would that white racial identity look like? Would there or could there be a white racial identity that was not merely "a politically constructed category parasitic on blackness"?[20] My experiences suggest that when white respondents are given counterarguments that demonstrate that racial inequality still exists they *modify* many of their positions.[21]

While critical of my own work for bracketing a narrative of whiteness within a reactionary and conservative framework, Henry Giroux asks how, as antiracist researchers and educators, we might provide: "the conditions for students to address not only how their 'whiteness' functions in society as a marker of privilege and power, but also how it can be used as a condition for expanding the ideological and material realities of democratic public life."[22]

The conditions required to think ourselves out of an oppositional understanding of whiteness means breaking the racial template which seduces researchers into asking questions which merely reproduce a "commonsense," neoconservative definition of whiteness and race relations based on whites' perceived marginalization. Those who wish to "abolish the white race" or define whiteness *only* as a source of power equally shared by all whites, level the social, political, and economic differences among whites while creating a simple racial dichotomy which is easily and routinely manipulated politically.[23]

Data does not "speak for itself" nor does it "emerge" in a vacuum. Who we are (and appear to be in a specific context) influences the questions we ask, the responses we get, and the scholarship we produce, which is reproduced by yet another cohort of graduate students. Some of this scholarship finds its way into *Newsweek,* the *Wall Street Journal,* or as a discussion topic on *The Oprah Winfrey Show* or *Montel,* where it becomes part of our collective understanding of race relations. I was reminded of this trickle-down understanding of race relations by a white male in a focus group. He insisted that Rodney King was a threat to the police officers who savagely beat him because he kept moving when he was on the ground. "If you want to know what is really going on," he told the group, "You gotta watch Rush [Limbaugh]."

Unfortunately, the counternarratives that might challenge the existing racial status quo go in large part unexplored. A colleague from a working-class background who was familiar with my work told me the purpose of my project was to demonstrate that working-class whites are racist. I would, as others had done before, paint a portrait of working-class whites as racists. This was not my intention, although his prediction was fairly accurate. I was steered toward a version of whiteness that had been framed by the narrow binary ways in which many researchers choose to explore racial identity construction and had accepted the script that had been provided to my respondents.

Beyond White Essentialism

An agitated white male in a focus group, typical of many I interviewed, complained that whites are the new minority group in the United States. Talking about the treatment of blacks, Mike explained to me: "It's not like they're discriminated against anymore, it's like the majority is now the minority because we are the ones being discriminated against because we are boxed in. We can't have anything for ourselves anymore that says exclusively white or anything like that. But everyone else can. You know what I mean."

Throughout my research white respondents generally embraced the belief that the U.S. class system was fair and equitable. Most respondents argued that those who delay gratification, work hard, and follow the rules will succeed, irrespective of color.[24] Many white respondents felt the leveled playing field argument has rendered affirmative action policies a form of reverse discrimination and source of resentment. Jennifer Hochschild calls this "whites' quandary." "Whites are more sure that discrimination is not a problem," that blacks can succeed, that self-reliance pays off, that blacks now "control their own fate" *and* whites feel that their life chances have eroded.[25] This was how my respondents were able to define themselves as victims. As the above quote by Mike explains, it is whites who are "now the minority." Like the white stories I outlined earlier, the whites-as-victim perspective can be added to the ever-growing list of those situations, attitudes, or injustices that make up the "white experience."

Like many other young whites from modest backgrounds, Mike defined himself as the racial "other." He viewed himself as lacking agency in a world where he was marginalized because of his race. This perception lends itself to the development of defensive strategies based on an essentialist understanding of whiteness. What, many of my respondents asked me, would blacks do if we wore a "It's a white thing. . . . You wouldn't understand" t-shirt? My point here is not to examine whether whites can be the subaltern, the racial outsider in a white society, or the other "other." My question concerns the shift from a racial identity that is invisible to one made explicit and the way this process may essentialize whiteness. Michael Omi and Howard Winant explain that "a racial project can be defined as racist if and only if it creates or reproduces structures of domination based on essentialist categories of race."[26] While ostensibly concerned with social justice and racial equality it is unclear to what extent white studies, as a racial project, can embrace an antiessentialist epistemology or methodology.

Much of the work being done in white studies embraces an essentialist standpoint in two ways. First, we have allowed a narrative of whiteness to emerge which has been molded by a reactionary political and cultural climate with a vested interest in defending the racial status quo. We might challenge the tendency for white respondents to validate and justify white privilege by inverting the questions we ask, so that respondents are forced to think of the structural advantages that accrue to them because of their skin color. How might a white informant respond to the question that requires him or her to consider how a fifty-year-old, white-collar black or Asian woman might view their whiteness? Do we ask questions which challenge our respondents to think about race as a political category, or do we reproduce, normalize, and continue to make whiteness invisible by uncritically validating the version of whiteness we expect to hear? White studies is in a position to explore counternarratives of racial identity construction which imply that whites have agency in the way they define themselves, and suggest that they might take responsibility for, or at least have a fuller understanding of, racial privilege in the United States.

This is of course a double-edged sword. To not talk about the ways in which whiteness retains its invisibility and hence its power is to "redouble its hegemony by naturalizing it."[27] However, to talk about whiteness as a visible, meaningful identity with definable particularizing qualities, is to treat this category as if it were real. It is unclear at the time of this writing whether "white studies" will embrace a critique of whiteness that challenges racial hierarchy through an explicit antiessentialist discourse, or whether it will become the vehicle through which a sophisticated, critical essentialism is articulated.

Survey Given to 514 Students at a Large Urban University

The entire original survey was thirteen pages. For this publication I have only included those questions that explicitly address white identity construction. Questions on race and residence, standard background variables, social networks and race, interracial dating, social distance scales, and the strength of ethnic identity measures have been omitted.

For a complete copy of the survey please contact me at: The Department of Sociology, Georgia State University, Atlanta, GA 30303–3083, or cgallagher@gsu.edu.

1. What is your racial/ethnic background? _____

2. What percentage of the U.S. population is:

   White   _____ %

   Black   _____ %

   Asian   _____ %

   American Indian _____ %

3. Think for a moment about the neighborhood or area where you were raised. When I am in the area where I was raised:
(check one)

   _____ I sometimes think about my race

   _____ I often think about my race

   _____ I never think about my race

If you answered "sometimes" or "often" what are the situations that make you think about your race?

_____

If you answered "I never think about my race" what kinds of events in your neighborhood would make you think about your race?

_____

4. When I was in high school:
(check one)

_____ I sometimes thought about my race

_____ I often thought about my race

_____ I never thought about my race

If you answered "sometimes" or "often" what were the situations that made you think about your race?

_____

_____

If you answered "never" why might that be the case?

_____

_____

5. In the course of my school day at Urban University:

_____ I sometimes thought about my race

_____ I often thought about my race

_____ I never thought about my race

If you answered "sometimes" or "often" what were the situations that made you think about your race?

_____

_____

6. In the course of your school day at Urban University in what situations are you likely to think about your race? (check all that apply)

_____ on public transit

_____ in the dorms

_____ in the classrooms

_____ in Student Activities Center

_____ in the library

_____ driving to Urban University

_____ dealing with the administration (bursar, financial aid)

_____ when I am a numerical minority in a class

_____ when I am interacting with students from different racial backgrounds than my own

_____ parking off campus

_____ when I interact with faculty

_____ at fraternity/sorority parties

_____ staying late on campus

_____ sporting events

_____ eating lunch on campus

_____ being approached by the homeless

7. What other Urban University situations or specific encounters on campus are likely to remind you of your race?

_____

_____

8. Are there any situations on campus that you find threatening?

_____

_____

9. What percentage of the Urban University population is:

White _____ %

Black _____ %

Asian _____ %

Other _____ %

10. Do you think more about your race since attending Urban University?

_____ yes _____ no _____ no opinion

APPENDIX 2
Focus Group and Individual Interview Schedule

1. General background questions: age, place of birth.
2. Where were you raised? What was your neighborhood like? Was it integrated?
3. How would you define your class background?
4. What was the class background of the family in which you were raised?
5. How do you define yourself ethnically?

   What is it—single, multiple, hybrid, symbolic?
   What meaning do you or does your family attach to your ethnicity?
   Are these things ethnically important: holidays, food, dating, neighborhood dynamics?

6. What does it mean to be white in the United States in 1999?
7. Are you conscious of being white? When?
8. In what situations do you think about being white?
9. What would you define as white culture?
10. Why do some whites feel threatened about the current state of race relations?
11. How is being white different from being black or Asian?
12. How is being white similar to being black or Asian?
13. What objects would you place in a museum of white history?
14. Define yourself politically.
15. What does that mean?
16. Once again, what does it mean to be white?

NOTES

I would like to thank France Winndance Twine for editorial guidance and comments on earlier versions of this chapter.

1. See Charles A. Gallagher, "White Reconstruction in the University," *Socialist Review* (1995) 94 (1/2): 165–88.

2. Norman Denzin, *The Research Act: A Theoretical Introduction to Sociological Methods* (Englewood Cliffs, N.J.: Prentice Hall, 1989).

3. John Lofland and Lyn H. Lofland, *A Guide to Qualitative Observations and Analysis*, 2d ed. (Belmont, Calif.: Wadsworth, 1984).

4. John H. Stanfield II, "Ethnic Modeling in Qualitative Research," in *Handbook of Qualitative Research,* edited by Norman Denzin and Yvonna Lincoln (Thousand Oaks, Calif.: Sage, 1994).

5. Maxine Baca Zinn, "Field Research in Minority Communities: Ethical, Methodological, and Political Observations by an Insider," *Social Problems* (1979) 27 (2): 209.

6. Ibid.

7. I am indebted to Kevin Delaney for helping me develop the idea of white stories.

8. Stuart Hall, "The Whites of Their Eyes: Racist Ideologies and the Media," in *Silver Linings: Some Strategies for the Eighties,* edited by G. Bridges and R. Brunt (London: Lawrence and Wishart, 1981).

9. Henry A. Giroux, "Racial Politics and the Pedagogy of Whiteness," in *Whiteness: A Critical Reader,* edited by Mike Hill (New York: New York University Press, 1997), p. 294.

10. See Matt Wray and Annalee Newitz, eds., *White Trash: Race and Class in America* (New York: Routledge, 1997).

11. Richard Dyer, *White* (New York: Routledge, 1997); Alastair Bonnett, "Constructions of Whiteness in European and American Anti-Racism," in *Debating Cultural Hybridity: Multi-Cultural Identities and the Politics of Anti-Racism,* edited by Pnina Werbner and Tariq Modood (London: Zed Books, 1997), pp. 173–92.

12. Ruth Frankenberg, *White Women, Race Matters: The Social Construction of Whiteness* (Minneapolis: University of Minnesota Press, 1993).

13. David Roediger, *Toward the Abolition of Whiteness: Essays on Race, Politics, and the Working Class* (New York: Verso, 1994).

14. John Hartigan, Jr., "Locating White Detroit," in *Displacing Whiteness: Essays in Social and Cultural Criticism,* edited by Ruth Frankenberg (Durham: Duke University Press, 1997), p. 204.

15. Barbara Flagg, "Transparently White Subjective Decision Making," in *Critical White Studies: Looking Behind the Mirror* edited by Richard Delgado and Jean Stefancic (Philadelphia: Temple University Press, 1997), p. 220.

16. Ian F. Haney López, *White by Law: The Legal Construction of Race* (New York: New York University Press, 1996), p. 157.

17. Henry A. Giroux, "White Squall: Resistance and the Pedagogy of Whiteness," *Cultural Studies* (1997) 11 (3): 383.

18. See Ashley W. Doane, Jr., "Dominant Group Ethnic Identity in the United States: The Role of 'Hidden' Ethnicity in Intergroup Relations," *Sociological Quarterly* 38 (3): 375–97.

19. See Charles A. Gallagher, "Redefining Racial Privilege in the United States," *Transformations* 8, no. 1 (spring 1997): 28–39.

20. Cornel West, "The New Cultural Politics of Difference," in *The Cultural Studies Reader,* edited by Simon During (New York: Routledge, 1993), p. 212.

21. Paul M. Sniderman and Thomas Piazza, *The Scar of Race* (Cambridge: Harvard University Press, 1993). Sniderman and Piazza found that whites were quite willing to change their minds about racial policy issues when presented with a counterargument.

22. Henry A. Giroux, *Channel Surfing: Race Talk and the Destruction of Today's Youth* (New York: St. Martin's Press, 1997), p. 108.

23. See *Race Traitor,* edited by Noel Ignatiev and John Garvey (New York: Routledge, 1996).

24. See Charles A. Gallagher, "White Racial Formation: Into the Twenty-First Century," in *Critical White Studies: Looking Behind the Mirror,* edited by Richard Delgado and Jean Stefancic (Philadelphia: Temple University Press, 1997).

25. Jennifer L. Hochschild, *Facing Up to the American Dream* (Princeton: Princeton University Press, 1995), p. 68.

26. Michael Omi and Howard Winant, *Racial Formation in the United States: From the 1960s to the 1990s* (New York: Routledge, 1994), p. 71.

27. Cited in David Roediger, *The Wages of Whiteness: Race and the Making of the American Working Class* (New York: Verso, 1991), p. 1.

Chapter 4

White on White
Interviewing Women in U.S.
White Supremacist Groups

Kathleen M. Blee

Recent scholarship points to a peculiar aspect of whiteness in intensely race-conscious societies such as the United States. White identity is based on distinctions from those marked as nonwhite, and is always in danger of challenge. Thus whiteness is at once intensely significant and ultimately meaningless. As Ruth Frankenberg (1993: 231) comments, "whiteness can by definition have no meaning: as a normative space it is constructed precisely by the way in which it positions others at its borders. . . . Whiteness is in this sense fundamentally a relational category" (see also Ignatiev 1995).

The unstable quality of white identity creates particular challenges and problems for research with white respondents, especially when issues of race are paramount in the research. In this chapter, I reflect on some of the methodological issues posed in a larger study that explores the extent and nature of women's active role in white supremacist and organized anti-Semitic activity in the United States. I approach this study as a white woman engaged in a study of white women who have dedicated their lives to the promotion of white racist goals. Although race would not seem paramount in such research since I am a racial insider on the surface, nonetheless neither I nor my respondents considered each other to be racial equivalents. I am guided by Marjorie DeVault's (1995) important insight that race and ethnicity are often relevant to the research enterprise, even when not explicit. As DeVault (1995: 613) argues, "'hearing' race and ethnicity in our talk with informants requires active attention and analysis." As others doing research in societies that are both similar and different from their own (Beoku-Betts 1994; Edwards 1990; Zavella 1993) have found, the location of a researcher both inside and outside the meaning-structure of those being studied is potentially revelatory, even as it poses methodological difficulties.

My research is guided by an interest in understanding the impact of the recently increasing numbers of women members on the direction, vitality, goals, and tactics of the modern organized racist movement and in developing new strategies to counter the growth of racist activities in the United States. Only within the past few decades have women become a significant force in contemporary racist groups. With the exception of the massive Women of the Ku Klux Klan movement in the 1920s (Blee 1991) and the smaller profascist "mother's movements" that were active during World War II (Jeansonne 1996), until the 1970s visible, public, organized racism and anti-Semitic activity in the United States has been largely conducted by men. Before that time, most racist organizations—including the Ku Klux Klan movements of the pre- and post-1920s—had excluded women from membership and relegated white women to being symbols of that which organized racism purported to protect: innocent white womanhood. Women played private domestic roles in early organized racist groups as the emotional support for male intimates engaged in racist activism, and as the primary conduit by which children learned racist principles at home. They also participated in racist collective action and in short-lived racist groups, especially those focused on issues of education or neighborhood such as the mobilizations against school integration (Roy 1998; Wrigley 1998). But rarely were women active in sustained organized racist groups.

Since 1970, and particularly in the 1990s, women have played a more public role in organized racism. Anxious to bolster membership and to cultivate members who will remain in the racist movement over the long term, many white supremacist and anti-Semitic groups have begun to accept women as members. In the 1990s, a number of groups have even allowed women to serve as spokespersons and as leaders, although generally only at low levels of the organizational hierarchy. As a result, the composition of organized racism has begun to change, with women and teenaged girls constituting an estimated 25 to 50 percent of *new* recruits to some groups.

Despite this organizational change, there is virtually no research on the impact of the influx of female members on organized racism today. Virtually all studies of racist activity assume even now assume that women participate only in peripheral, meaningless roles, largely as the wives and girlfriends of male racist group members, despite evidence that this assumption is not always true (Blee 1996).

The research from which this chapter is drawn is an effort to remedy this scholarly lacuna. By studying the women who are involved in contemporary organized racist groups directly, I treat women's roles in racist groups as a question to be investigated rather than assuming women's marginality in the racist movement. Such an approach makes it possible to assess changes in organized racism resulting from women's increased public role. Given the changing gender composition of the racist movement, the focus on women's participation may also alter the understanding of what tactics are effective against the spread of organized racism.

One part of this research is based on structured interviews that I conducted between September 1994 and October 1995 with thirty-four women who are current activists in racist and anti-Semitic groups in various regions of the United States. (Other aspects of this research, not discussed in this paper, include unstructured life histories, analysis of group propaganda, and organizational ethnographies.) Given the paucity of information about the landscape of organized racism in the United States or about those who are active participants in this movement, a first step in the interviewing methodology involved the establishment of a general sampling frame from which I could select respondents. For this, I subscribed for a one-year period to publications by every self-identified racist, anti-Semitic, white supremacist, Christian identity, neo-Nazi, white power skinhead, and white separatist organization that I could find in the United States that was currently publishing material. I found more than one hundred groups in every region of the country, from the lists of racist/anti-Semitic groups in the archives of a number of national antiracist and anti-Semitic organizations and from archival collections on right-wing extremism at Tulane University and the University of Kansas. The publications included newsletters, magazines, flyers, Internet postings, and web pages. I also had access to musical recordings, fax messages, television and radio programs, and taped recordings of a number of telephone "hate lines." The resulting set of publications by racist groups was analyzed to determine which groups had significant numbers of women members or women in visible or leadership roles. From this list, I then selected approximately thirty groups that varied by region of the country and type of racist/anti-Semitic activity and contacted them (or, if known, women in these groups) for interviews.

Because I was interested in making this study as representative as possible of the landscape of organized racism today, I targeted the most active segments of the modern racist/anti-Semitic movement in a search for respondents. These included (1) white power "skinheads," loosely structured gangs of teenagers and young adults who model themselves after similar earlier groups in England and Canada and who practice intense violence against peoples of color, Jews, immigrants, and those they perceive to be gay or lesbian (Hamm 1993); (2) the "Christian Identity" sects, a network of quasi-theological communities that regard Jews and African-Americans as the offspring of Satan and white Christians as the true lost tribe of Israel (Barkun 1994); (3) neo-Nazi and white supremacist groups who trace their ideological lineage to Hitler and who typically favor complete separation between white Aryans and others; and (4) the Ku Klux Klan, a set of groups now splintered into at least a dozen competing Klans, many with recent strategic alliances to neo-Nazi and white power skinhead groups.

Once I had established the list of groups from which I wanted to find respondents, I arranged to contact individual members in a variety of ways. For a few groups, I used pre-existing personal and professional contacts established during my earlier research on the 1920s Ku Klux Klan. For other groups and members, I sought out referrals from racist activists, journalists, researchers, family and friends of group members, and other sources. Even police authorities proved to be good sources of contacts for groups such as white power skinheads whose young teenaged members ironically often rely on the police officials assigned to monitor them for guidance and assistance in the face of economic and interpersonal problems.

I was not able to use snowball sampling, the method of relying upon initial respondents for referrals to subsequent respondents, although this is the sampling method of choice for most studies of difficult-to-locate populations. Within the racist movement in the United States there is tremendous internal friction. The Ku Klux Klan has split numerous times over personality and financial conflicts as well as political differences. Other racist and neo-Nazi groups have similar histories of internecine conflict, resulting in complicated histories of interpersonal hostility even within politically allied organizations. Such fractionalized relationships made respondent-generated suggestions of other respondents too restrictive since respondents would not be likely to suggest the names of antagonists or members from competing groups.

The group of respondents I eventually contacted and who consented to be interviewed included fourteen who were in some leadership position and twenty who were simply active members of racist/anti-Semitic groups. The oldest respondent was ninety; the youngest was sixteen. The median age was twenty-four. Respondents lived in fifteen different states, with the greatest concentrations in Georgia (6), Oklahoma (5), Oregon (4), and Florida (4), and were dispersed across region, with eleven from the South, ten from the West Coast, ten from the Midwest, and three from the East Coast. I interviewed fourteen women who were non-skinhead neo-Nazis, while six were members of various Ku Klux Klan groups, eight were white power skinheads, and six were members of Christian Identity or related white/Aryan supremacist groups.

Racial Navigations

Delicate issues of race and racial dynamics infused the research process. Of course, the explicit subject of this research was race, especially issues of racial identity and racist activism. Race was clearly central to the lives of my informants, many of whom had experienced family ostracism and substantial financial decline to devote themselves to the practice of white, Aryan supremacy. It might seem that I—a white woman—would encounter relatively unproblematic racial dynamics in interviews with these women. In fact, complicated issues of race arose between me and the interview subjects from the earliest stages of the research process and continued to affect both the dynamics and the quality of the study. Occasionally, intrusions of race dynamics inhibited the research, but more often issues of race between myself and the respondents shed new light on the racial meanings and racial identities of these women.

Race existed as an element of tension and contestation in the framing of my interviews in several ways. First, very early in the research process I learned that I must be aware of issues of identity labeling during even the initial communication between me and the groups from which I hoped to locate women to be interviewed. When contacting groups seeking names of women members and when talking with individuals whom I wanted to interview, I used the self-referential language found in the group literature, referring to members as "racists," as advocates of "white power," as "white supremacists," or as adherents to Christian Identity, in line with the language of their group's propaganda.

Such caution in the choice of language was necessary because modern racist groups have intricate rhetorical preferences as to how they identify themselves and how they differentiate themselves from other groups that an outsider might see as similar. For example, some Klan members and groups are content to be called racists. Other Klan chapters and members insist, against all the evidence, that they do not promote racist practices or ideas but are only interested in protecting the white race. These groups preferred to be known as "white separatists" or as advocates for whites.

Knowing the correct rhetorical codes for each group or splinter group was important in order to establish myself as knowledgeable in the racist movement. It was also one step toward demonstrating that I was not a spy dispatched by the police or by antiracist groups such as the Southern Poverty Law Center or the Anti-Defamation League of B'nai B'rith, since many racist activists (incorrectly) see the opposition as holding monolithic views of the racist movement and thus unable to correctly distinguish between the possible group labels.

The dynamics of group labeling also had a more problematic side. Some informants perceived my efforts to take seriously and abide by the rhetorical codes of their group as implying some acceptance on my part of racist politics. Thus, my efforts to comply with the language rules of the racist movement to gain an entry into racist groups and achieve some level of rapport with potential respondents also risked conveying false information about my racial politics.

Such rhetorical concessions on my part also raised some ethical questions. When researchers act in accord with the obviously false rhetorical conventions of racist groups, does that risk furthering the credibility of the racist movement itself? For example, I initially raised questions with respondents about their political motivations and activities. Some women, particularly those from Christian Identity groups, objected to the formulation of their actions as "political," preferring to see themselves as directed by spiritual concerns. This formulation also served to disavow the consequences of their actions on the larger society, part of the Christian Identity effort to assert a racist/anti-Semitic agenda immune to legal scrutiny. Although I gave no indication of support for the agenda of Christian Identity, nonetheless my choice of language meant that I had forgone a direct challenge to at least one aspect of their racial agenda.

Second, racial negotiation was evident in the discussion of political and ideological differences between me and these respondents. With one exception, every person I contacted by letter or by phone to arrange interviews assumed that I was white and Christian. (The former is true; the latter is not.) In part, this was due to an assumption that only white Christians would be willing to risk the danger of meeting racist activists, many of whom openly espouse violence against Jews, African-Americans, and other racial and ethnic minorities. However, the expectations about my racial and religious identity also reflected the overwhelming assumption—shared within the racist movement and throughout much of mainstream U.S. culture—that anyone not identified to the contrary must be white and Christian. Marking myself as a university professor further increased their expectations that I would be white. Racial activists' lack of contact with Jews, Muslims, and members of other religions also increased the expectation that I would be Christian.

Along with these predictions of my racial identity, respondents had distinct expectations about my racial allegiance. This intensified when I met informants to arrange for face-to-face interviews. At no point did I imply that I was sympathetic or a likely convert to the viewpoint of the group. Rather, I emphasized that my views were likely to be quite at variance with theirs, but that I was committed to presenting my interview subjects in an accurate and fair manner. (I use the term "interview subject" rather than "informant," as the latter term has a very negative connotation in the organized racist movement as someone who secretly provides information to the authorities.) My decision to be explicit and clear about the ideological gulf that separated me from my respondents and the impossibility that I could be converted to their worldview resulted in part from my ethical concern for honesty in the research process. Also significant, though, was the danger of violence I might face by posing as a member or potential convert to a racist group, since legal actions against such groups and their members have often been based on information garnered from the testimony of infiltrators and informants.

However, simply communicating one's ideological differences with informants does not obviate all ethical and political dilemmas. Rather, conveying the message that my own politics were firmly established and antithetical to those of my respondents was more a process than a completed act in some of the interviews. Most respondents seemed satisfied that I could have a fair but nonsympathetic stance toward their groups. As one woman, a young activist in a Christian Identity group, put it, "I don't know what your political affiliations are but I trust that you'll try to be as objective as possible. We don't often get that." However, as discussed below, other respondents persisted in efforts to convince me of the validity of their positions or my responsibility to advance the goals of white people. This occurred throughout the interview and even subsequently, through letters to me insisting that I should "do my duty to the white cause."

Third, racial issues emerged in the negotiation over legal consent to the interview. Respondents in social science research typically seek assurance of confidentiality or anonymity to prevent their views or characteristics from being made public. In contrast, racial activists are interested in promoting their group and their ideology in any possible forum, including through academic work. Thus, issues of racial loyalty arose in the process of obtaining signatures on the forms giving consent to the interview. Respondents struggled to add language requiring that I use the actual names of their groups, and sometimes their own (official, organizational) names in any publication resulting from this research. Although the forms that seek consent from interviewees for research interviews are infused with institutional, legal language, several of the racist activists in this study regarded the issue of consent differently—not as a legal contract, but as a measure of my racial commitment. These respondents challenged me to advance "the cause" by using my access to academic publications to promote racist ideas. Such verbal challenges implicitly drew on our unacknowledged racial commonality and assumed that, as members of the same racial group, we would have similar racial agendas despite my protestations to the contrary. Here, they perhaps capture one of the most difficult ethical dilemmas in researching groups whose agendas we deplore: that scholarship has the power to publicize even as it scrutinizes. So when an older Ku Klux Klan woman who had agreed to be interviewed, told me, "Thanks for writing an article that might inspire others," I was convinced that my decision to disguise actual groups and individuals was the correct one.

Racial negotiation did not end when the interviews were arranged. Instead, subtle issues of race pervaded the interviewing process. To illuminate these dynamics, I discuss two very different interviews from this research which highlight some of the issues common to this peculiar form of white-on-white interviewing.

Hitler's Family

The first interview was one I conducted with Jan,[1] a middle-aged woman from Maine. Jan was active in the Hitler Family (HF), a small underground group with several chapters across the country that advocates Nazi principles, modified for the modern United States. The HF claims that its main ideological principle is Aryan solidarity within the nation which, they argue, requires the exclusion of non-Aryan immigrants from the United States. Further, they distinguish between individuals and races according to their degree of social, spiritual, and intellectual evolution, with Aryans regarded as the highest stage of human evolution. Non-Aryans are portrayed in largely animalistic terms, as violent, uncooperative, and materialistic.

Although many of their members currently live in cities, the HF glorifies the rural countryside as the place where Aryan principles can develop. Like other groups in the neo-Nazi movement, the HF encourages its members to relocate to environmentally pristine (and majority-white) areas. This practice has fueled the migration of a number of neo-Nazi activists and groups to the states of the Pacific Northwest, especially Idaho, eastern Washington, and western Montana. The HF and others, hoping for extensive white supremacist settlement of this area and eventual succession from the United States, denote this as the "Great Northwestern Territorial Imperative."

The HF is also active in Holocaust denial and insists that claims that 6 million Jews perished at the hands of the Nazis are inflated due to postwar Jewish efforts to extract reparations from Germany and other Aryan countries. Instead, they insist that far fewer Jews died during World War II and that these deaths were largely the result of the shortages of food and medicine due to Allied blockades of Germany during the war.

Like most Nazi-oriented groups in the United States today, the HF adopts the symbols and rhetoric of Hitler's Germany. Its literature prominently displays swastikas and symbols of ancient Nordic religions and trumpets what it sees as the glories of Hitler's regime, especially Hitler's efforts to strengthen the Aryan race. Although operating largely underground, the HF does publish and sell a variety of pamphlets and books, ranging from texts of Hitler's speeches to analyses of the contemporary U.S. political situation according to Nazi principles.

My interview with Jan was arranged through a contact in a related neo-Nazi group who told her about my project and persuaded her to participate. At the beginning of the interview, Jan expressed suspicions about my research. In particular, she was concerned that her group be differentiated from other aspects of the racist movement, insisting that the HF was "less focused on hate" than other white supremacist groups. As she put it, "The other ones are vicious and they are not philosophical at all." This statement reflected Jan's underlying belief that there is a gradation within the white race, and that followers of the HF are among the most intellectually sophisticated and highly evolved within the movement. Thus, whiteness—which is presented as an undifferentiated category of racial identification and loyalty in the propaganda of most racist groups—is a much more complicated and internally stratified label for Jan. She attributed her view of the differences within the white race both to her upbringing and to her assessment of contemporary racist politics.

First, Jan noted that she was unable to see whites as equal because she was raised to consider some white ethnic groups as different, and worse, than others.

> My parents lived in a big Greek section [of the city] and they didn't like them. [They said,] "They're different from us, you know?" I found that to be true when I did date Greek guys. I noticed that they had different ways. . . . An outsider has a worse time trying to figure out how to handle these guys.

Jan was not claiming—as some other racist activists would—that Greeks were nonwhite or less white than other ethnic groups. Rather, she was arguing that because Greeks and other whites were fundamentally different—although both white—she was an outsider to the culture of Greek men. Later, she similarly disparaged Italians, this time by noting that the term "America" was difficult for her to accept because it implicitly commemorates Christopher Columbus.

> I don't like that term "American" because I think that [laugh] you know America is named after an Italian map maker.

Straining for the appropriate language, Jan seized on "tribe" to denote how it was possible to have such variability within a single race of whites.

> I see myself as a kind of Aryan tribalist. One tribe can vary a lot from the next.

Jan's delineation of ethnic differences within the white race was greatly at odds with the propaganda published by the HF and other racist groups, most of which portray whites as a homogeneous race which can be unified by raising racial consciousness and political action. To the extent that ethnic differences are addressed in this propaganda, typically these are used rhetorically to exclude certain groups from the umbrella of whiteness rather than to delineate groups within the white race. Thus, before the Klan opened its doors to Catholic members in the 1970s, Klan chapters occasionally suggested that Italians were not truly members of the white race but existed in a racial netherworld both because their purported darker skin color prevented them from being truly white and because their assumed Catholic faith prevented them from being fully loyal to the white race. Such a difference between Jan's racial reasoning and the portrayal of race in racist group propaganda is not unusual. Indeed, racist group members typically display more complicated understandings of race than are presented in literature meant for mass consumption (see Blee 1998).

Jan's graded view of whiteness was also related to her evaluation of the contemporary white supremacist movement. Far from glorifying the racist movement, as the literature of her group does, Jan had a very negative opinion of most racist activists.

I think most of the people who call themselves part of the movement are people who have been attracted to a stereotype, what they think it means. . . . They just act like white trash.

Jan's complicated views of race and racial activism also affected the racial dynamics of the interviewing process. Early in the interview, Jan interrupted herself and commented: "I'm just assuming you're [my kind of] white. I could be wrong here." When I responded with a quizzical look, she continued, "It [whiteness] covers a lot of territory, you know. There's all kinds." In this exchange, Jan was seeking assurance not only that I was within her acceptable range of white ethnic groups, but, implicitly, that I would maintain my initial commitment not to betray her even if I was not "the right kind of white." However, since I made no efforts to talk about my racial and ethnic background, Jan eventually dropped the subject and returned to her original point.

A later effort to assess my commitment to her kind of whiteness involved Jan's discussion of an acquaintance, a woman she described as having "had bad experiences with minorities" but being nonetheless unwilling to do anything about it. She characterized this woman as white but—due to her reluctance to act on behalf of white people—nearly a traitor to whiteness. "White people who would never make a stand over any issue like race," Jan argued, "are too afraid to have anyone call them a racist or get any bad publicity [even though] they do agree." Again, the issue of whether I was a "race traitor" or a "race loyalist" hung over the interview, marking another gulf between us that I was unwilling to bridge.

White Warriors

The second interview I had was with Lisa, a leader in a violent white power skinhead group, the White Warriors (WWs), whom I contacted through another member of her group. Lisa had an extensive personal history of violent actions. She had completed one prison sentence for assault. At the time of our interview, she was in prison again, having been convicted of being an accessory to murder. Lisa claimed to be in her late twenties, but appeared younger. She sported several visible tattoos, including one explicitly symbolic of white power. In contrast to the fairly cordial tone of my interview with Jan, my interactions with

Lisa were tense and frequently antagonistic. Lisa's language was full of racial expletives and obscenities and it was difficult to keep her focused on the questions I was asking.

Lisa had been involved with the White Warriors for about three years, a long commitment by the standards of white power skinheads whose affiliations to particular groups and even to the white power skinhead movement tend to be quite short-lived. Although she had not joined any other racist or anti-Semitic groups, Lisa had friends who were members of the Ku Klux Klan and neo-Nazi groups and Lisa herself had attended parties and rallies of these groups.

It was difficult to learn about the beliefs of the WWs through the interview because, like other skinheads, Lisa was reluctant to discuss her group's ideas and politics to any significant extent. In part, this might have reflected both a personal and an organizational distrust of outsiders, including scholarly researchers. But at least as significant a factor in Lisa's reluctance was her shallow ideological understanding, a common feature among white power skinheads. It is action and relationships between people, not argumentation or relationships between ideas, that are important to white power skinheads. Action (especially threats, fighting, and violence) and friends (other white power skinheads) are what sustain skinhead groups over time.

Like other white power skinhead groups, the WWs do not publish a regular newsletter or other forms of propaganda. Rather, an understanding of the ideology of the WWs has to be pieced together through its occasional flyers, and the clothing, tattoo insignia, and music predilections of its members—a set of cultural markers at least some of which are wielded for shock value rather than to represent the actual opinions of activists. Given the difficulty in summarizing the WWs' philosophy, it is possible only to say that it involves a violent antipathy to all African-Americans, Jews, Muslims, a vitriolic hatred of gays and lesbians, and a confrontational, ganglike antagonism toward everyone outside the WWs, occasionally even other white power skinheads.

The negotiation of race in my interview with Lisa was much more challenging than in the interview with Jan, although the result was much the same. Lisa became quite impatient when I began the interview by telling her about the goals of my research. When I brought up my standard speech about the ideological gulf between me and those I was interviewing, Lisa cut me off and would not let the interview return to this point. Instead, she hurled challenges at me at scattered points of the interview while preventing an answer. The following exchange was typical of this pattern:

> *KB:* At that time, were you associated with certain [racist] groups? You don't need to tell me which groups. But were you associated with certain groups?
>
> *Lisa:* Yes.
>
> *KB:* What kind of groups?
>
> *Lisa:* White supremacy, neo-Nazi, the belief in anarchy. *I can't stand Jews. Are you a Jew? I can't stand Jews* because they're the ones that said "Crucify Jesus," okay? I don't believe in government because it's mostly ruled by the fucking Jews anyway.

Note that Lisa countered my inquiries into her group affiliations by raising a challenge about my own ethnic and religious identification, *"Are you a Jew?"* bracketed between statements of her antipathy toward what she feared I might secretly be, *"I can't stand Jews."* Yet Lisa would not allow me to answer.

Moreover, like other racist activists I interviewed, Lisa did not believe that racial categories are fixed in all circumstances. Rather, she presented race as somewhat fluid and chosen. To Lisa, people adopt and can change their racial allegiances, racial identities, and even racial categorization, depending on their actions and beliefs. Thus, one reason that she did not probe for an answer to the inquiry, *"Are you a Jew?"* was because the answer could only be revealed through my actions toward her and others like her. Throughout the interview with Lisa other examples of this reasoning presented themselves—Hispanics in her prison whom she regarded as "really white," because they hated other Hispanics or African-Americans; an African-American friend whom she saw as white because he shared her white power skinhead beliefs, and even participated in assaults on other African-Americans.

Lisa's discussion of her own racial identification also involved change over time. In her youth, Lisa related, she saw herself as white. Later, when she discovered that white people had stolen land from American Indians, she decided that her intense sense of victimization meant that she was really partly Indian.

> This [country] was Indian territory. This was their country. White man took it over and I'm 3/4 Indian, so it pisses me off.

And later in the interview:

> *Lisa:* "I was denied my Indian heritage and I did grow up as a white
> person."
> *KB:* "Denied by?"
> *Lisa:* "My father. I wish that I would have been raised as a Cherokee."

When pressed, however, Lisa vacillated about her current racial identification:

> *KB:* "As a white supremacist don't you think white people have done
> a lot of terrible things to the Indians historically?"
> *Lisa:* "That's why I don't like most white people, but I choose white
> people over [other racial groups]."

Further, Lisa's ideas about race depended on an assessment of racial
loyalty. Just as her African-American friend became white through his
commitment to a white agenda, so too did people gain or lose racial
identities by their actions. One particularly striking example of this involved Lisa's discussion of why she had agreed to be interviewed for
this research while another white supremacist woman in her prison declined to be interviewed.

> I think it's really fucked up that Sarah would tell all her shit about
> white supremacy and all the things that go along with it yet when me
> and her were sitting in front of . . . a black lady, the [prison] superin-
> tendent [who asked,] "Will you talk to a lady from a university about
> white supremacy?" [Sarah] stands up, [and says,] "I'm not saying
> shit about my Aryan beliefs." And [she] walked out.

Immediately after, Lisa's disdain toward Sarah for her reluctance to
be interviewed was redirected toward me. My statements of ideological
difference now became evidence of my disdain for her and all white
people and my alleged cowardice about expressing my true racial beliefs to the African-American prison superintendent.

> At least I ain't ashamed of [being in favor of white power]. I'll tell
> them about what I think, you know. I'm the only one that [is] open
> about it. And it pisses me off about you. The two of you [Sarah and
> I], deep down, you suck up to [African-Americans].

Conclusion

This brief examination of some of the perils and insights involved in research on white racial activists by a white researcher suggests at least a few general themes about white-on-white interviewing practices. In particular, this research confirms what others have also found—that researchers can simultaneously be "insiders" and "outsiders" to the culture and meaning-systems of those they seek to study. My role as a white person conveyed access and a basic level of rapport with white racist activists that would have been impossible for a nonwhite researcher to achieve. However, both access and rapport between me and my respondents were attenuated by recognition, both on my part and on the part of my respondents, that my political stances and academic position meant that I was by no means a true insider to the world of white racial politics. However, such barriers to racial identification and interviewing rapport were also the means whereby I was able to "hear" the complications of racial understandings that my respondents were reporting. It was by pointing to my status as a racial outsider, in spite of my outward racial markings as white, that these racist activists were led to explain the intricate ways in which they fashioned their racial identities and the means by which they assigned racial identities to others.

NOTES

This research was supported by a grant to the author as a Research Professor at the University of Kentucky.

1. All names of individuals and groups are pseudonyms. Details that would identify individuals and groups have been changed.

REFERENCES

Barkun, Michael. 1994. *Religion and the Racist Right: The Origins of the Christian Identity Movement.* Chapel Hill: University of North Carolina Press.

Beoku-Betts, Josephine. 1994. "When Black Is Not Enough: Doing Field Research among Gullah Women." *NWSA Journal* 6 (3): 413–33.

Blee, Kathleen M. 1991. *Women of the Klan: Racism and Gender in the 1920s.* Berkeley: University of California Press.

———. 1996. "Becoming a Racist: Women in Contemporary Ku Klux Klan and Neo-Nazi Groups." *Gender & Society* 10 (6): 680–702.

———. 1998. "Reading Racism: Women in the Modern Hate Movement." In *No Middle Ground: Women and Radical Protest,* edited by Kathleen M. Blee, pp. 180–98. New York: New York University Press.

DeVault, Marjorie. 1995. "Ethnicity and Expertise: Racial-Ethnic Knowledge in Sociological Research." *Gender & Society* 9 (5): 612–31.

Edwards, Rosalind. 1990. "Connecting Method and Epistemology: A White Woman Interviewing Black Women." *Women's Studies International Forum* 13 (5): 477–90.

Frankenberg, Ruth. 1993. *White Women, Race Matters: The Social Construction of Whiteness.* Minneapolis: University of Minnesota Press.

Hamm, Mark S. 1993. *American Skinheads: The Criminology and Control of Hate Crimes.* New York: Praeger.

Ignatiev, Noel. 1995. *How the Irish Became White.* New York: Routledge.

Jeansonne, Glen. 1996. *Women of the Far Right: The Mother's Movement and World War II.* Chicago: University of Chicago Press.

Roy, Beth. 1998. "Goody Two-Shoes and the Hell-Raisers: Women's Activism, Women's Reputations in Little Rock." In *No Middle Ground: Women and Radical Protest,* edited by Kathleen M. Blee, pp. 96–132. New York: New York University Press.

Wrigley, Julia. 1998. "From Housewives to Activists: Women and the Division of Political Labor in the Boston Antibusing Movement." In *No Middle Ground: Women and Radical Protest,* edited by Kathleen M. Blee, pp. 251–88. New York: New York University Press.

Zavella, Patricia. 1993. "Feminist Insider Dilemmas: Constructing Ethnic Identity with Chicana Informants." *Frontiers: A Journal of Women Studies* 13 (3): 53–76.

Chapter 5

Doing My Homework
The Autoethnography of a White Teenage Girl

Lorraine Delia Kenny

Working in the Fields of Color Blindness

Midway through fieldwork at my adolescent alma mater, the Shore-ham-Wading River (SWR) Middle School on Long Island, the girls' varsity basketball team made it to the sectional finals.[1] SWR was matched up against Amityville, a team hailing from a town consider-ably closer to New York City than SWR and from a school district whose student population is two-thirds African-American (Brown 1994: A35). The SWR team was entirely white, while the Amityville team was black. It was an away night game and SWR parents and teachers came out in full force, as did the Amityville community. Con-sequently, the fans were divided along racial lines, with white SWR fans occupying one section of the bleachers and the black Amityville supporters the other. I sat among the SWR spectators, chatting with the parents, teachers, and district superintendent (and father of one of the players) who had come to cheer the girls on. As both teams were warm-ing up, the talk around me turned to "how *big* the Amityville girls are" compared to "our *skinny* girls." Here big and skinny displaced the ob-vious: black and white.

Once the game started, both teams' fans responded vociferously as the girls dribbled up and down the court. The match was charged. Amityville's defense effectively kept the SWR girls out from under the basket. As the game progressed, the SWR girls became increasingly frustrated. As a result, they began to slam into the Amityville players and hold onto the ball too long before they attempted to get it by an Amityville girl to an SWR teammate. The refs called foul after foul against SWR, and Amityville kept using their penalty shots to put the ball in the basket, hence increasing their lead over SWR. About halfway into the game, a ref called the first foul on an Amityville girl, bringing the SWR crowd to its feet cheering, and the mother of the best player on the team shouting: "It's about time, ref. I was beginning to think you were color-blind."

Ostensibly, this mother was referring to the teams' uniforms: SWR in blue and gold; Amityville in red and white. However, the underlying racial connotations of this outburst were hard to simply ignore. The whiteness and blackness of the two teams stood in starker contrast than their school colors. Regardless, no one around her—including or especially, as the case may be, myself—responded. Instead, her comment seemed to hang in the gymnasium air for a split second, while we, the SWR crowd, regained our composure and got on with rooting for our skinny white daughters. SWR's enthusiasm and ref bullying were to no avail; our girls eventually lost to Amityville by 12 points, 46 to 34.

As indirect as this racial outburst may have been, in my months in the field I had rarely witnessed such a clear demonstration of SWR's racial culture at work. The "color blindness" here was not so much the ref's, who was clearly just doing his job, as the SWR parents', who aspired to maintain a kind of social color blindness while all too obviously remaining deeply color, or more specifically, racially conscious. Their race consciousness, however, was not about their own middle-class whiteness—certainly not directly—and the ways they racialized their daughters (and sons), so much as it was about avoiding the topic altogether. This is a community with foundations and investments in a culture of avoidance (Baumgartner 1988; Lipsitz 1995). They had moved to this quiet, effectively homogeneous community to get away from the culture of conflict they imagined a diverse metropolitan setting to harbor. But this was also, to a degree, a community that fancied itself to be, at the very least, "tolerant" of difference. They were not actively, publicly bigots; they didn't have to be. Their lives of privilege had, up until recently, rarely been challenged. And the recent crisis points, tied to a complicated shift in the tax base, were economic, not racial.[2] The culture of avoidance they practiced manifested itself in terms of race as "color/power evasiveness" (Frankenberg 1993): a belief in the merits of liberal democracy wherein success and failure are individualized, not institutionalized. In this respect, race, especially whiteness, was not the SWR community's problem.

I, on the other hand, had returned to my hometown precisely to study this phenomenon. In inflammatory terms, the very groundwork of my study sets me up as a potential race traitor: if whiteness, or at least middle-class whiteness, maintains its social hegemony through a kind of measured silence and anonymity, as numerous theorists of whiteness have suggested (see below), an ethnographer of whiteness necessarily seeks to break this code and hence give the lie to white privilege. I had come home to articulate that which normally cannot and should not be said, and I had come to do this not simply as an outside observer, one who could claim a kind of distance from her object of study, but as a prodigal daughter deeply implicated in her own whiteness who personally and intellectually owes much to the community she left behind. Studying the culture of avoidance (or more specifically, middle-class whiteness) in one's hometown poses a series of methodological and ethical dilemmas that in many ways became the subject of my autoethnography. For these dilemmas constitute not only my ethnographic practice but also the race culture I sought to articulate.

The Ethnographic Dilemma of Hometown Whiteness

In recent years, studying one's hometown and writing an autoethnography have been taken up within anthropology as a form of disciplinary critique. Writing about one's "home" presumably disrupts the self-other dynamics that have typically left their imprint on ethnographic knowledge (Fabian 1983). But not everyone's hometown posits the same anthropological relationships and questions. In *Fictions of Feminist Ethnography*, Kamala Visweswaran calls on anthropologists to do their "homework." She asks, "Why is it that despite recent critiques of place and voice in anthropology, we have yet to turn to our own neighborhoods and growing-up places?" (Visweswaran 1994: 104). This chapter—and the larger study it comes out of (Kenny in press)—is my attempt to begin this process of "home" study, but specifically in terms of hegemonic racial and class-based practices. And here lies a twofold dilemma: one part anthropological, the other a dilemma of identity, self-recognition, and ethics. In studying my hometown, I became a native anthropologist of sorts. Native in the sense that this was my "growing-up place," and yet not so native in that this was a normative and not an "exotic" culture I had come to study. When Lila Abu-Lughod asks, "What happens when the 'other' that the anthropologist is studying is simultaneously constructed as, at least partially, a self?" (Abu-Lughod 1991: 140), she writes of native or seminative anthropologists who return to their growing-up places or ancestral homelands to study the non-Western/nonwhite other (e.g., Abu-Lughod 1986, 1993; Kondo 1990; Kumar 1992; Limón 1994; Visweswaran 1994). Despite the collapsing of anthropological distance that such studies entail, these anthropologists are still more recognizable as anthropologists than, Abu-Lughod suggests, as "Americans who study Americans" (1991: 139), by which she means, as I read her, white middle-class Americans studying white middle-class America. The native or near-native anthropologists that Abu-Lughod and others have considered are still studying anthropology's others, while the white, middle-class, prodigal daughter ethnographer studies a self that up until recently—with a few exceptions (e.g., Schneider 1980; Varenne 1986; Nader 1988)—was inconceivable as a direct object of anthropological inquiry (see Ortner 1991).

Beyond disciplinary frameworks, whiteness and middle classness pose their own ethnographic challenges. Not only are they not a ready-made anthropological other, they are not a readily recognizable self. Recent theorists of race have argued (see especially Dyer 1988; Frankenberg 1993; Morrison 1992) that whiteness in the United States—especially in its middle-class, heterosexual configuration—occupies a hegemonic position precisely because it cannot and will not speak its own name. Or, as Toni Morrison writes, "whiteness, alone, is mute, meaningless, unfathomable, pointless, frozen, veiled, curtained, dreaded, senseless, implacable" (1992: 59). This general understanding of whiteness leaves the white, middle-class, Western anthropologist studying an intentionally invisible home from within, a normative platform of invisibility. As an ethnographer of middle-class whiteness, I needed to devise methods for naming the unnamable, marking the unmarked, seeing the invisible, and analyzing why normative whiteness depends so much on not being recognized as a racial and social category. And I had to do all this from within my own supposedly self-evident whiteness as well as from within the anonymous whiteness that enshrouded the SWR community.

This was a blindingly white-on-white world and ethnographic expedition. Between 1982 and 1993, the year I began my fieldwork, the SWR school population went from being 98 to 95.9 percent white. Moreover, out of a class of about 160 students, the eighth grade I studied had one African-American girl and four Asian kids, at least two of whom had been adopted by white families. The nonwhite teachers at the middle school were equally few and far between; though the principal was African-American, his teaching staff of about fifty instructors included only three African-American women, no Asians, and no Latinos. This was, statistically at least, an overwhelmingly white population and as such a fairly typical suburban community.[3]

These numbers, however, are only skin deep. What is most significant about racialized communities for anthropologists and for others interested in the cultural meanings of race and the social and political effects of those meanings is not so much the percentage of whites and nonwhites who live in them but the everyday practices that racialize them. Playing the numbers game involves taking the path of least *and* most resistance. The current battle over the fate of affirmative action policies in the United States makes the limitations of this approach all too apparent; the ideals of the civil rights movement will not be met by quotas alone, and quotas are the first things to go when policies come under popular, governmental, or legal scrutiny. Herein lies the difference between studying whites and studying whiteness. Whiteness is a set of social, economic, and historical practices on the quotidian and systemic levels. It is, in other words, about cultural content rather than skin color.

In "Brown-Skinned White Girls," France Winddance Twine offers a compelling ethnographic account of how racial categories are markers of upbringing and context. Her subjects were African-descent (biracial) women, identified as white while they were growing up in their middle- and upper-middle-class, predominantly white, suburban communities. It was not until later in their lives—in the wake of puberty with its turn toward heterosexual dating or as students in a multiracial university setting—that they came to see themselves or were socially positioned by their peers and other institutional forces as nonwhites (Twine 1997). In the process of analyzing their stories, Twine begins to fill in the blanks of hegemonic whiteness, giving content to this otherwise abstract and formatively elusive concept. To be white in her study is to be color-blind, race neutral, and/or to conceive of one's self as racially invisible; it is to possess a certain "purchasing power" or access to the material privileges commensurate with a white middle-class lifestyle; it is to see oneself as an individual rather than as a member of a racialized or ethnic community; it is to feel comfortable around white-skinned, middle-class people, to not feel (racially) self-conscious or to engage in self-censorship, or as bell hooks describes it, to not "wear the mask," pretending to "be comfortable in the face of whiteness only to turn [around] and give expression to intense levels of discomfort" (hooks 1992: 341).

The whiteness Twine begins to delineate in this study is clearly class based and located within a specific social milieu, underscoring the degree to which whiteness is not a unified and fixed category but situational and multiply inflected by other social conditions, including gender, region, age, generation, and status, in addition to class. In his work on whites in Detroit, John Hartigan Jr. emphatically argues for the heterogeneity of whiteness, also demonstrating how class operates to give different communities of whites more or less access to the privileges commonly associated with white skin within the racially hierarchized social order of the United States (see especially Hartigan 1997a and 1997b). Both these studies shift the academic discussion of whiteness onto local anthropological ground, calling for more complex understandings of the cultural geography of race and its concomitant landscapes of power, privilege, and disadvantage. While Twine's work is based on interviews with newly race-conscious, African-descent, suburban-raised women speaking of their "white" childhoods in retrospect, and Hartigan's analyses of whiteness emerge out of an extensive ethnographic study of three differently positioned white communities within one geographic region, both rely methodologically and theoretically on tropes of distance and difference (be it temporal and interracial in the case of Twine, and intraracial or class-based in the case of Hartigan) to articulate the local content of whiteness in their respective fields.

This methodological and epistemological turn is de rigueur when it comes to social scientific and even commonsense analyses of race, especially in discussions of whiteness where the object of study is predicated on a myth of invisibility. The only way to make whiteness visible is to show it in conflict with or in contrast to what it is not. The literature on whiteness abounds with such examples: in *White Women, Race Matters,* Ruth Frankenberg (1993) frames her informants' life stories in terms of issues of racism and their experiences with interracial sexual relationships and child rearing. Douglas E. Foley, in his own autoethnography *The Heartland Chronicles* (1995), studies "racial relations" between the whites and the Mesquaki Indians in his hometown of Tama, Iowa. And other notable texts look at the historical dimensions of the role that racial differences and racism plays(ed) in the formation of whiteness (Blee 1991; Breines 1992; Roediger 1991; Stoler 1991; Ware 1992).

In my study of my own homegrown, middle-class, Long Island whiteness, I could not turn to these analytical tools. Not only was the other intimately intertwined with the self, and hence the analytical distance between observer and observed collapsed, but the historical raison d'être of suburbia itself shuns difference. Places like SWR rest on a legacy of white flight from the so-called other America: the nonwhite, ethnic, urban, and/or rural underclass (Jackson 1985; Lipsitz 1995). They are ontologically, if nothing else, the anti–other America.[4] I knew that I had been racialized in this fairly isolated suburban community not by being told or shown that I was not nonwhite or not other. The basketball mom notwithstanding, expressions of race and racism were and are kept in check in this polite, largely Christian, middle-class enclave. This is a community of intentional sameness. The tropes of difference are held at bay, disavowed, avoided, or at the very least disguised, translated into less direct vocabularies, like "skinny" and "big."

Though middle-class consciousness of race had shifted in the intervening years since I grew up in Shoreham, indeed Long Island itself was no longer the pristinely white bedroom community of New York City that it had once fashioned itself to be (Kelly 1993; Schemo 1994), the race question at SWR was still, to a large degree, whitewashed and avoided: we have no race problem here.[5] The principal, one of the few consistently openly race-conscious voices in the community, himself balked at the idea that I would study race or more specifically whiteness under his jurisdiction. In a letter he sent me prior to my arrival at the school, he wrote, "You ask . . . 'How do girls learn to be white. . . ?' I don't understand what this means! Aren't girls born white? What kind of questions would you be asking to determine how kids 'learn to be white.'. . . The more I think about it, the more inappropriate it seems to conduct racially based research on students in a public school setting" (personal correspondence, August 20, 1993).

I was not going to find a way to rename racial practices in a field that was privileged enough not to recognize itself racially, indeed went to great lengths to avoid doing so, by falling back on obvious constructs of difference and distance. This was a field of similarity. And I was, to a large degree, in the same field. I also needed an analytics that worked from within the homogeneity, one that would intensify this shade of whiteness rather than artificially contrast it with other ways of being white or nonwhite. And I needed to teach myself to see that which I had been trained not to notice. I needed to pay attention when my own anthropological questions met with resistance. For in these encounters I was being reeducated into the culture of avoidance. I also looked at how the culture of avoidance operated specifically in relation to questions of race. In its zeal to avoid or evade its own social and racial positioning, how did this community negotiate the race question if and when it did surface? Ultimately, I had to ask, what is this culture of avoidance avoiding?

Cultures of Avoidance

Deracializing Whiteness

My official arrival into the field would be marked by a series of semiformal presentations about my project. Teachers wanted me to introduce myself to their classes, and the principal wanted me to speak about my work to a parent liaison committee that met once a month or so to discuss their concerns about their children's educations with the middle school administration. In addition, the principal sent a memo to eighth grade teachers explaining my presence in the school, vaguely stating that I would be "gathering data on 8th grade female students" and emphasizing that any material I would subsequently publish would respect their anonymity. This was a community that was small enough to notice when a "stranger," even a known stranger, was among them and suspicious enough to need to know what this insider-outsider's intentions were. They liked to know what was going on, but only up to a point.

The breaking point, I had already gathered from the principal's prefieldwork correspondence, had something to do with race. The principal's reactions to my proposed research would turn out to be an anomaly only in terms of degree and directness. Explaining to my various SWR audiences that I was there to study what girls learned about being white, middle class, and female by growing up in a place like Shoreham-Wading River elicited some notable responses that efficiently taught me in fairly stark terms the boundaries of public discourse and the limits of self-awareness in this town. The girls' parents and teachers mainly wanted to hear my thoughts on girls and self-esteem, girls and math and science, and girls and the media, all common topics on TV talk shows, in women's magazines, and on prime time news programs at that time. Eighth graders, on the other hand, didn't want to know I was studying "girls." When I introduced myself to a small group of students for the first time, they became visibly and audibly uncomfortable when I explained that I was studying how *girls* grow up in a white, middle-class community like SWR. The boys giggled and the girls looked horrified. The teacher advised me to tell future groups that I was studying how *kids* grow up at SWR. I heeded her advice, applying it in conjunction with the lessons I had learned from my correspondence with the principal, and proceeded to keep things as vague as possible whenever kids or adults asked me exactly what I was doing as I roamed the halls, wandered out to the playing fields, or went with the girls to the movies or to eat tacos at Taco Bell or burgers and fries at McDonald's (two of their favorite fast-food eateries).

These seemingly minor linguistic discomforts were more than just semantic idiosyncrasies. They indicated who this community was and how they came to articulate and rearticulate themselves in their children. That the parents and teachers, many of whom lived as well as worked in this school district and were themselves parents of teenage girls or twenty-something women, wanted to talk about gender did not suggest that this was the only term in my list of topics that posed a problem for them individually or collectively. Instead it was the term they found most acceptable to talk about. Naming gender was a way of *not* naming race and class generally or whiteness and middle classness more specifically. The eighth graders, on the other hand, more directly articulated their disturbance. Race and class were not hot button issues for them, while gender, or more specifically, sexuality was. However, they did not express their uneasiness around this topic in a confrontational manner; their giggles and silences were pleas to me to drop the topic rather than explore it with them further. Both the adult and teen cultures in these instances were practicing the art of avoidance, one subtler than the other.

When it came to race and class, the kids didn't so much avoid these topics as simply not take much notice of them. One day an English and Social Studies teacher read a clipping from the *New York Post* about a nearby school that, following complaints from Native American groups, had just stopped rehearsals for its theatrical production of Peter Pan. The kids responded by saying things like, "I think they're taking things way too seriously." And "Oh, *puhleaze,* it's just entertainment!" When the teacher asked, "Do Indians like being called 'redskins'?" One girl, Christine, exclaimed, "Do we mind being called white?"[6] The tone of her voice answered her own question. "No, why should we?" And her choice of pronouns clearly articulated, in both senses of the word, the collective racial identity of the room. When Christine ended the conversation on such a definitive racial note, there were no nonwhite-skinned kids in the room. But even if the class were not composed of a sea of white faces, I suspect that Christine's comment would still have gone not only uncontested but unacknowledged, at least not openly. Here, being white (and middle class) meant being born into the privilege of not consciously taking one's race and class too seriously. For the white-skinned SWR eighth graders, race was a nonissue. As for the nonwhite-skinned kids, I never heard them openly articulate a position on race. Either they chose to turn a deaf ear, or having been born, raised, and educated in this community they had not yet come to articulate a nonwhite consciousness. Or else they were either not comfortable or not interested in discussing these matters in my white presence (cf. Twine 1997). Regardless of motive, the effect was uniform: the teen culture, like the parent culture at SWR, bypassed issues of race and class in their day-to-day interactions with each other.

Teaching Tolerance

Though race and class were not really supposed to be mentioned in public or in polite company, the school did make an effort to cobble together a multicultural curriculum of sorts. This was, after all, a post-pc, post-Crown Heights, post-Rodney King and the Los Angeles uprising world, to name just a few recent, high-profile public events focused on race that could not be easily avoided even by the most evasive of white liberal sensibilities.

The one school-based program on race that I observed was part of an extracurricular teaching tolerance program in which students elected to participate, called Bringing Unity to Youth, or BUTY (pronounced "beauty") as the kids and teachers referred to it.[7] BUTY consisted of a "cultural exchange" between the SWR and Riverhead middle schools. Only a twenty-minute drive east of Shoreham, Riverhead is probably the district closest to SWR with the largest nonwhite population: in 1992–93, of the nearly four thousand students attending Riverhead schools, 30.6 percent were black, 0.8 percent were Asian, 1.9 percent were Hispanic, and 66.5 percent were white (Brown 1994: A35). The economic disparities between Riverhead and SWR were also pronounced. Unlike isolated, virtually commerce-free, and family-oriented Shoreham-Wading River, Riverhead has an extensive commercial center and is a county seat replete with a Department of Motor Vehicles, a New York State Supreme Court building, and a county jail. Colloquially, Riverhead is known for being "rougher" than Shoreham or Wading River. Until the opening in late 1994 of a complex of outlet stores on the eastern edge of Riverhead, the SWR community did most of its shopping west of Shoreham, avoiding the Riverhead experience altogether. Now they are drawn to the outlets, but not much further. Likewise, few SWR kids have regular contact with Riverhead kids, and those that do, do so to the chagrin of their parents. In the beginning of May, under the auspices of BUTY and its multicultural agenda, about thirteen Riverhead kids, almost all of whom were African-American, came to SWR, and at the end of the month, about twelve SWR kids (and I), all of whom were white, went to Riverhead. In both settings, kids were paired with an indigenous student and "shadowed" him or her for the day.

At SWR, the preparation leading up to the exchange was fairly perfunctory. About a week before the Riverhead students were scheduled to come to SWR, the community service coordinator in the school, Mrs. F., met with the SWR kids participating in the program to go over the logistics and give them a sense of context for the exchange. For some this would be their second year visiting Riverhead with BUTY. When Mrs. F. asked them what the differences were between the two schools, kids noted that Riverhead had a cafeteria; students had to stay inside during lunch; there were security guards; and there was yellow tape in the hallway, which everyone had to walk to the right of. Then some kids started talking about how Riverhead students had reacted to SWR the year before: "They thought our school was small and boring." "They kept *axing* us where all the blacks were." A comment that prompted Jean and Jessica to add: "When we were in Brooklyn showing [our slide show] 'BJ/3,' kids *axed* us that. We said it was our community. It's not that we kick them out."[8] Instead of addressing Jean and Jessica's comment directly, Mrs. F. persisted in her earlier vein of questioning: "What are the differences between you and them?" To which someone replied, "They're big." The meeting ended with Mrs. F. trying to get SWR kids to think about how to start conversations with their Riverhead visitors, and how to make them feel welcome. Tommy said he'd ask them if they liked Pearl Jam (a popular, white, grunge band at that time). Lisa suggested, "We can pay for their pizza." Both comments could have opened up discussions about whiteness and class, especially in terms of questions of cultural tastes and aesthetics (Bourdieu 1984), but the period was over and everybody moved on to their next scheduled activity.

On the day Riverhead kids visited, they walked around SWR saying things like, "This school is like a museum; we don't have couches and stuff," asking, "What y'all can do to get detention?" and explaining how they got three days' detention for having a water pistol, which meant they stayed after school and sat in a room and couldn't talk to anyone from 2:30 to 4:00.[9] In a pithy moment, one Riverhead kid went up to the stacks in the library and dramatically ran his hand along the top shelves. "See, you got dust," he said, displaying his smudged fingertips, a comment I took to be a biting piece of social commentary, that is, you all may have money and privilege but that doesn't mean you don't have your own "dirt" like everyone else. No one seemed to appreciate or understand his humor. When Riverhead kids passed a black SWR student in the hall (all 1.1 percent of them), they would say hello. Sue and Lisa noticed this practice, concluding in a somewhat offended manner, "Hey, they're counting the number of black kids in the school."

What they and the rest of the SWR kids didn't seem to notice was what Riverhead kids knew that they didn't know. In social studies class, Mr. R. just happened to be going over the early 1960s and the civil rights movement, using Billy Joel's lyrics to "We Didn't Start the

Fire" and corresponding slides as a basis for the discussion. When Mr. R. asked, "Who defeated the world champion boxer Sonny Liston?" most of the Riverhead kids' hands went up. "Mohammed Ali." No SWR kids had a reply. When Malcolm X's picture came on the screen, again Riverhead kids could tell his story in detail, while only some SWR kids knew anything about him. Later in the class when Mr. R. asked if anyone knew who Warren Christopher was, or who the current Secretary of Defense was, no one—neither Riverhead nor SWR kids—knew the answer, though to the latter question, SWR's Bill replied, "Oh, he's the guy with that long name." He was referring to General Shalikashvili, the Chairman of the Joint Chiefs of Staff at that time; Bill was the resident war and military trivia junkie. The Riverhead visit ended soon after this history/current events lesson. Despite the pretenses of their meeting, as far as I could tell little was exchanged between the SWR and Riverhead kids in the course of that day's visit. To the contrary, much was left unsaid and unanswered.

In writing about her own education in the third world and subsequent transformation into a first-world scholar, Mary E. John notes, "Education is obviously a process by which we learn to avow and remember certain knowledges and devalue and forget others" (John 1989: 55). As a result, John suggests, we forge our subjectivities through a curriculum of "sanctioned ignorances" that at the very least avoid the more difficult questions. Though the context of John's observation differs dramatically from that of the SWR kids' lives, the educational process seems to travel beyond obvious borders. Not knowing about the civil rights movement, Mohammed Ali, or Malcolm X may indeed be "sanctioned ignorances" for SWR kids. This was no doubt not the first time they had been "taught" about the civil rights movement. I had seen posters and other educational materials around the school in sixth-, seventh-, and eighth-grade classrooms that illustrated nonwhite histories and white history in relation to nonwhite histories. And I probably would have found similar materials in the district's elementary schools. I knew, for example, that at least one eighth-grade girl understood enough about the history of slavery and emancipation to jokingly call me her "little Harriet Tubman" when I ushered her past the hall monitors into a world of relative freedom from adult supervision in the academic wings during lunch activity one day. The salient questions here are: What or who has sanctioned these white middle-class kids' ignorances? And to what end? In remaining ignorant of nonwhite histories what do they not learn about their own history of whiteness?

Ostensibly, the SWR-Riverhead exchange was designed to disrupt such sanctioned ignorances. To this end, SWR would complete the experience by joining Riverhead kids on their home turf. On the morning SWR kids went to Riverhead, Jean said she was sick and that the boy she had been paired with from Riverhead made her uncomfortable when he was at Shoreham. Jessica was convinced she was going to get "jumped." And Lisa complained that going to Riverhead had been "boring" last year, "You have to sit in class all day long."

The contrasts between SWR and Riverhead couldn't have been greater. Every Riverhead classroom had a set of "rules," "consequences," and "rewards" posted in the front of the room that students were supposed to follow. These included things like "Be in class and seated when the bell rings," "Always keep your textbook covered," "Do not talk during the lesson," "Remain in your seat," and "No food, drink, or candy in class." The science lab had an additional sign: "We are all expected to dress appropriately for school. Weapons, drugs, alcohol, and foul language may not be displayed." In most classes, kids sat in assigned seats in rows. And they rushed between class periods, making sure that they stayed to the right of the yellow line on the floor. For the most part, Riverhead kids did not talk in classes, as opposed to the cacophony of SWR life, which also, by the way, often included lots of eating of snacks and lunches and drinking of sodas, boxed juices, and milk during and between classes. Riverhead teachers brusquely reprimanded kids who spoke out of turn, saying things like, "The next person who doesn't behave in class will get detention," while SWR kids, often suffering with few or no consequences, jumped into class discussions without waiting for a teacher to call on them; such behavior was more in line with the pedagogical culture at SWR than not. SWR kids were encouraged to be active participants in their educations and to distinguish themselves as individuals. Lunch at Riverhead was regimented, surveilled, and loud. Sixth graders ate lunch during sixth period (around 10:50); seventh graders ate during seventh period (around 11:30), and eighth graders ate during eighth period (around 12:10). In the lunchroom, kids sat at metal picnic-style tables with attached benches and talked very loudly while teachers and teachers' aides stood vigil by the exits. At SWR, on the other hand, kids brought food from home, which they could heat up in the microwaves in the various classrooms, or an advisor, another teacher, or I took them out to lunch at the local pizza place or bagel shop or nearby fast-food restaurants. When they stayed at school, SWR kids ate in their advisories—a smaller, more intimate version of what traditionally passes for homeroom in most U.S. secondary schools—and had a half hour of free time before eating to catch up on their work or hang out with their friends either inside or outside the school building. Clearly, the white middle-class SWR students were being disciplined to be individuals, to be their own managers, and to be comfortable with supposedly benign and nearly invisible forms of authority, while their Riverhead counterparts were being taught to stay in line (literally as well as more broadly), to follow orders, and not to question authority.

In addition to the social regulations of Riverhead school life, Riverhead pedagogy was worlds apart from SWR's. In English class at Riverhead the teacher instructed kids to read paragraphs from a textbook on Greek mythology out loud for forty minutes, an activity I never witnessed at SWR. Indeed, few SWR classes used textbooks at all. More often than not, SWR's English classes consisted of kids working on individual writing projects. And once a week, teachers devoted a period of class time to silent reading, whereby the kids, teachers, and any visitors would read for forty minutes from a book of their choosing. SWR kids kept reading logs and English journals that kept track of and elaborated on class activities. In art class in Riverhead, everyone worked from kits on the same project. The girl I was paired with was making a rabbit pillow, the girl next to her a heart-shaped one. In SWR art rooms, kids worked on elaborate projects of their own design, ranging from ceramic sculptures to silver jewelry to wood furniture. Overall, none of the Riverhead rules, consequences, awards, or activities resembled life at SWR. These differences were not lost on either the SWR or Riverhead students, though their significance remained unexamined.

On the van ride back to Shoreham, the kids exchanged stories. Lisa said she got called a "white heifer," a slang, she said, for "white trash," or what amounts to a slang of a slang. Regardless, she seemed pleased by the fact that she had gotten a lot of guys' phone numbers.[10] Jim had to spend most of the day in detention because his partner kept getting in trouble. Bob fell asleep in social studies. Christine noticed that there was a white side and a black side to most rooms. And they all started imitating the way Riverhead kids talked, saying things like "playin," "sweatin," and "Whatsup!?" Meanwhile, Mrs. F. continued to drive the van in near silence, choosing not to use the kids' spontaneous reactions to their day to facilitate a discussion on the significance of race and class.

Such was the extent of the "cultural exchange." As far as I knew, there was no follow-up activity. Once the SWR kids got back to Shoreham, some went off to basketball practice, others went home to hang out with friends, watch TV, talk on the phone: the usual. No adult organized a critical conversation about what they had just experienced or about how their perceptions fit into a larger racial and economic picture. Doing so would have meant facing the SWR kids' whiteness and privilege head on. It would have meant unpacking Jean and Jessica's statement: "We said it was our community. It's not that we kick them [black people] out." It would have meant unsanctioning their ignorances, asking them to look at what they don't know, and to notice patterns in the gaps in their knowledge. Teaching tolerance in this offhand manner more accurately meant teaching avoidance. It meant teaching them to be unconsciously race conscious. And it further sanctioned certain kinds of ignorance over others. This was, to say the least, a multiculturalism of inconsequence, much like the one Paul Beatty satirically describes in his fictional memoir about growing up black in a white neighborhood.

> I was the only 'cool black guy' at Mestizo Mulatto Mongrel Elementary, Santa Monica's all-white multicultural school. My early education consisted of two types of multiculturalism: classroom multiculturalism, which reduced race, sexual orientation and gender to inconsequence; and schoolyard multiculturalism, where the kids who knew the most polack, queer and farmer's daughter jokes ruled. (Beatty 1996: 172)

A multiculturalism that was more than superficial would ask, what kind of multiculturalism did Lisa learn as she was being called a "white heifer," or Christine internalize when she noticed that kids segregated themselves into black and white contingents? Or more to the point, what kind of multiculturalism was this when their own group facilitator chose to ignore rather than discuss further their observations and experiences vis-à-vis this so-called exchange? In the context of teaching tolerance, SWR whiteness became defined by what SWR kids didn't know and didn't know they didn't know. In effect they were being taught to disavow differences, to not speak about them beyond the neatly confined excesses of their white peer culture. Instead of teaching kids to speak about race—theirs and others'—with any sense of the histories of privilege and disadvantage that imbue it, teaching tolerance reinforced the community's sanctioned silences and evasions. The biggest evasions here, however, were not about who the Riverhead kids were and why, so much as who the SWR kids were and why. By learning to disavow differences the SWR kids were learning not to notice their own whiteness and their own positions of relative social privilege.

Learning to Live with Contradictions

The lesson, however, is confusing at the very least. Here was a program designed to expose kids to, and teach them about, difference retreating into its own whiteness/sameness. While the frameworks of difference and distance appear central in the above examples, a multiculturalism of inconsequence ostensibly collapses the analytical perspective. There is no space for comparisons and conflict, practices that demand a certain amount of self-awareness. Instead, the culture of avoidance that operates in place of a racially (self-)cognizant culture is a culture of learning to live passively with contradictions and look past hypocrisies. While these hypocrisies surfaced in various venues throughout my fieldwork, the biggest burden with which this community lives is the encroaching sense that their own privilege is less than secure and costs them dearly when it comes to managing their children's lives (see especially note 2).

White flight to suburbia meant gaining the privilege to own one's single-family home and hence purchase a piece of middle-class privacy. Being an ethnographer of privacy, especially as a prodigal daughter who was socialized in this very social economy meant that I had to tread fine lines between what was public, what was private, and what could be articulated as white middle-class cultural practices, when those practices were themselves defined by their closed-door status. The girls and their parents seemed fully aware of the ways in which I could move between what was known and what was hidden about their lives and often tested the limits of my position as a privileged insider-outsider. I was told things I wasn't supposed to know by girls about other girls or about their own families. Parents would ask me to keep an eye on their daughters and to let them know if anything was amiss, while at the same time keeping me at a perfunctory distance when I came to pick their daughters up or attempted to hang out with them in the sanctity of the family home. One parent actually joked about how I had just missed the daily beating he administered to his children. While I had no reason to suspect that his humor had any bearing on reality, I took his comment as a reminder that I was treading on delicate territory and that I was perceived as someone out to expose their inner lives.

As a result of this border crossing between the public and the private, as well as the inside and the outside, there are things I know about this brand of middle-class whiteness that I have been asked to keep to myself. Some of these things do not seem particularly private to me in my guise as ethnographer, though a teacher, student, or parent have categorized them as such, and as a former (or perhaps more accurately "recovering") native, I can empathize with their impulses. Moreover, there are things I know about this whiteness that I keep in check through my own volition, unsure of how to write about it without putting myself in jeopardy; litigation stands as a viable option in an affluent culture of avoidance when the very terms of that culture are broken. This issue of the privilege of white privacy at times left me speechless, caught up within the constitutive silences of middle-class whiteness: the silences I have described throughout this chapter have been mine as much as the SWR's faculty and parents. And in writing about them now, I am in a sense betraying hometown confidences. At times the culture of middle-class whiteness easily had its way with me. Part of my job as a prodigal daughter ethnographer was to lie in wait for those moments when I was most caught up in the hegemony, when I wanted to say things or intervene in the culture of avoidance but chose instead to remain silent. In part, I did this because I didn't want to jeopardize my hometown advantage, which positioned me as someone the community would confide in or occasionally slip up in front of. But I also did this because I didn't feel comfortable breaking the hometown rules, rules with which I am thoroughly conversant and by which I live, to one degree or another.

When it came to a multiculturalism of inconsequence, I had to confront the ethics of not naming white privilege, theirs and my own. As an ethnographer, attempting to follow the processes of disavowal and avoidance that go into making a white middle-class sensibility, I couldn't name the unnamable without destroying the evidence, without bringing into the public domain that which was meant to remain private and anonymous. However, as a prodigal daughter working largely within the confines of an educational institution my responsibilities seemed less foregone. This dilemma would surface periodically as I sat in classrooms and listened to white history being presented as neutral or overheard kids misrecognize their own racial and class positionings. For the most part I remained complicit, taking note of the sanctioning of ignorances for later ethnographic consideration.

Now I am faced with the process of unsanctioning the ignorances—my subjects' and my own—and hence of violating the ethics of a culture of avoidance. In telling the story of SWR whiteness, I am not telling it within the codes of the culture of privilege I came to study. This leaves me caught within a contradiction of my own making: as an ethnographer of middle-class whiteness in a culture of similarity, I seek out what this culture attempts to avoid and what its members hold private, and I look for the ways they construct and live with the contradictions these practices necessarily wrought. In writing about this brand of whiteness, I am violating my subjects' and my own (dubious) privilege not to speak their/my own name. Such is the risk and the value of doing one's homework.

NOTES

1. This chapter is based on fieldwork conducted during the 1993–94 school year. I would like to thank the students, teachers, administrators, and parents who welcomed me into their community and made this project possible.

2. While I was in the field a battle over the school budget brought on by the demise of the Shoreham Nuclear Power Plant was gaining full steam. Since the Nuclear Regulatory Commission revoked the Long Island Lighting Company's jurisdiction over the plant in 1991, the utility has attempted to hold the SWR school district responsible for millions of dollars in back taxes, money they claim they overpaid when the plant was overassessed. The SWR school district is largely a product of these taxes. The middle school and high school campuses were built with this money, with little expense spared. The community willingly put up with the threat of having a nuclear power plant in their backyard—or more accurately, simply avoided thinking about the consequences of having a radioactive behemoth as a neighbor—because it was economically beneficial to them. Now with the tax base literally pulled out from under them,

the community is caught up in a vicious battle over the fate of the school system. Educationally this has meant a lot of retrenchment, which has gone hand in hand with large staff layoffs and other cutbacks. In the fallout from the plant closing, the once model school district struggles to survive. The privilege of not having to worry about their children's educations has literally come home to haunt them. What is most striking about this battle over taxes versus nuclear power versus taking one's child's upbringing and education for granted is that the bottom line is and always was money. I discuss this issue more fully in *Daughters of Suburbia* (Kenny in press).

3. In "The Possessive Investment in Whiteness: Racialized Social Democracy and the 'White' Problem in American Studies," George Lipsitz notes, "by 1993, 86 percent of suburban whites [in the United States] still lived in places with a black population below 1 percent" (1995: 374).

4. I use the negative descriptor to hold onto the ways in which suburban whiteness is historically raced. The other is more of a trace than a reality in a place like Shoreham-Wading River. It is the cultural practices that attempt to erase or evade that trace that I attempt to follow in the lives of my subjects.

5. This was not an uncommon suburban phenomenon. In "Facing Big-City Problems: L.I. Suburbs Try to Adapt," Diana Jean Schemo points out that though more and more African-American and Latino people moved to suburbia in the 1990s (nationally, in 1994, one black person in three lived in the suburbs) "lily-white communities tend not to become integrated." Furthermore, during this same time period on Long Island, 95 percent of its black residents lived in 5 percent of the census tracts (Schemo 1994).

6. All the kids' and teachers' names have been changed throughout this essay.

7. Before I knew exactly what BUTY was, I thought the kids were referring to some kind of school-sponsored cosmetology program, a club that would have seemed out of place in this middle-class community that prided itself on sending 95 percent of its graduates to college.

8. BJ/3, otherwise known as "The Fire Burns On," is a slide show set to the tune of Billy Joel's "We Didn't Start the Fire," a popular song covering world history between 1949 and 1989. As part of a social studies unit in Mr. R.'s class, kids rewrote the lyrics to "Fire" so that the new version chronicles historical events occurring in their lifetime (1979–93) and then compiled a slide show visually representing the same period. Throughout the year, Mr. R. took kids to present BJ/3 at different schools and conferences.

9. These comments predate the recent spate of lethal shootings in white high schools and middle schools in such far-flung places as Bethel, Alaska, and Jonesboro, Arkansas. How these events figured in the consciousnesses of the kids at SWR and Riverhead and how the authorities responded would be a sig-

nificant test case for the culture of avoidance; one I cannot, unfortunately, address here.

10. Like the basketball mom that started off this discussion of the culture of white middle-class avoidance, Lisa is a rule breaker. She was new to the school and spent most of the year fighting with her mother and teachers. One prominent way she had of getting her mother's attention was to pursue relationships with lower-class non-SWR kids, especially boys. Leading her mother to break the social codes of avoidance and accuse her of "dressing like white trash," among other things.

REFERENCES

Abu-Lughod, Lila. 1986. *Veiled Sentiments: Honor and Poetry in a Bedouin Society.* Berkeley: University of California Press.

———. 1991. "Writing against Culture." In *Recapturing Anthropology: Working in the Present,* edited by Richard G. Fox. Santa Fe, N.M.: School of American Research Press.

———. 1993. *Writing Women's Words: Bedouin Stories.* Berkeley: University of California Press.

Baumgartner, M. P. 1988. *The Moral Order of a Suburb.* New York: Oxford University Press.

Beatty, Paul. 1996. "Taken Out of Context." *Granta* 53 (spring): 167–94.

Blee, Kathleen M. 1991. *Women of the Klan: Racism and Gender in the 1920s.* Berkeley: University of California Press.

Bourdieu, Pierre. 1984. *Distinction: A Social Critique of the Judgment of Taste,* translated by Richard Nice. Cambridge: Harvard University Press.

Breines, Wini. 1992. *Young, White, and Miserable: Growing Up Female in the Fifties.* Boston: Beacon Press.

Brown, Peggy. 1994. "On LI, Race Looms Large." *Newsday,* May 20.

Dyer, Richard. 1988. "White." *Screen* 29 (fall): 44–64.

Fabian, Johannes. 1983. *Time and the Other: How Anthropology Makes Its Object.* New York: Columbia University Press.

Foley, Douglas E. 1995. *The Heartland Chronicles.* Philadelphia: University of Pennsylvania Press.

Frankenberg, Ruth. 1993. *White Women, Race Matters: The Social Construction of Whiteness.* Minneapolis: University of Minnesota Press.

Hartigan, John, Jr. 1997a. "Establishing the Fact of Whiteness." *American Anthropologist* 88 (3): 495–505.

———. 1997b. "Locating White Detroit." In *Displacing Whiteness: Essays in Social and Cultural Criticism,* edited by Ruth Frankenberg. Durham: Duke University Press.

hooks, bell. 1992. "Representing Whiteness in the Black Imagination." In *Cultural Studies,* edited by Lawrence Grossberg, Cary Nelson, and Paula Treichler. New York: Routledge.

Jackson, Kenneth T. 1985. *Crabgrass Frontier: The Suburbanization of the United States.* New York: Oxford University Press.

John, Mary E. 1989. "Postcolonial Feminists in the Western Intellectual Field: Anthropologists and Native Informants?" *Inscriptions* 5: 49–73.

Kelly, Barbara. 1993. *Expanding the American Dream: Building and Rebuilding Levittown.* Albany: State University of New York Press.

Kenny, Lorraine Delia. In press. *Daughters of Suburbia: Growing Up White, Middle Class, and Female.* New Brunswick: Rutgers University Press.

Kondo, Dorinne K. 1990. *Crafting Selves: Power, Gender, and Discourses of Identity in a Japanese Workplace.* Chicago: University of Chicago Press.

Kumar, Nita. 1992. *Friends, Brothers, and Informants: Fieldwork Memoirs of Banaras.* Berkeley: University of California Press.

Limón. José E. 1994. *Dancing with the Devil: Society and Cultural Poetics in Mexican-American South Texas.* Madison: University of Wisconsin Press.

Lipsitz, George. 1995. "The Possessive Investment in Whiteness: Racialized Social Democracy and the 'White' Problem in American Studies." *American Quarterly* 47 (3): 369–87.

Morrison, Toni. 1992. *Playing in the Dark: Whiteness in the Literary Imagination.* New York: Vintage Books.

Nader, Laura. 1988. "Up the Anthropologist—Perspectives Gained from Studying Up." In *Anthropology for the Nineties: Introductory Readings,* edited by Johnetta B. Cole. New York: Free Press.

Ortner, Sherry B. 1991. "Reading America: Preliminary Notes on Class and Culture." In *Recapturing Anthropology: Working in the Present,* edited by Richard G. Fox. Santa Fe, N.M.: School of American Research Press.

Roediger, David. 1991. *The Wages of Whiteness: Race and the Making of the American Working Class.* New York: Verso.

Schemo, Diana Jean. 1994. "Facing Big-City Problems: L.I. Suburbs Try to Adapt." *New York Times,* March 16.

Schneider, David M. 1980. *American Kinship: A Cultural Account.* Chicago: University of Chicago Press. Originally published in 1968.

Stoler, Ann Laura. 1991. "Carnal Knowledge and Imperial Power: Gender, Race, and Morality in Colonial Asia." In *Gender at the Crossroads of Knowledge: Feminist Anthropology in a Postmodern Era,* edited by Micaela di Leonardo. Berkeley: University of California Press.

Twine, France Winddance. 1997. "Brown-Skinned White Girls: Class, Culture, and the Construction of White Identity in Suburban Communities." In *Displacing Whiteness: Essays in Social and Cultural Criticism,* edited by Ruth Frankenberg. Durham: Duke University Press.

Varenne, Hervé, ed. 1986. *Symbolizing America*. Lincoln: University of Nebraska Press.

Visweswaran, Kamala. 1994. *Fictions of Feminist Ethnography*. Minneapolis: University of Minnesota Press.

Ware, Vron. 1992. *Beyond the Pale: White Women, Racism, and History*. London: Verso.

Chapter 6

Masters in the Field
White Talk, White Privilege, White Biases

Jonathan W. Warren

Race Problems

When I teach methods courses I often lecture from Charles Wagley's *Race and Class in Rural Brazil*. This edited volume of extremely rich ethnographies, originally published in 1952, always proves an effective means of illustrating how a researcher's assumptions and experiences affect not only what he or she sees and records but also the conclusions drawn from his or her data. These case studies are an ideal pedagogical tool for making this basic methodological point because they detail what contemporary North American students almost universally recognize as strong indicators of racism. Yet Wagley maintains that "Brazil has no 'race problem' in the same sense that exists in many other parts of the world" (1952: 7).

For example, one of the chapters in this book is based on fieldwork that Marvin Harris conducted in Minas Velhas, an old gold mining town located in the south-central mountain region in the state of Bahia. Harris observed that political and economic power were starkly racialized in Minas Velhas. The seventeen adults who "appear to be pure Caucasoid," he reported, "are all plantation owners, and all of them also have residences in the city of Salvador (ibid.: 23). There are no people in [the] two lower class strata who are considered 'pure' white. A few are considered *brancos da terra* but the great majority are Negroes, mulattos, and others of various degrees of race mixture" (ibid.:

24). Not surprisingly, given this racial hierarchy of power, he also discovered a fertile terrain of symbolic racism:

> In Minas Velhas, the superiority of the white man over the Negro is considered to be a scientific fact. . . . A school textbook used in Minas Velhas plainly states the case: "Of all the races the white race is the most intelligent, persevering, and the most enterprising. . . . The Negro race is much more retarded than the others. . . ." None of the six urban teachers (who are all, incidentally, white females) could find ground to take exception with this view. They all contended that in their experience the intelligent Negro student was a great rarity. When asked to explain why this should be so, the invariable answer was: *É uma caracteristica da raça negra* (It is a characteristic of the Negro race). . . . Once when a small group of men was asked what Negroes were like, one of them, the mayor's son, shook his head and replied: "Everyone knows what a disgraceful creature the Negro is! But there's something I don't understand and want you to tell me. How did this curse ever come into the world in the first place when Adam and Eve were both white?" (ibid.: 51–52). Some specific features of the Negro stereotype are . . . : 1) The Negro race is subhuman and inferior to the white race, 2) The Negro does and ought to play a subservient role to the white, 3) The Negro's physical features, including physique, physiognomy, skin color and body odor are utterly displeasing. (Ibid.: 56)

During my lecture I continue on in this manner citing example after example of the racial imaginings and disparities documented in this book. I then note, to the students' surprise, that Wagley concluded that "Brazilians have an important tradition to cherish in their patterns of inter-racial relations. . . . It almost might be said that 'race relations' do not exist in Brazilian society. This nation of people born of marriages between three racial stocks, and formed out of slaves and their masters, has developed a society in which in the relationships between people 'race' is subordinate to human and social values" (ibid.: 8, 14). Thus the editor of this volume reasserts the trope of the Brazilian racial democracy despite—at least in the eyes of contemporary North Americans—his and the other contributors' findings.

Students are perplexed by Wagley's conclusion, given the empirical realities described. I used to ask them to remember Wagley's own historical background—he came from a North American context of an-tiblack terrorism and state-enforced segregation in which even the minutia of daily life were racially codified and policed. I would then cite a few Jim Crow laws to underscore this point.

> *Pool and Billiard Rooms*—It shall be unlawful for a Negro and white person to play together or in company with each other at any game of pool or billiards. (Alabama)

> *The Blind*—The board of trustees shall . . . maintain a separate build-ing . . . on separate ground for the admission, care, instruction and support of all blind persons of the colored or black race. (Louisiana)

> *Circus Tickets*—All circuses, shows, and tent exhibitions, to which the attendance of . . . more than one race is invited or expected to at-tend shall provide for the convenience of its patrons not less than two ticket offices with individual sellers, and not less than two entrances to the said performance, with individual ticket takers and receivers, and in the case of outside or tent performances, the said ticket offices shall not be less than twenty-five feet (25) apart. (Louisiana)

> *Wine and Beer*—Any person licensed to conduct the business of sell-ing beer or wine . . . shall serve either white people exclusively or col-ored people exclusively and shall not serve to the two races within the same room at any time. (Georgia)

> *Textbooks*—Books shall not be interchangeable between white and colored schools, but shall be continued to be used by the race first using them. (North Carolina)

> *Intermarriage*—All marriages of white persons with Negroes, Mulat-tos, Mongolians, or Malays hereafter contracted in the state of Wyoming are and shall be illegal and void. (Wyoming)

With this as the referent, I explained, one can imagine how Wagley may have seen a racial democracy in Brazil—a nation in which racial segregation was not legally codified (or at least not nearly to the same degree), where "race mixing" was the espoused official solution to the "Negro question," and where working-class and middle-class whites did not form a bloc of antiblack terrorism. Thus, against the backdrop of "a caste like society with rigid barriers between the racial groups," it was understandable that Wagley judged Brazil to be a nation with a "proud . . . tradition of racial equality" (1952: 7, 8).

Post–Jim Crow Blind Spots

Over the years I have become less satisfied with this explanation for the simple reason that I continue to encounter the writings of white U.S. scholars who—much like Wagley—either state or imply that racism is of minimal significance in Brazil. That is, a number of researchers in the post–Jim Crow era still theorize about Brazilian society as if it were a racial democracy. For example, in her award-winning book *Death without Weeping,* Nancy Scheper-Hughes (1992) studied "patterns of nurturing" in the context of extreme economic deprivation in north-eastern Brazil. Her basic argument is that in the "shantytown" where she conducted research, poor women and men with very young children frequently had to decide whether or not the children were likely to survive. Subsequently, she asserts, they chose to expend attention, affection, and precious resources (such as food, water, and medicine) on those children they deemed "thrivers." "The survivors and keepers were nurtured," she writes, "while the stigmatized or 'doomed' infants were allowed to die . . . 'of neglect'" (ibid.: 342).

However, in her analysis Scheper-Hughes does not address the premium placed on "whiteness" in Brazil although countless researchers have found that this has a dramatic effect on who is considered "attractive," "intelligent," "valued," and the like (Andrews 1991; Burdick 1998b; Degler 1971; Hanchard 1994; Nascimento 1989; Patai 1988; Simpson 1993; Skidmore 1993; Twine 1998; Wagley 1952). For instance, Figueira (1990: 64) discovered in interviews with 204 Afro-Brazilians in Rio de Janeiro that "positive qualities are liberally attributed to whites a high percentage of the time (75% of the cases). And the negative qualities are liberally attributed to blacks also a high percentage of the time. The tendencies indicate that there exists a general opinion (amongst both whites and Afro-Brazilians) of the 'inferiority' of blacks and the 'superiority' of whites." For a majority of the Afro-Brazilian interviewees, whiteness signified "friend," "studious," "intelligence," "beauty," and "wealth," whereas blacks were associated with "jack-ass," "pig," and "thief" (ibid.: 64).

The negative connotations of "blackness" are so ubiquitous in Brazil that "more African looking" Brazilians are noted for whitening their racial position when possible[1] as well as seeking "whiter" partners in order to produce "more beautiful children" (Twine 1998: 91).

Stories about parents giving preferential treatment to lighter-skinned children are not hard to find. Take, for instance, the story of a working-class woman in the Baixada who gave birth to twin girls, one of whom was much darker and nappier-haired than the other. When the daughters were older, according to a neighbor, the mother assigned household chores to the darker-skinned one, while making sure the lighter one had ample time for schoolwork. "Only the *pretinha* (black girl) is like a servant in the house," a neighbor explained. "She's the one who does everything: cleans the house, washes the clothes, makes the food; while *branquinha* (the white girl) gets to study, read the newspapers, magazines." Another family's story was more dramatic. A mother of two daughters, one with nappier hair than the other, constantly fussed over the beauty of the softer-haired one. "You should see what she does," reported a neighbor, "the one with the nice hair is always nicely dressed, her clothes are always cleaned and ironed, and she always gets her way. The older one— ha!—she would go about with her hair uncombed, because her mother would not comb it. . . . And the older girl was never dressed as well, or in clean clothes, or ironed. Then came the incident. "One day, that woman took an electric razor and shaved off every hair on the nappy-haired girl's head," recounted the neighbor, sighing deeply. "When we objected, she just said: 'That hair was wrong, it had to go.' Just one day, the girl comes home, and unsuspecting, gets her hair shaven: she was bald!" The woman telling me the story looked at me sadly. "So this girl comes next door, crying, crying, crying until all she could do was sob." (Burdick 1998b: 43–44)

Given the meaning attributed to certain physical characteristics in Brazil, it is puzzling that Scheper-Hughes failed to examine how these racist attitudes may have impacted parents' perceptions of whether a baby was "already wanting to die" and thus "given-up-on." This is especially perplexing since she had no alternative or competing explanations. "And so after all is said and done," she concedes, "I still do not know exactly what prompts a mother or father to conclude that a baby is a victim of child sickness or child attack and is therefore under a death sentence" (Scheper-Hughes 1992: 393). In avoiding a discussion of racism in this context, Scheper-Hughes took what might have been an excellent opportunity to illuminate "this traditional practice of letting go" and turned it into yet one more affirmation of the putative insignificance of race.

Kottak's book *Prime-Time Society* (1990) provides another example of how white non-Brazilian scholars continue not only to avoid the issue of racism to the detriment of their analyses but also expend effort in reinterpreting facts that could potentially be upsetting to the hegemonic belief in the racial democracy. In his analysis of the "cultural effects" of U.S. and Brazilian TV, Kottak devotes only a few pages to the subject of race. This alone gives the reader the erroneous impression that the racial effect of Brazilian TV on "human social behavior" is of minor or secondary consequence. Moreover, in the small number of paragraphs in which Kottak addresses race, he observes, "Although Brazil is sometimes called a racial democracy, blacks, who are just as obvious in the Brazilian as in the American population, are much rarer on Brazilian than American TV. . . . Traditionally, blacks, when present on Brazilian television at all, played the same kinds of menial roles they played in real life. (This was also true of American blacks' movie and television roles through the 1950s.) Dark-skinned Brazilian actors mostly still play cooks, maids, drivers, and thugs" (ibid.: 61–62).

Though one of his stated objectives is to outline the cultural impact of TV on Brazilian society, he fails to do this with regard to race. The absence of a discussion or analysis of the significance of a predominantly white TV land encourages the idea that this racialization has little if no affect on Brazilian culture. More remarkably, one is actively discouraged from interpreting the predominance of white images as an indicator of white supremacy. Although the passage quoted above implies that the "racial democracy" may be erroneous or is at least suspect, the reader is directed away from such an interpretation. For example, the statement that "blacks are just as obvious in the Brazilian as in the American population" is curious because it suggests that persons of noticeable African descent form a much smaller percentage of the Brazilian population than they actually do. Conservative estimates would put the number of persons of visible African descent—phenotypes which do not appear on Brazilian TV—at around 50 percent of the population, in contrast to 13 percent of the U.S. population. Thus, by *not* juxtaposing the paucity of "dark-skinned characters" against the predominance of "dark-skinned" people in Brazilian society, Kottak's statement has the effect of diminishing the antiracist impact that a description of an all-white television land could have had.

However unwittingly, Kottak does not stop here in his efforts to downplay the racist implications of a white TV land. Almost immediately after raising the issue, he writes, "the poverty that affects a disproportionate number of dark-skinned Brazilians means that there are relatively fewer trained black actors there than in the United States" (Kottak 1990: 62). This statement invites a class-reductive analysis. That is, the reader is encouraged to believe that the paucity of dark-skinned characters has to do with poverty and not with racism. This nonracial account of the racialization of television is particularly problematic given the strong predisposition in Brazil toward denying racism by explaining racial disparities exclusively in terms of class discrimination (Twine 1997a, 1998; Winant 1994). For example, Turner (1991: 73) observed amongst Brazilian university students, "When acts of social discrimination were admitted, the explanation supported by the students was [that] the occurrences were based upon class perceptions rather than upon racial identification."

In what amounts to his final attempt to minimize the degree of racism in Brazil, Kottak views the lack of "dark-skinned characters" as a result of the absence of a distinct and coherent "black" social identity from which a push for collective betterment could emerge. While I would not disagree with this argument, I find it noteworthy that Kottak is able to make this claim but somehow strip it of its capacity for antiracist critique. There is no coherent "black community," he argues, because racial categories are more fluid than in the United States. Although certainly true, he does not mention that one of the principal reasons for this "fluidity" has to do with the racist practices of "whitening," by which "dark-skinned Brazilians" actively attempt to distance themselves symbolically, culturally, socially, and biologically from "blackness." And, even more surprising, nowhere in his analysis does he intimate that the producers, directors, persons controlling casting, and the like—no doubt most of whom are white—may be racist and thus likely to play a pivotal role in ensuring that Brazilian TV remains an all-white domain. Instead, he attributes the absence of nonwhites on television solely to the inability of racial subalterns to mobilize—a failure ascribed *not* to racism but rather to a fluid categorical system.

It should be evident, then, that the explanation I offer my students for the conclusions reached by Charles Wagley and other ethnographers in the 1950s cannot account for the fact that a number of contemporary U.S. scholars continue to presume that white supremacy is not that significant or serious an issue in Brazil. We have seen how, even in the post–Jim Crow era, a number of white researchers either avoid the issue of racism altogether and thus effectively communicate that it is a nonissue or seem to bend over backward to reinterpret and reframe evidence that could disrupt the racial democracy imagining. Clearly one cannot blame these oversights and defensive maneuverings on an apartheid point of reference. How can we explain why so many white researchers from Europe and North America (to the detriment of their scholarship as well as the cause of racial justice) have so uncritically accepted and reproduced the notion that Brazil has a minor if any "race problem," despite overwhelming evidence that race is a key axis of power significantly affecting social formation in Brazil?

White Convictions

On December 19, 1997, the theme of the Derek McGinty radio talk show was "Race Issues in Brazil." In the introduction to the program Carlos Lins da Silva (the senior correspondent of the Brazilian newspaper *Folha*) and France Winddance Twine outlined several aspects of Brazilian racial inequality. For example, although nonwhites constitute a majority of the population, they make up a very small percentage of the university student population. There are only a handful of "dark-skinned" government officials, and corporate boardrooms are all-white domains (see Burdick 1998b: 1). Also mentioned was the racial hierarchy of desirability discussed earlier and the fact that employers frequently refuse to hire nonwhites for nonmanual jobs (see Andrews 1991). In response to this elementary sketch of Brazilian racism, a number of U.S. whites phoned in to express their frustration with the "tenor" of the conversation. Kyle—a native of Maryland who had lived for several years in a small town in the state of São Paulo—was representative of the U.S. white callers.

[Brazilians] are wonderful. That's why I moved to Brazil. I've never seen anyone discriminate in any way . . . not even any innuendoes. It's all gradations of color. I think what got me upset with the tenor of this program . . . the professor is basically right on all of her points, but we're laying an American overlay on a Brazilian situation. It's not South Africa of years ago. Just two quick examples. I've listened to your program many times and you'll talk about racial issues and somebody will say, "I'm a white guy walking down the street and I'll see a black guy and I'll feel bad or I'll feel intimidated." I walk down the street in São Paulo—the third largest city in the world—I see dark-skinned people coming. . . . I don't give it a thought. And another thing, I have a professor friend down there (. . .)—his specialty is popular culture—I shocked the devil out of him a couple of years ago . . . he didn't realize this, in the U.S. some whites can get beat up or killed even just for the color of their skin. He'd never heard of such a thing. I think what the tenor of this program could do is kind of perpetuate divisive racial issues which could be very destructive in Brazil—it's kind of like an ethnoimperialism if you will.

Interestingly, Kyle did not take issue with the content of the discussion—"the professor is basically right on all her points." Nonetheless he was "upset" by the interpretation that Brazil was a deeply racist society. Hence his comment, "It's not South Africa of years ago" (South Africa had not been previously mentioned). His barometer of the racial climate seemed to be based not on whether power was racialized nor the degree of antiblack racism, but rather on his comfort level as a white person with "dark-skinned" people. And since as a white person, he did not feel threatened, intimidated, or bad when passing nonwhites on the street (which he apparently did in the United States), it seemed difficult for him to think of Brazil as anything but a racial democracy—even when presented with some very convincing evidence to the contrary.

I suspect that Kyle's sentiments are representative of many U.S. whites because I have encountered similar reactions by several of my students and colleagues. Whenever I teach a course on race in Brazil, to take one example, students readily understand that the absence of nonwhites from political and economic power and the pervasiveness of derogatory stereotypes of people of African descent are signs of racism. But invariably a few white students, who have spent time in Brazil, become notably distressed by the portrayal of Brazil as a nation in which racism is a significant problem. It is noteworthy that like Kyle above, they *never* dispute the structural and symbolic racism detailed in class but nonetheless consider absurd the implication that Brazil is a white supremacist nation. The reasons for their convictions are usually very thin. The sorts of remarks they make are, "Yeah, but it doesn't feel that racist in Brazil." Unable to make a more substantive argument to support their position, they often become defensive, resistant, and sometimes openly antagonistic. Clearly, something about their personal experience in Brazil makes them very reluctant to accept what the other students regard as an obvious conclusion about the state of Brazilian race relations.

I have often run into a similar attitude with some of my North American colleagues. In 1995 I was conducting research in Brazil with the support of a Fulbright fellowship. In March that year all the fellows met in the capital city, Brasilia. During this several-day-long retreat we were encouraged to discuss our research projects with one another. Since one facet of my research focused on racism and antiracism, many of my conversations revolved around these issues. Overall, I found my white peers—in contrast to the one U.S. black who attended the retreat—very resistant to thinking of Brazil in terms that did not fit into the racial democracy narrative. In response to my contention that racism was just as serious an issue in Brazil as it was in the United States, they made the following sorts of statements:

> It seems so much better here than in the States. I can go to Afro-Brazilian events here and feel like my race doesn't matter. I feel like they see me as an individual and not as a white. In the U.S. blacks would peg me as just another white person. (Twenty-nine-year-old white man)

> I love it here. The people are so sensual. I feel like I'm getting in touch with my sensuality. It's so open here. There isn't that hostility like in the U.S. where if you just look at a black person they immediately get an attitude. There isn't that racial tension here. It's so much better. (Twenty-five-year-old white woman)

Taken together with Kyle's comments and the reactions of my students, at first glance it may seem that these people are simply self-centered—given that they evaluate the degree of racism on the basis of their ease and satisfaction around nonwhites. Put less generously, this may simply be a case of whites feeling more secure because "blacks know their place." In fact, a popular Brazilian adage says, "there is no racism in Brazil because blacks know their place." However, although white comfort is certainly one of the reasons why North American whites tend to minimize or completely ignore the significance of race in Brazil, it is a comfort less rooted in blacks' "knowing their place" than in blacks' "taking their place." For example, blacks certainly "knew their place" in the Jim Crow South, given the level of white surveillance and violence. But I doubt my students and colleagues would have concluded that the southern United States was a nonracist space. Instead, as I will detail, the "ease" felt by U.S. whites in Brazil is grounded in a particular symbolic context in which whiteness is esteemed and desired.

In addition to white comfort, the other reason whites have too often overlooked the significance of race has to do with the fact that whites actually experience the racial democracy as genuine. They sincerely believe that "race doesn't matter." At the phenomenological level the racial democracy is "true" for many U.S. whites. It is viscerally "correct." Thus the verisimilitude of the racial democracy is such that it is extremely difficult for these individuals to think of Brazil as a white supremacist nation. And obviously, if the representation of Brazil as a racist nation rings hollow to their ears—as it does for many whites who have spent time in Brazil—then white scholars would fail to take racism seriously even when it is germane to their analyses and has such important political implications.

White Talk

In *White Women, Race Matters,* Ruth Frankenberg argues that "for many white people in the United States . . . 'color-blindness'—a mode of thinking about race organized around an effort to not 'see,' or at any rate not to acknowledge, race differences—continues to be the 'polite' language of race" (1993: 142). It is believed that "to notice 'color' is not a good thing" (ibid.: 145); "to be caught in the act of seeing race [is] to be caught being 'prejudiced.'" (ibid.: 145). Frankenberg's point, then, is that many white North Americans—and I would guess that this is much more typical of middle- and upper-class whites—are coached to think about race by not thinking about race.

In not discussing race, in working to not recognize it, many U.S. whites also, of course, tend to direct their attention away from racism. That is, in being race-evasive there is a concomitant pull toward being power-evasive with regard to race (Frankenberg 1993). For example, Jennifer Simpson observes that many "educated whites" actively attempt to ignore, forget, or deny racism through what she terms "selective hearing," "creative interpreting," and "complicitous forgetting." "I hear (White) people employ these rules in so many situations and with such ease that I realize the rules are not only unwritten, they are unrealized. 'Oh, I didn't mean it that way,' 'Don't take my words so seriously,' 'I don't think that's what he was saying,' are all ways of rewriting the story, writing racism out of the (remembered) story" (1996: 377). Thus, "white talk," as Simpson calls it, is based on learning *not* to acknowledge or perceive the links between phenotype and power; on pretending one has transcended the multiple ways one's ideas, values, expectations, emotions, and practices are shaped by race.

A further characteristic of white talk involves imagining oneself as raceless—as being race neutral. "Being raised white and middle class," Twine writes, "emerged as being linked to learning to privilege specific ideological positions, namely the tendency to self-identify first as an individual with no links to a specific racialized or ethnic community." For example, Mimi, "the daughter of a Chinese American father and a mother of Chinese and African descent from the West Indies" who was raised in a middle-class white northern Californian suburb, well described this aspect of the white idiom of race:

> [My family] is not racist. But they're very assimilated. They're not prejudiced, but in terms of their ideals, their standards, I think they've adopted white ideals and white standards. You know those sorts of people who are "race neutral.". . . They don't see [racial identity] as defining them at all. . . . They try to ignore differences, and when I say to people "I'm black," I'm saying, "I am different and I want you to notice and not act like it's not an issue." And not to

discriminate against me for it but to recognize and appreciate it. (Twine 1997b: 223)

Thus many nonblack North Americans attempt not only to be color-blind—that is, they "try to ignore [racial] differences"—but also to think of themselves as individuals without a racial position. White talk, then, entails a deracialized conception of self.[2]

Scholars of whiteness have also noted that there is an affective corollary to white talk that pivots around a "flight from feeling" (Frankenberg 1993). In an effort "to 'not see' race difference despite its continued salience in society and in [one's] own life," individuals often divide the "discursive terrain into areas of 'safe' and 'dangerous' differences, 'pleasant' and 'nasty' differences" (ibid.: 149). Within this idiom of race there is often "a selective attention to difference, allowing into conscious scrutiny—even conscious embrace—those differences that make the speaker feel good but continue to evade by means of partial description, euphemism, and self-contradiction those that make the speaker feel bad [such as] the naming of inequality, power imbalance, hatred or fear" (ibid.: 156–57).

Conflict avoidance is thus a component of white talk. Ironically, this can turn antiracist practices into markers of racism. If the assumption is that tension and conflict are "bad" (i.e., are affective signifiers of racism), then antiracist practices—which are likely to generate animosity, tension, negative feelings, and the like—will be misinterpreted as racist. As we shall see, this white idiom of race prevails in Brazil. As a consequence, when the 1992 rebellion in Los Angeles erupted—in response, at least in part, to the racist "justice" system in the United States—Brazilians with whom I spoke almost universally interpreted it as a sign that "racism was worse in the United States than in Brazil." It was evident that conflict was automatically taken to be an indicator of the degree of racism. Remarkably, none of those I encountered in Brazil stopped to consider that the absence of conflict and contestation could be a sign of even poorer racial conditions in that country.

Racist Sensibilities

In contrast to the dominant mode of thinking about race among white North Americans, the descendants of slaves in the United States tend to have a race-cognizant idiom of race. In general, U.S. blacks acknowledge the existence of racial inequality and white privilege (Essed 1991; Feagin and Sikes 1994; Carroll 1997). That is, they much more readily comprehend the difference that race makes in peoples' lives and are less inhibited about recognizing that white supremacy is a significant factor shaping contemporary U.S. society. Moreover, there is an emphasis on what Simpson (1996) calls "back talk"—on recognizing, analyzing, and contesting racism when and wherever it manifests itself.

"Blackness," then, entails a different language of race in the United States than does "whiteness." Black subjectivities are linked to a different discursive and material practice of race which Whitney, a woman of African descent who was raised by white adoptive parents, came to learn as she became black in her late teens. Through her relationship with her black boyfriend, she began to learn how to decode racist assumptions and everyday articulations of racism—something she was not equipped to do, given her rearing in a middle-class white cultural milieu:

> Raishan was talking to this [black] woman at the bank. And she goes, "Yea, when you make your millions." And this white woman, who also worked at the bank, overheard them. And she goes, "How is he going to make millions, he's not a rapper or an athlete." See, that's a racial statement because she doesn't think that blacks could—are capable of doing anything except for being a rapper or an athlete. But I wouldn't have caught on to that if I hadn't been more aware like I am now . . . in high school I would not have caught on to that. I'm more cued to that type of thing. I'm a different person now. (Twine 1997b: 236)

In addition to having a more advanced understanding of racism, researchers have also documented that "confrontation is a common strategy [employed by U.S. blacks] for dealing with the racist attitudes and actions of white Americans" (Feagin and Sikes 1994: 281). In Rebecca Carroll's interviews with black teenage girls, the failure to engage in "back talk" was frequently interpreted as a moral weakness. It was considered one's responsibility to confront and challenge racist occurrences when they surface. The following response by Lanika, a seventeen-year-old black girl from Alabama, to what she perceived as a racist comment, illustrates this point.

I work at a music store after school and on the weekends. I have this one male coworker who is white, and he goes to the same school that my sisters go to. The atmosphere in that store is real laid back, and me and my coworkers can talk to each other and joke around. One time when we were just about to close the store, I had a line of people at my register and so did this white coworker of mine. While we're working the register, he started talking to me about this white guy who had come to the store the other day and was acting black. He said to me, "Yeah, you know, this guy listened to black music, he talked black, and when I leaned in to give him his CD, he even *smelled* black!" Well, I'll tell you, all the people in both of our lines just sort of stared at him, and I was really offended and embarrassed. It was too late to drop it at that point, so I asked him, "What exactly do you mean he *smelled* black?" And he was like, "You know, that smell; black people have a certain smell." So me and a couple of my black coworkers—in front of the customers—just had to go off on him! He told us we were taking it the wrong way and I wondered what other way there was to take it. I was like, "Why don't you tell me about this smell? Maybe because I'm black, I can't smell it, so maybe you better describe it for me. Because shoot, I'd like to know about that smell." He got real apologetic after that.

The next day at work, he and I had a little conference with the manager. I told the guy that I wasn't trying to hold anything against him, because I don't like for there to be friction or static in a working environment but he was out of line. His defense was that he had black friends in school with whom he was always cracking these sorts of jokes and they never took offense. Clearly he was making an attempt to prove he wasn't racist, yet the way he went out of his way to tell me about his black friends and what they were like told me that he might not be racist but he sure is prejudiced. I tried to explain to him that he may well have black friends who are comfortable with him and the things he says, but that as a white person, his making a comment about black people having a certain smell in front of customers and coworkers was both inappropriate and stupid. He had only been working at the store for about a month and maybe he didn't know better. But if he had given it some thought, he probably wouldn't have said it to begin with. Language goes a long way; you have to be careful with it, especially when you're talking about race. (Carroll 1997: 29–30)

This was clearly not "white talk." Not only did Lanika publicly scold her colleague for his comment but she also took the issue to the manager. In fact, when juxtaposed with those socialized into the white idiom of race, Lanika had an incredibly sophisticated racial analysis demonstrating, among other things, an understanding of rhetorical strategies to mask one's complicity with racism and the significance of context for the meaning of terms and expressions.

What is unique and fascinating about Brazil when compared to the United States, is that the descendants of slaves—except for those who identify as Indian (see Warren in press)—often deploy an idiom of race similar to the one found among U.S. whites. U.S. blacks, for example, frequently link themselves to "black people" and their historical experience with slavery and race exploitation. For instance, Jo-Laine, a fourteen-year-old "light-skinned, black" girl from Brooklyn, clearly saw herself as connected to slaves and their descendents:

> Being part of black culture feels very good to me. I heard or read Maya Angelou say once, "I am the hopes and dreams of slaves." I love that, and that's how I feel, too. I feel so proud, and even though I know that no matter what I do or say, there will always be somebody who's going to try and put me down or make me feel like less of a person than they are, all I have to do is think about how far we've come. It was worse for my parents and my parents' parents, but if they could do it, then I know I can go out in the world, hold my head high, and make even more changes for my own children. (Carroll 1997: 37)

In contrast, ethnographers have documented that *pardos* (the census category for nonwhites who identify as "mixed-race") and black-identified Brazilians, usually emphasize their white ancestors and tend to characterize the past as either free of racial conflict or unknown when constructing their family lineage and community histories. For example, Scheper-Hughes (1992: 90) discovered that the residents of a shantytown in northeastern Brazil who were "the descendants of a slave and runaway slave-Indian (*caboclo*) population . . . [did] not think to link their current difficulties to a history of slavery and race exploitation." In a poor, urban community in Rio de Janeiro Sherriff found that "very few informants in fact, were able to recall hearing stories about the slavery era, although the grandparents and great grandparents of a number of the older people I knew had in fact been slaves" (cited in Twine 1998: 119). And in both rural and urban areas in southeastern Brazil most persons of color would simply tell me that they did not know if their ancestors had been slaves; nor if slavery had ever existed in the region in which they lived. Consuela, a nineteen-year-old self-identified *mulata* resident of a *favela* (a poor, predominantly nonwhite neighborhood) in Rio de Janeiro, was typical in this regard:

> *JW:* "Who were your ancestors?"
> *Consuela:* "I don't know."
> *JW:* "Do you know if you're the descendant of slaves?"
> *Consuela:* "I don't know. Nobody ever said anything. All that I know is what I learned in school. Everything that I know about blacks is because of school because that is the stuff of history, so we have to learn about that, about blacks and slaves."
> *JW:* "Do you know if you're a descendant of Africans or Indians?"
> Consuela: "No one here at home knows."
> *JW:* "Of Europeans?"
> *Consuela:* "It appears that the father of my mother was Italian. Her mother was black and Spanish—something like that, but they never told me much about the black side. But she always talked about her father being Italian and her grandmother being Spanish." (Warren in press)

Unlike Jo-Laine, Consuela was clearly not raised in a world in which the slave experience and her personal connection to slavery were discussed. In Brazil the descendants of slaves do not typically draw strength, pride, or a sense of community—as Jo-Laine did—from their ancestors' experiences with slavery. Instead they tend to view it as something to be forgotten, minimized, or denied. The effect is that historical articulations of racism—such as slavery, colonization, and apartheid-like practices—disappear. Not only does racism—not to mention nonwhites—often get erased from family, community and national genealogies, but the same holds true for the contemporary moment as well. In the words of Rebecca Reichmann, "Racial discrimination is endemic in Brazilian society. Yet mystification and denial of racial differences are widespread" (1995: 35). As with white talk, white supremacy and white privilege are "disallowed or submerged discourses" for both whites and nonwhites in Brazil (Scheper-Hughes 1992: 90). Underscoring this point, Twine writes,

> There are few subjects, if any, in Vasalia [a small town in southeastern Brazil] that are more difficult to discuss in private or public than racism. During my field research I never witnessed anyone initiate or engage in public discussions of racial inequality. When I attempted to raise this issue I was immediately silenced by residents who accused me of being a racist for simply calling attention to what I perceived to be racial disparities in employment, education, housing, and political representation" (1998: 139).

Besides denying or minimizing racial discrimination, researchers have found that the descendants of slaves frequently employ a number of "defensive discourses . . . to avoid recognizing white supremacy" (ibid.: 86). For example, in interviews with eighty-three poor Brazilians in Rio de Janeiro, most nonwhites (except for "lifelong blacks" who represent less than 2 percent of the Brazilian population) reported that they

> had never *personally* witnessed color prejudice or discrimination . . . ; among those who [said that they had], the offense had been witnessed *somewhere else,* not "here," and the examples given usually had to do with a dismissive attitude on the part of a wealthy white toward a poor black. Then informants would move on to insist that what such examples really illustrated was "social," not "racial" prejudice and that, after all, among the poor themselves there was neither. (Burdick 1998a: 142)

Among working-class Afro-Brazilians in Vasalia, Twine encountered the same tendencies to reduce racism to "social" or "class" discrimination and to contain racism spatially by locating it outside of the local community. Nonwhites were so resistant to the suggestion that their town was racist that a number of them preferred to invoke essentialist ideas about black inferiority. For instance, note the response of Jorge, a twenty-two-year-old Afro-Brazilian, to the question: "How would you explain the fact that all of the bank employees [in Vasalia] are white?"

> I think that it must be because of this. Blacks haven't been able to obtain those jobs because they lack intelligence/knowledge. Their I.Q. is

not high enough to get the job. It must be because of their I.Q. because they have the opportunity, because the exams are open to everyone. In the state of Rio, it's an open exam. If a black person passes the exam, he is hired. Blacks are not prevented from taking the bank exam. (Twine 1998: 77–78)

Interestingly, even on those few occasions when racism was acknowledged to be at work, blacks and *pardos* in Vasalia rarely if ever discussed them with their family or friends:

The Afro-Brazilians I interviewed all reported that they had *never* discussed their experiences of racism with their family members or friends. I lived with a working-class Afro-Brazilian family for ten months. During the entire time of my field research I never heard them mention racism or engage in serious discussions of racial inequality. . . . *None* reported having ever discussed racism with any of their family members or friends. What is surprising is that even in their homes . . . they still do not engage in discussions that could assist their family members and themselves in collectively coping with racism. (Ibid.: 139. Emphasis in original)

In addition to discussing, sharing, and analyzing instances of racism only infrequently, the descendants of slaves prefer to answer racism with silence (Hanchard 1994: 63; Sherriff 1997; Burdick 1998a: 142; Twine 1998). That is, Brazilian blacks and *pardos* tend to respond to perceived racism via withdrawal or by changing their behavior—rarely by challenging racism or by suggesting that the behavior of the individual who was racist should change. Keep in mind Lanika's willingness to immediately confront what she perceived as a racist statement when reading Hemerson's (a twenty-five-year-old black man from Belo Horizonte) reaction to a clear racial slight.

Hemerson: "One time I was working as a representative selling books. I arrived at a house of a person and I offered him a book. Instead of politely taking the book he asked what I was wanting. He said to me, 'Get out of my door nigger. I don't like niggers.' I left without saying anything and feeling sad."
JW: "Why did you stay quiet? Why didn't you challenge him?"
Hemerson: "I prefer to stay quiet. We [blacks] avoid discussion . . . it

is much better. Because if he offends you and you feel offended, you are going to speak with him and he is just going to offend you even more. So it is preferable to just remain quiet. It is better to leave than to remain and listen to more. If you stay, you just get even more upset and then it could even become physically aggressive. You feel that pain in the heart, but that passes. But the moment it becomes physically aggressive, everything changes. And like always, 'A black never does anything reasonably, he has to do things in excess.'" (Warren in press)

There is, thus, a large degree of overlap in the racial idioms of white North Americans and nonwhite Brazilians.[3] Their language of race is typically color- and power-evasive. "Color" must be ignored. The issue of racism is to be avoided or reinterpreted when possible. Conflict and confrontation are to be shunned. In fact, by the logic of this paradigm it is "racist" to bring up race and to challenge racism. This is why antiracist scholars in Brazil are often positioned as "racists" if they raise the issue of racial inequality. By racializing power and naming white privilege—the hallmarks of race-cognizant thinking—the individual committed to a color-blind perspective is unsettled. Such discursive practices violate the etiquette of silence and can be interpreted as racist because one is asserting race when one *should,* if one is not a racist, be attempting to overlook it.

Imagine, then, how U.S. whites, with sensibilities heavily informed by "white talk," are likely to experience Brazil. During their interactions with nonwhites racism is never mentioned. They are told—as I have been assured on numerous occasions by Afro-Brazilians—that racism, if it exists, is a minor issue in Brazil. In fact, nonwhites go out of their way to avoid discussions of race—let alone white supremacy. Naturally U.S. whites are apt to feel more comfortable in this context, because they speak a similar language of race.

As we have learned, in the United States the descendants of slaves are more likely to engage in "back talk." Thus among U.S. blacks attention is more likely to be called to a white person's racial privilege. With a higher degree of racial literacy—given that race is dealt with and not ignored—more statements are apt to be interpreted as racist and overtly rebuffed. In this context, it is much more difficult to feel that "race doesn't matter," as if one were merely a "raceless" individual. One of the Fulbright fellows, recall, experienced this world as "more racist" because he felt he was "pegged as just another white person." Those versed in white talk are likely to be troubled by U.S. blacks pointing out that whites have racial privilege, that they are not "racially neutral," and that they have been affected by the racism that saturates society. Such people feel "deindividualized." Their self-understanding of themselves as "race neutral" is called into question, and their idiom and concomitant etiquette of race violated by facing up to these truths.

The point, then, is that U.S. whites are likely to experience Brazil's racial democracy as real. This narrative resonates for them because they can feel that race is irrelevant even in the presence of nonwhites. Their markers of racism, such as tension, are not present. Their experiences with U.S. blacks, in contrast, are much more disconcerting for them because they must contend with race-cognizant discourses in which they are racialized, racism is openly discussed, and even subtle articulations of white supremacy are challenged. This explains why whites recognize the United States as "racist" but not Brazil. At a visceral level, Brazil's racial democracy is experienced as accurate. Thus, even when presented with overwhelming evidence to the contrary, they are intuitively reluctant to describe Brazil as racist and are open to alternative explanations of social formation that do not lean on white supremacy as a critical variable.

The Emotional Dimensions of White Privilege

As we have learned, it is difficult for U.S. whites to view Brazil as racist because phenomenologically they experience it as nonracist. But this is only part of the reason why whites tend to minimize racism in Brazil. In this final section I will argue that in addition to the racial democracy "feeling real," there is *a desire* to "believe it real." That is, U.S. whites often become emotionally invested in sustaining the imagining of Brazil as a racially meritocratic society. This sentiment is akin to that outlined by Antonio Sérgio Alfredo Guimarães (1995: 208): "Any study of racism in Brazil must begin by reflecting on the very fact that racism is a taboo subject in Brazil. Brazilians imagine themselves inhabiting an anti-racist nation, a 'racial democracy.' This is one of the sources of their pride and, at the same time, conclusive proof of their status as a civilized nation." According to Guimarães, Brazilians are attached to the racial democracy narrative because it gives them ground to claim moral and social superiority as Brazilians. That is, it is one of the few arenas in which they believe they have surpassed Europe and the United States—their referent of "civilization." Given this belief and their satisfaction with it, they are reluctant to envision their nation as one riddled with racism.

For reasons to be discussed below, racism can become a taboo subject for U.S. whites as well. Like Brazilians they also often have an emotional stake in the racial democracy and are consequently defensive about portrayals of Brazil as a white supremacist nation. In the examples given earlier, we saw that though the facts of white supremacy were not disputed, there was nonetheless an unwillingness to label Brazil racist. Remember Kyle who "basically agreed with the points of the professor," but regarded a discussion of these points as "divisive." For reasons he did not provide, he considered it an instance of "ethnoimperialism."

Curiously, I have heard other foreign whites level this charge against scholars and activists who are working to further antiracism in Brazil. For example, in May 1995 I attended a race symposium in Rio de Janeiro. During one of the sessions a white Englishman, then a professor of sociology at the Universidade Federal do Rio Janeiro and chief coordinator for a Rockefeller-funded Program for the Study of Race and Ethnicity in Brazil, attacked the other scholars and activists on the panel for speaking about the need to encourage Afro-Brazilians to identify with their "Africanness" (instead of privileging their "Europeanness") in order to destigmatize the meaning of "blackness" in Brazil. He accused them of trying to impose U.S. black thinking on Brazil, and of not appreciating the positive aspects of race relations in Brazil. He argued that it was illogical to self-identify as black if one was of minimal African descent (as if there were an objective way to racially identify people), and he implied that the antiracist scholars and activists were imperialistic, bowing to the ideological pressures of black North Americans. He rhetorically asked the Brazilians in the audience whether they wanted to become like the United States where there is all that "hostility, animosity, and separation."

In the previous section I argued that part of the reluctance to conceptualize Brazilian society as laden with racism stemmed from particular sensibilities grounded in white talk. Nevertheless, if criticism of discussions of white supremacy—such as those expressed by Kyle, my

Fulbright fellows, and the white Englishman—were motivated exclusively by the fact that such a portrayal of Brazilian society did not resonate with their phenomenological impressions, then their defensiveness to counterinterpretations would probably not be quite so constant and unwavering. That is, one would expect more ease in discussing racism, more urgency in addressing the issue, and more serious consideration of particular antiracist strategies. Thus there appears to be more at work here than merely a violation of one's sensibilities vis-à-vis race.

A hint as to what this may be is provided by the purported concern with "divisiveness" and "hostility." Although white terrorist organizations are not nearly as pervasive in Brazil as in the United States, Brazil is very hostile to persons whose phenotype signifies Africanness. As has been well documented, blacks face an onslaught of symbolic violence that has significant material consequences: police brutality, economic and political disenfranchisement, second-class service in stores, banks, hotels, restaurants, and the like. It would appear, then, that the concern of whites must rest, at least in part, with the place—or more accurately the potential displacement—of whiteness in Brazilian society. In short, it has to do with white comfort and its potential erosion.

When compared to the United States, white privilege in Brazil—especially in nonwhite spaces—is much greater. Whiteness holds much more currency generally but in particular with blacks and *pardos,* as compared with U.S. blacks. We have already seen that most nonwhites in Brazil view whites as aesthetically more desirable than themselves. Consequently, as Tatiana (a fifty-one-year-old Afro-Brazilian *dona da casa* (homemaker) married to a dark-skinned black man) argues below, this is why Afro-Brazilians express a strong preference for lighter-skinned or white Brazilians as their spouses.

It is to have *more beautiful* children, more beautiful grandchildren. The parents do this in order to have more beautiful children. To have [children with] hair that does not require much work to keep it neat, because straight hair is much easier, isn't it? There are many [black] people that prefer white spouses. My [black] father-in-law, the father of [my black husband] prefers white spouses. My [black] father-in-law, the father of [my black husband] prefers that his children marry whites. (Twine 1998: 91. Emphasis in the original)

In contrast, most U.S. blacks—such as the seventeen-year-old black girl cited here—prefer to date other blacks:

> I can't see dating a white guy. My boyfriend now, he goes to public high school. He's black. There are only six black guys at my school. I don't really know why I wouldn't think about dating a white guy. I guess for me personally, because I try to read and find out about my history as much as I can, it's pretty hard for me to get beyond the image of white slave masters raping their black women slaves. It's an image that really sticks out in my mind and has obviously had a scarring affect on me. (Carroll 1997: 31)

In addition to dating preferences, U.S. blacks typically do not valorize relationships with whites, and are frequently indifferent to whites or privilege blackness (see Ogbu 1995). In fact John Hartigan, Jr. (1997: 186), found that blacks in Detroit, Michigan, think of whites as a pollutant. In Brazil much the opposite tends to be the case. As we have seen, blacks and *pardos* often see and treat whites as desirable or special (see Warren 1997). A number of scholars have even documented an inordinate degree of deference toward white people. For example, Harry Hutchinson (1952: 34), a U.S. white who conducted research in a small town in Bahia, observed,

> The white is addressed by the formal *o senhor,* while he in return addresses all others by the popular *você*. The white may also receive the very informal and affectionate form of address *yoyó* (for a man) or *yayá* (for a lady), which was traditionally used by slaves for their masters. Interestingly enough, it is usually the darkest of the *pretos* (even the most independent of them) who generally use this form of greeting. *Vossa Excelência* (Your Excellency) is also heard frequently when people of low status of an older generation address an "aristocratic" white.

While conducting fieldwork in Pernambuco, Scheper-Hughes noted that even as a very young woman she was referred to as *Dona,* a formal title of respect usually reserved for middle-aged and elderly women. I had a similar experience in southeastern Brazil in that older nonwhites would sometimes refer to me as "*o senhor*" which simultaneously conveys "mister" and "master." But no elderly whites, regardless of their class status, referred to me as "*o senhor.*"

Even if nonwhites do not call a white "master," there is no question that whites are held in high regard. Obviously, white privilege exists in the United States as well (McIntosh 1992), but in Brazil I experience it as much greater. In the more than two years I have spent in Brazil, I have frequently been told "how beautiful" I was. This was communicated to me with such reverence that it was clear that besides my whiteness it did not really matter how I looked. My skin and eye color (hazel) and the texture of my hair (straight) seemed to be the exclusive criteria used to evaluate my physical appearance.

Non-Brazilian whites I met in Brazil often told me stories which illustrated that they were experiencing their whiteness in a similar manner. One morning I had breakfast in Salvador, Bahia, with a white engineer from Seattle. In the United States he would not have been considered of even average appearance. Yet here he seemed to be in a wonderful dream that he could not believe was real. He told me countless stories of Brazilians telling him how *bonito* (beautiful) he was, and of attractive women approaching him and telling him that he was a *gatão* (a stud).

Another example of the increased level of white privilege was the general sense of empowerment I experienced. In the United States I usually perceive my phenotype as something that does not disqualify me—as something that helps to ensure that I will be treated as an individual. However, in Brazil I experienced whiteness as granting me immediate access. I recall feeling as if simply being white was enough to get almost any job I desired, regardless of my qualifications.

A story that a white colleague from Chicago once told me may help to illustrate this point. One afternoon he was learning to roller blade in a park in São Paulo. Suddenly a *mulata* approached him and asked if he would roller blade in a commercial they were filming that day for a soft drink or snack food. When he pointed out that he was merely a novice roller blader, she said that that was not a problem because he had the look they were seeking. Not surprisingly, all the other recruits for the commercial were white.[4] I bring this story up here because I think it doubtful that in the United States one would be placed in a commercial simply because one was white. Again, I do not want to suggest that white privilege is not relevant in the United States, but only to underscore how whiteness can be even more potent in Brazil.

In addition to white privilege being more accentuated in Brazil—in particular when nonwhite contexts are compared—it is simultaneously, as Twine (1998: 66) has noted, more "doxic." That is, white supremacy is much less remarkable and thus more invisible. As mentioned, nonwhites rarely discuss race and racism. In fact, they tend to employ race-evasive discourses; they prefer to frame social inequality in class terms and favor discourses and identities which minimize or deny the role of race and racism in contemporary Brazilian society (Sherriff 1997; Twine 1998).[5] Consequently, one's privilege as a white person is rarely, if ever, discussed or referred to, even in nonwhite social spaces. One's whiteness may never come up in discussion except to affirm how attractive one is. Therefore a white person, even in nonwhite circles, will likely experience race as either "not that significant" or as something positive.

An analogous situation is that of the European and North American sex tourists in developing countries like Thailand. Not only can these tourists get a lot more for their money, but they are also able to more easily convince themselves that they are not sex tourists. As Julia O'-Connell Davidson writes, "Certainly, the Mr. Average type does not wish to see himself as a punter. Pattaya is 'fantasy island' precisely because when a 22 year old woman approaches him and puts a slim arm around the rolls of fat bulging over the waistband of his trousers or strokes his balding head and tells him that he is a sexy man, he can convince himself that it's true" (1995: 51). Similarly in Brazil, not only are white researchers able to get a lot more for their whiteness, but they can also more easily delude themselves into believing that they are not white—that they are "just an individual."

Given the nature of whiteness in Brazil as compared to the United States, it is evident that Brazil is a racial paradise for whites, in that they enjoy an incredible degree of uncontested white privilege. In Kyle's words, "It's wonderful." Whites can more easily indulge in racial privilege without guilt because white privilege is naturalized and unmarked in nonwhite spaces. Hence the motivation to adopt official and popular discourses that affirm the absence of racism. The Brazilian racial terrain provides powerful incentives for "going native," for accepting and defending elements of the myth of racial democracy. The great sense of pleasure that many whites report experiencing in Brazil is contingent, at least in part, on the belief that there is no race problem. Thus it is not surprising that a number of whites resist imagining Brazil as racist by minimizing or disallowing the significance of race.

Conclusions

I have examined how racial sensibilities and affective experiences can shape the production of knowledge and power. More specifically, I have argued that because of white talk and white privilege, a number of foreign scholars, U.S. whites in particular, have tended to minimize the significance of racism to the detriment of their analyses. Given the ubiquitous nature of European colonization as well as its accompanying racialisms, it is likely that the imagined superiority of whiteness and the pervasiveness of color- and power-evasive discourses of race are not confined to Brazil alone. Consequently, many of the characteristics of the Brazilian racial terrain outlined above are likely to feature in the cultural landscapes of other national contexts as well. It follows that the methodological pitfalls to which white scholars versed in white talk often succumb in Brazil can also trip up researchers concerned with other regions of the world. It is thus my hope that this essay will help sensitize scholars to these perils so that they may improve their scholarship and avert complicity with white supremacy.

NOTES

1. The widespread occurrence of "whitening" in Brazil is indicated, among other things, by the way a number of nongovernmental agencies chose to expend their energies and resources in the year prior to the 1991 census. With funding from the Ford Foundation, these NGOs launched a campaign under the slogan "Não deixa a sua côr passar em branco. Reponda com bom censo." ("Don't let your color pass into white. Respond with good sense.") The fact that these organizations chose to mobilize around the issue of whitening and spend precious resources countering it, testifies to its prevalence as a practice.

2. A noted consequence of this deracialized conceptualization of self is that race and racial justice usually come to be regarded as matters of concern only for individuals who "have a race"—putatively unlike themselves.

3. The one important exception to this is Indianidentified Brazilians (see Warren in press).

4. This was not surprising because the vast majority of images on TV in Brazil are white (Kottak 1990; Simpson 1993).

5.

Racism is a disallowed and submerged discourse in Northeastern Brazil, so that every bit as much as Wolf's (1982) European peasants, these are a people "without a history." They call themselves simply *os pobres* [the poor] and they describe themselves as *moreno* (brown), almost never as *preto* or *negro* (black). They are "brown," then, as *all* Brazilians, rich and poor, are said to be "brown." In this way, the ideology of "racial democracy," as pernicious as the American ideology of "equality of opportunity," goes unchallenged, uncontested, into another generation. (Scheper-Hughes 1992: 90. Emphasis in the original)

REFERENCES

Andrews, George Reid. 1991. *Blacks and Whites in São Paulo, 1888–1988*. Madison: University of Wisconsin Press.

Burdick, John. 1998a. "The Lost Constituency of Brazil's Black Movements." *Latin American Perspectives* 25 (1): 136–55.

————. 1998b. *Blessed Anastácia: Women, Race, and Popular Christianity in Brazil*. New York: Routledge.

Carroll, Rebecca. 1997. *Sugar in the Raw: Voices of Young Black Girls in America*. New York: Crown Trade Paperbacks.

Degler, Carl. 1971. *Neither Black nor White: Slavery and Race Relations in Brazil and the United States*. New York: Macmillan.

Essed, Philomena. 1991. *Understanding Everyday Racism: An Interdisciplinary Theory*. Sage Series on Race and Ethnic Relations, vol. 2. Newbury Park, Calif.: Sage.

Feagin, Joe R., and Melvin P. Sikes. 1994. *Living with Racism: The Black Middle-Class Experience*. Boston: Beacon Press.

Figueira, Vera Moreira. 1990. "O Preconceito Racial na Escola." *Estudos Afro Asiáticos* 18: 63–72.

Frankenberg, Ruth. 1993. *White Women, Race Matters: The Social Construction of Whiteness*. Minneapolis: University of Minnesota Press.

Guimarães, Antonio Sérgio Alfredo. 1995. "Racism and Anti-Racism in Brazil: A Postmodern Perspective." In *Racism and Anti-Racism in World Perspective*, edited by Benjamin Bowser, pp. 108–226. Newbury Park, Calif.: Sage.

Hanchard, Michael. 1994. *Orpheus and Power: The Movimento Negro of Rio de Janeiro and São Paulo, 1945–1988*. Princeton: Princeton University Press.

Harris, Marvin. 1952. "Race Relations in Minas Velhas: A Community in the Mountain Region of Central Brazil." In *Race and Class in Rural Brazil*, edited by Charles Wagley, pp. 47–81. Paris: UNESCO.

Hartigan, John, Jr. 1997. "Locating White Detroit." In *Displacing Whiteness: Essays in Social and Cultural Criticism*, edited by Ruth Frankenberg. Durham: Duke University Press.

Hutchinson, Harry W. 1952. "Race Relations in a Rural Community of the Bahian Recôncavo." In *Race and Class in Rural Brazil,* edited by Charles Wagley, pp. 16–46. Paris: UNESCO.

Kottak, Conrad Phillip. 1990. *Prime-Time Society: An Anthropological Analysis of Television and Culture.* Belmont, Calif.: Wadsworth.

McGinty, Derek. 1997. "Race Issues in Brazil." In *The Derek McGinty Show.* December 19, American Public Radio: Washington, D.C.

McIntosh, Peggy. 1992. "White Privilege and Male Privilege: A Personal Account of Coming to See Correspondences through Work in Women's Studies." In *Race, Class, and Gender: An Anthology,* edited by Patricia Hill Collins. Belmont, Calif.: Wadsworth.

Nascimento, Abdias. 1989. *Brazil: Mixture or Massacre: Essays in the Genocide of a Black People.* Dover, Mass.: Majority Press. Originally published in 1979.

O'Connell Davidson, Julia. 1995. "British Sex Tourists in Thailand." In *(Hetero)sexual Politics,* edited by M. Maynard and J. Purvis. London: Taylor and Francis.

Ogbu, John. 1995. "Cultural Problems of Minority Education: Their Interpretations and Consequences—Part 2: Case Studies." *Urban Review* 27 (4): 271–97.

Patai, Daphne. 1988. *Brazilian Women Speak: Contemporary Life Stories.* New Brunswick: Rutgers University Press.

Reichman, Rebecca. 1995. "Brazil's Denial of Race." *NACLA Report on the Americas* 28 (6): 35–44.

Scheper-Hughes, Nancy. 1992. *Death without Weeping: The Violence of Everyday Life in Brazil.* Berkeley: University of California Press.

Sherriff, Robin. 1997. Untitled. Ph.D. diss., City University of New York.

Simpson, Amelia. 1993. *Xuxa: The Mega-Marketing of Gender, Race, and Modernity.* Philadelphia: Temple University Press.

Simpson, Jennifer S. 1996. "Easy Talk, White Talk, Back Talk: Some Reflections on the Meanings of Our Words." *Journal of Contemporary Ethnography* 25 (3): 372–89.

Skidmore, Thomas E. 1993. *Black into White: Race and Nationality in Brazilian Thought.* Durham: Duke University Press. Originally published in 1974.

Turner, J. Michael. 1991. "Brown into Black: Changing Racial Attitudes of Afro-Brazilian University Students." In *Race, Class, and Power in Brazil,* edited by Pierre-Michel Fontaine. Los Angeles: Center for Afro-American Studies, University of California.

Twine, France Winddance. 1997a. "Mapping the Terrain of Brazilian Racism." *Race and Class* 38 (3): 49–61.

———. 1997b. "Brown-Skinned White Girls: Class, Culture, and the Construction of White Identity in Suburban Communities." In *Displacing*

Whiteness: Essays in Social and Cultural Criticism, edited by Ruth Frankenberg. Durham: Duke University Press.

Twine, France Winddance. 1998. *Racism in a Racial Democracy: The Maintenance of White Supremacy in Brazil.* New Brunswick: Rutgers University Press.

Wagley, Charles. 1952. *Race and Class in Rural Brazil.* Paris: UNESCO.

Warren, Jonathan W. 1997. "Ó Fardo de Não Ser Negro: Uma Análise Comparativa do Desempenho Escolar de Alunos Afro-Brasileiros e Afro-Norte-Americanos." *Estudos Afro-Asiáticos* 31: 103–24.

———. In press. *Contesting White Supremacy: Indian Resurgence in Brazil.* Durham: Duke University Press.

Winant, Howard. 1994. *Racial Conditions: Politics, Theory, Comparisons.* Minneapolis: University of Minnesota Press.

Wolf, Eric. 1983. *Europe and the People without History.* Berkeley: University of California Press.

Chapter 7

Racism, Eroticism, and the Paradoxes of a U.S. Black Researcher in Brazil

Michael G. Hanchard

"I believe that Brazilian Coca-Cola is better than American Coca-Cola," a black Brazilian across the table from me in the state of São Paulo calmly told me on the night before the 1988 presidential election, as he brought his soda can down resolutely on the table. Aside from the can of Coca-Cola, we were linked by two mutual friends from the city of São Paulo. On this particular night my two friends, both black (and members of the Worker's Party) were trying to convince this man and his family to vote for Luis Inacio Lula da Silva instead of the right-wing candidate, Fernando Collor de Mello, who eventually garnered the presidency.

My friend Marcos, eyeing the interaction at the table, warned me with a raised eyebrow to keep cool. I sipped a few drops of my own Coca-Cola, allowed it to linger on my taste buds like a vintage wine, and declared, "You might be right. This does taste better than U.S. Coca-Cola. Why do you think this is so?" "Because Brazil has everything," the man, obviously satisfied with my response and warming up to the subject, stated. "All the ingredients that go into Coca-Cola Brasileira are better, fresher, and probably made with less chemicals than the ones in the United States." "More natural," I added. "Yes!" he stated triumphantly. Marcos, within earshot, looked at me and smiled.

This incident serves to illuminate several issues I would like to address in this essay, issues which emerged during my fieldwork in Rio de

Janeiro and São Paulo, Brazil. With the exception of a single white person, the wife of the man I mentioned above, everyone in the house considered themselves black. As a U.S. citizen, I was in a minority. Though each family member I spoke with considered themselves negro, none were political activists or college educated. They provided a living counterpoint to claims made by some Brazilianists that terms like *negro* and *raça negra* are largely part of the lexicon of college-educated activists involved in the black movement, and not the parlance of working-class Afro-Brazilians (Sansone 1996; Fry 1995–96).

Second, Brazil's *comunidade negra* or black community was, like most designated "black" communities, politically, economically, and normatively diverse. Terms such as "the black community" conceal as much as they reveal, for the internal complexity of such communities cannot be defined by phenotype. There is not one black community but several, a complex array of people and positions informed by the complexities of race, nation, class, gender, sexuality, and region. In turn, I had not one relation to this particular black community but several. As a U.S. African-American male, I occupied several positions simultaneously. Depending on the observer, I could be an interloper or intimate friend; an "American" first and a black second; a male researcher to be viewed with gendered suspicion, or a black male who could serve as a platonic friend; a political progressive or sometimes (though rarely) an automatic embodiment of U.S. imperialism; a black scholar with much to learn, but also with something to offer the black activist community in the form of "outside knowledge." My own identity as a U.S. citizen could be correlated with the best or worst the United States had to offer to the rest of the world, independently of my actual cultural origins, ideological affinities, or—in the case of soda—consumption patterns. During my three years of intermittent fieldwork in Brazil, I had to develop a way of responding to and defending myself against this correlation by emphasizing different aspects of my identity.

I would like to believe that no single characterization fully depicted who I was (or am), either. These depictions, as I came to discover, told as much about the gazes of black, brown, and white Brazilians as they did about me. Instead of the common—and often trite—reflections by field researchers on their increased self-knowledge due to sojourns in the field, I shall focus on facets of my experience in Brazil wherein I was an object of knowledge. As a black male researcher, my presence evoked a variety of reactions in activist and intellectual circles, family and familiar gatherings, as well as my neighborhoods of residence. My position as an erstwhile ally, object of suspicion, confidant, interlocutor, teacher, and student had as much to do with Brazilian race relations and Brazilian views of blackness in the United States and elsewhere, as it had to do with me as a solitary individual.

My blackness did not provide automatic entry into people's homes or conversations. At the same time, it provided me with what Raymond Williams has referred to as structures of feeling (Williams 1977), a basis of experiential knowledge that enabled me to grasp what was being offered as sources of information in the stories people would tell about themselves and the world they found themselves in. By comparing these stories with ones I was more familiar with, I was able to attempt to decipher my experiences with the *communidade negra*.

In order to provide an ethnoscape (Appadurai 1996) of my periods of fieldwork in Brazil, I will focus on the conditions under which I worked and conducted my daily life, which might be useful to subsequent generations of U.S. African-American scholars conducting research about African-descended peoples in the New World and beyond.

Rio de Janeiro, 1988

After a preliminary trip in 1985, I arrived in Rio de Janeiro for my first leg of fieldwork in September 1988. Having several Cariocan friends (residents of Rio) who lived in New York in the 1980s helped me tremendously in developing personal and professional contacts. Ironically, my first contact with a black activist and intellectual in Rio, Julio Cesar Tavares, was made via a former student of his who considered him brilliant, even though she disagreed completely with his vision of Brazil as a racist society. "We are not a racist society: we have race mixture," she would repeat to me during my first months in Brazil, often in the company of her friends (mostly white and middle class, *classe media*) and family (white).

After settling into an apartment in Flamengo, a neighborhood just north of downtown, I spent most of my weekdays doing research at the Center for Afro-Asiatic Studies at Candido Mendes University. Carlos Hasenbalg, then director of the Center, graciously allowed me to work there. Professionally cordial, personally distant, he had seen my type before, as I would soon discover. A foreigner himself (Argentine), Carlos had been director of the center for several years before my arrival. He and the staff hosted many U.S. citizens as well as other foreigners who came to Brazil as tourists, entrepreneurs, academics, and other prognosticators with solutions to racism, the national debt, capitalist underdevelopment, and the like. I painfully watched the staff elegantly endure impromptu lectures from a foreign (usually U.S.) visitor who, after a few days in Zona Sul,[1] the most elite section of Rio de Janeiro, discovered that racism did indeed exist in Brazilian society, and pointedly wanted to know what was being done about it. In a matter of only a few days, they had solutions to a problem that neither the Center members nor the average black and brown Brazilian appeared preoccupied with. Though I was certainly not one of those foreigners, I underestimated the degree to which my own movements and interactions would be informed and structured by the behaviors of some of my national predecessors.

During those fall months of 1988, I was largely ignored by the staff of Candido Mendes for reasons I could not at first fathom. There would be glances, hellos, and goodbyes, but infrequent invitations to lunch or social events outside the intellectual confines of my project. I could not help but juxtapose my sense of isolation against those meetings with foreign "experts" and wonder if the latter performances constituted the distance between myself and the staff of Afro-Asiaticos during the months of September, October, November, and December. In planning my return to Rio the following year, I decided to stay there for only a month, conduct as many interviews as possible, and spend my remaining time in São Paulo. My experiences seemed to confirm the common sense about Rio de Janeiro often stated by non-Cariocans in Brazil: "Cariocans will promise you the friendship, the world, but will never invite you to their home." São Paulo, by contrast, was always presented to me as a more serious city, with a people outwardly distant but internally passionate. "Paulistas are cold at first, less friendly than the Cariocas, but if they decide that you are their friend, they will take you into their home," friends from São Paulo as well as other parts of Brazil told me. My friends from São Paulo seemed the very embodiment of this observation, helping me to find an apartment, making contacts for interviews, and taking me to the best *feiras* (markets) in the city.

However, Carlos Hasenbalg greeted me enthusiastically upon my return to the Centro de Estudos Afro-Asiaticos. After the formal exchange of pleasantries, he inquired about my intended stay. "Probably a month, if you don't mind," I offered. "Only a month? Why? You can stay as long as you like. I can give you an office, phone to use. No problem." With that, my second research sojourn to Rio de Janeiro was immediately extended. I decided to stay for four months, and promptly moved into the designated "visiting scholar" office the following day.

Why the difference? I asked myself. A change of heart? A bad year for the Center? Perhaps the memory of whatever faux pas I had committed had faded from recollection? I soon found the answer to my questions in the comments of a boyfriend of one of the staff members. An officer in the navy, cheerful and intense, he invited me out for a leisurely lunch with his girlfriend. Over lunch, he explained the silence of the previous year. "You know Hanchard, you are an ok guy. I wasn't sure at first, but we like you. There aren't too many Americans coming through here that we like." "What do you mean?" I asked in between bites. His girlfriend continued, "You are a vegetarian, you are quiet, and you are Marxist." The first two were quite accurate. As for the third characterization I considered myself a Gramscian, but only a fool would quibble about a methodological and political detail at such a moment. Certainly there were other gringos who were vegetarians, but perhaps they had not met them. I had never been a boisterous type, but I considered this a personal idiosyncrasy rather than a measure of national identity. Perhaps only loud gringos visited Rio. "Vegetarian, Marxist, quiet, speaks Portuguese, he *has* to be different from the other Americans," she exclaimed in recounting a discussion about me with other staff members at the Center. Her boyfriend nodded in assent. Taken individually, each trait would be insignificant, but when strung together and considered against a backdrop of instant remedies, open-toed sandals with white socks, and the resolute monolingualism of many U.S. citizens who had passed through Rio and spent time on its beaches, streets, and professional and academic offices, the four characteristics became a cluster of clues from which the staff members had begun to piece together a type of person they could not have conceived inhabiting the colossus of the north.

She also told me that it was she who had suggested to Carlos that I be made a visiting scholar upon my arrival. Conversations with several other staff members over the next few months confirmed her story. The staff had decided I was worth the risk, and would not upset the *clima* (climate) of the Center. After this encounter, I entered homes, shared *feijoada* (a Brazilian black-bean stew), and became more than just a visiting scholar to several staff members of the Center. It had come down to this: my daily behavior, mostly unobtrusive, spared me further isolation and possible embarrassment. My acceptance was predicated on the fact that I was not a boorish carnivore from the United States. It made sense. Gringos, whether via the IMF, the U.S. government, or the occasional tourist were always telling them what to do.

This was a truism about U.S. citizens abroad, canonized in Pearl S. Buck's *The Ugly American*. But how could I be a gringo? I had always assumed that ugly Americans were white, from a certain class and regional background. I had no difficulty imagining their domestic personal arrogance extending abroad, masters of the universe that they are. After observing U.S. tourists of all hues drive the hardest bargains in Havana and Salvador, Bahia, I decided that I had to distinguish myself from those "other" gringos. In other words, I had to distinguish my content (Michael Hanchard, etc.) from my form (*negro norteamericano*, black American). To many Brazilians, race was secondary to nationality.

São Paulo, 1988 and 1989

After the months of silence in Rio de Janeiro in 1988, I was ready for the change of scenery that São Paulo provided. Julio Cesar Tavares provided me with three contacts in São Paulo who would ultimately become not only my best friends in Brazil, but in life; Francisco Marcos Dias, Luis Paulo Lima, and Deborah Silva Santos. Those three, along with Thereza Santos, Hamilton Cardoso, and the late Wanderlei Jose Maria constituted my nuclear family in São Paulo. Not only did they give me an intense, sometimes brutal political education, but their acceptance of both my project and person enabled me to gain legitimation. Such legitimation carried both short- and long-term costs. Marcos, in particular, constantly corrected my Portuguese and made me the butt of endless jokes about "Americanos" and large black men, not to mention my limited dancing skills (by Brazilian standards) during my first two months in São Paulo. This was considered excessive even by members of this São Paulo family, but I tried to understand it as a ritual exercise. If I was going to study them, Marcos and others seemed to say without saying, then they were going to study me, to ensure that I neither disappointed nor betrayed them, and to prepare me for sometimes hostile audiences among activist communities.

My stay in Rio had seasoned me for the oscillating emotions and attitudes I encountered during fieldwork: interviewees could be noncommunicative in one context and garrulous in another, some activists and their families embraced me while others kept me at arm's length, arms folded across their chests, convinced of my duplicity with and personal embodiment of U.S. imperialism, especially its imperialists acts directed at Brazil. Some interviewees and their friends were eager for any information I could offer about the United States, especially the black struggle. However, tensions between militants from competing political parties and/or black movement organizations surfaced during awkward moments at parties and marches when it was discovered that the only thing two opposing activists had in common was a *negro norteamericano* who had interviewed them both.

However, I was surprised when Francisco Marcos Dias, one of the founding members of the Worker's Party and several black cultural organizations in São Paulo in the 1970s, suggested that I might have better luck with some hard left activists if I identified myself as Jamaican, rather than *um Americano,* an American. "They are not going to want to hear about your politics or your research project. Once they hear you are American, *acabou* (finished), he declared.

Both my parents were born in Jamaica, so it would not be altogether untrue if I made "being Jamaican" my primary personal identification. Yet this posed another dilemma: it might change how some people related to me, but how would it change how I related to them? I never got around to saying this, but I was always tempted to ask the suspicious ones if I should judge Brazilians on the basis of a dictatorship and Fernando Collor de Mello, the first civilian to be elected president after military rule. The condemnation always felt too easy, but I also had to acknowledge the power it gave the potential interviewee—he or she could determine whether I was worth conversing with.

Being caught in a lie would only worsen matters, I thought, in a poor attempt to hide the obvious. What would happen if it was discovered that I was born and bred in the United States? Like any offspring of first-generation immigrants in the United States, the distance between my parents' country of birth and my own could not be measured in miles or kilometers. In the attempt to avoid one form of association with the United States, would I be adopting another, more individually condemnable, association with lying and betrayal? I could at least try to show people the importance of distinguishing my own positions from those of the Reagan or Bush administrations, and in doing so demonstrate that like many Brazilian citizens, U.S. citizens often do not get the political and economic policies they deserve. In the end, I decided to refer to myself as a U.S. African-American and hope that all my qualifiers (Jamaican-descended, opponent of Ronald Reagan and George Bush's foreign policy in virtually every part of the world) would suffice as credible, honorable credentials.

This maneuver had methodological implications. I could not affect the "scientific" neutrality so coveted by many practitioners of my discipline in the United States. For these activists and their families, life did not fit neatly into categories of nationalist, individual self-interest. Movement militants were actually behaving in a manner opposite their individual self-interest, putting their lives and careers at risk for purposes of community and collective action. Like most political activists operating under politically repressive circumstances, political dissent could lead to public sanctions or worse.

In such an ethicopolitical context, I considered it naive and dishonest to claim neutrality. To my mind, racial inequality did exist in Brazil, and I *wanted* these activists to be heard and to succeed in persuading both elites and masses that their cause was a just one. More pragmatically, given the questions I was asked ("If you were Brazilian, who would you vote for? What do *you* think about Jesse Jackson? Louis Farrakhan?") any claim of neutrality would have undermined my own research efforts. If I had no opinions, why should they? Just another extractive, exploitative gringo.

I offered much of this explanation to Marcos and other members of my São Paulo community. If it was discovered that I was indeed an *Americano*, I could be accused of misrepresenting myself for some sinister purpose. Each self-description had its hazards. At stake, in the eyes of my friends and myself, were the long-term consequences of a half-truth-telling *negro norteamericano* doing research on the *movimento negro* (black movement) in Brazil. This could damage the future research projects of other black scholars, not just myself. Marcos, Luis Paulo, and Denise could be tainted by their association with me.

After the ritual hazing I received from Marcos, he let me know that he was fully aware of the broader implications of my presence in São Paulo. "White scholars from the States here are plentiful, but you are rare," Marcos frequently reminded me. He promised to assist me only on the condition that I return to Brazil after the completion of my research, circulate my work among black militants in Rio de Janeiro and São Paulo, and continue a dialogue with them long after my dissertation and book were completed. This was both the easy and the difficult part.

Implications for Scholarship

Listening to various activists, both men and women, recount personal and witnessed experiences of black marginalization in Brazil, I was reminded of the similarities between black activist experiences at various points along on the African diaspora route throughout the postcolonial Caribbean and Africa, as well as Europe and other parts of the New World. I listened to black women activists recount stories of single parenthood, isolation, and resentment by men threatened by their intellect, stories quite similar to those told by black women in Britain, the United States, Jamaica, and elsewhere where the range of opportunities is never commensurate with the range of talent in a given community.

While I could both recognize and empathize with these experiences and stories, they were not mine, nor those of any other African-descended people other than the ones I spent considerable time with. As a budding scholar and ultimately as a trusted friend of many black activists, I was nonetheless an outsider. For these reasons, I was disabused of any illusion that I could be the "voice of the powerless." Whether activists found my work useful for their own political purposes was another matter about which I could not be certain. My relation to the *movimento* and its people was never stable but highly contingent, self-implicating, and subject to change and reversal. The fact that at some point I was *their* object of study necessarily made me more self-conscious and hopefully more responsible.

These moments forced me to reflect back on my experiences in graduate school before leaving to conduct fieldwork. More than once had well-meaning professors and fellow students told me in the hallways of the politics department at Princeton that my preoccupation with black social movements could lead to the disciplinary perception that I was intellectually narrow, or worse, that I was not a "true" political scientist because I was too close to, and too normatively embedded in, my objects of analysis to be properly objective. Such commentary always astounded me because of its inherently parochial, segregationist views of black politics. In order to study the black movement in Brazil, I had to learn another language, culture, and political system and in so doing learn about a part of the world that was not my own. What was narrow about that? What was even more astonishing is that such comments were often made by people whose subjects included the U.S. Congress—a single institution in one country—which was apparently so broad and wide ranging that no such charge of normative bias or parochialism could be leveled.

One of the implicit criteria imposed on scholars of subaltern groups in the United States and elsewhere is what I shall call the "distance/separation" quotient. The degree of distance or separation between black scholars and their objects of study has been one of the main criteria for ascertaining the intellectual and scholarly merit of research produced by black scholars. In other words, the scholar, and not the field or phenomena, becomes the object of study. If a black scholar is deemed to be too close to her or his object, the charges of biased, nonscientific research are sure to follow. The possibility of affinity between researcher and subject matter is not seen as a research opportunity, but as a deficit. Ironically, black scholars in most multiracial polities represent a miniscule portion of a minority population, and an even more miniscule portion of any scholarly community. That these people could be presumed to automatically have special insight or access to another community of people, especially those of another nationality and culture, is naive at best. Ted Gordon eloquently reminds us of this in his autobiographical ethnohistory of African-Nicaraguans, *Disparate Diasporas* (Gordon 1998). That there is no such distance/separation quotient for white political scientists of elite backgrounds who study the U.S. Congress, for example, attests to the enduring assumption of the universal, objective position of white scholars in the social sciences in general, and in political science in particular.

Such assumptions rest on a Cartesian scientism that is all the rage in contemporary political science , which Sheldon Wolin aptly characterized nearly thirty years ago as "methodism." To quote Wolin, "The first methodistic act of the Cartesian was to purge the self of the opinions acquired by upbringing, education and common experience. The contemporary methodist performs the same act of divestment, except that he will use the language of social science" (Wolin 1969: 1070). Such assumptions have dire intellectual and ethicopolitical consequences for the histories and politics of minority groups. Rather than use one's experiential knowledge as a basis for understanding other societies, peoples, and political systems, methodism argues that methodologies precede political phenomena.

Gathering research on an understudied topic such as racial discrimination in Brazil in the 1980s required "tacit political knowledge" (ibid. 1969), knowledge that has not been formalized into a system and is ambivalent and ambiguous, and has contradictory meanings. Such knowledge is historically constituted and embedded in daily life, not ready-made in the form of "indicators." The process of "data collection" and knowledge formation in such research was initially more inductive than deductive. How does one make sense of a topic that had been considered a nontopic by scholars and the public alike? Twentieth-century black activism in São Paulo and Rio de Janeiro provided avenues of investigation into patterns of discrimination and inequality that had not only gone unresearched, but required scholars who were willing to pursue counterintuitive positions. To be sure, I was not the first U.S. African-American scholar or African scholar to do so. I had been preceded by Angela Gilliam, Michael Mitchell, J. Michael Turner, the Haitian Pierre-Michel Fontaine, and the Ghanaian Anani Dzidzenyo, among others. With the exception of Fontaine, whom I have never met, each of these scholars had been accused, at some point in their careers, of a built-in bias in their scholarship due to a presumption of automatic affinity between researcher and research subject.

The repression of the study of racial inequality in Brazil has been framed not by the discourses of science, but by the ideology of racial democracy. National peculiarity and specificity have been used to counter claims of racial discrimination, prejudice, and race-related violence. The careers of many Afro-Brazilian academics—such as Eduardo Oliveira de Oliveira and Guerreiro Ramos—were marked by the disapproval of the academic establishment which declared, among other things, that they were so fond of discussing the "pathologies" of black Brazilians that they were blinded to their own. The relative ease with which I moved within activist and black communities more generally in Rio de Janeiro and São Paulo was in contrast to my friendly but distant encounters with many white Brazilian academics, who looked upon the black movement and students of it with suspicion. U.S. African-Americans like myself were (and are) often perceived as "importing" ideas about racial discrimination to Brazil that do not correspond to Brazilian reality. Even with mounting data by the 1980s of unequal access to education, housing, health care, and other quality of life indicators, Brazilian educators and intellectuals in the state and in civil society like to point out how they are different vis-à-vis the United States, refusing to acknowledge that Brazilian and U.S. racisms are but different branches of the same tree.

Gendering Race and Diaspora

The gendered implications of my fieldwork in Brazil were myriad, experienced personally but also vicariously through my wife, who once got into a shouting match with a white middle-class woman in a Zona Sul self-service laundromat. Assuming that my wife was a black Brazilian woman, she began to order her about the laundromat and demanded that she remove her clothing from the machine to enable her to wash her own clothes since she was, after all, a busy woman, and assumed that my wife (Nancy Tartt) was merely a maid with an entire day to wash her clothes. The woman attempted to change her behavior once she discovered that my wife did not speak Portuguese and was from the United States, but it was too late. A shouting match ensued, in English and in Portuguese, wherein body language spoke more poignantly than words. The woman, who spoke some English, understood that she was being called a racist, and replied that this was a U.S. problem and not a Brazilian one. To be sure, the same incident might have occurred had my wife been a maid of any color in Brazil, though probably without the same outcome. I doubt such an incident would have occurred had my wife been white.

More directly, I came to understand the sometimes hidden structures of gender dynamics upon my arrival in Rio de Janeiro in 1988. One summer evening in 1988, I attended a party at the home of a British anthropologist. We had met through a mutual friend at a Luis Melodia concert at Circo Voador in Lapa, a section of Rio de Janeiro. The invitation to the party was friendly and unambiguous though nonetheless odd, for she forbade me to invite the person who had introduced us.

The latter was a *mulatto* Brazilian from Copacabana whom I had met on a basketball court in Flamengo and with whom I attended the concert. She did allow me to bring some other friend along, which I did. This friend was Julio Cesar Tavares, a *movimento* activist, scholar of linguistics and anthropology at the Federal University in Niteroi. Knowing neither the pretext nor the person, I had no idea what to expect at the party other than perhaps beer, food, music, dancing, and laughter.

I never would have imagined what I encountered at the anthropologist's house in Santa Theresa. Upon arriving, I was struck by the peculiar assortment of fest-makers: academics, activists, a few foreigners like myself—an intelligentsia, but not an elite. The male-female balance was weighted decidedly on the male side, and the majority of the men were *preto* (black) or *moreninho* (brown skinned). I did not consider this odd in light of the fact that it was a woman's party; assuming she was heterosexual or at least intermittently attracted to men, such an imbalance would have made perfect sense for her and similarly aligned female friends. Virtually all the artwork on the walls—an assortment of postcards, paintings, and advertisements of romantic and sexual couplings of white women with black men—depicted black men with white women. When linked to the party thrower and the overwhelmingly dark, overwhelmingly male presence at the party and the sight of the hostess dancing with several of these men who whispered entreaties into her ear at one point or another in a never-ending samba, whispered entreaties into her ear, to which she responded with a giggle or a shake of the head before sauntering over to another ardent dancer—I had the distinct feeling of déjà vu, although I certainly had never been to this person's house before nor seen these people. Robert Mapplethorpe? Gaugin? Carl Van Vechten's *Nigger Heaven*? Maugerite Duras? Jorge Amado? These were some of the figures that swam in my head for days, even years after that party. The party hostess was easily inscribed in the existing cultural, racial, and gender dynamics in Brazil in a way that I would never be. Because of my own subject position, it was impossible for me to see her simply as someone just having a good time, as I am sure some readers will infer from the description above.

I watched the scene for several minutes, oblivious to all around me, until she called out to me from the dance floor and said, "Come on out and dance, Mike, don't be uptight." I was not the only wallflower, so I can only guess that I appeared singularly uptight amidst the nondancers. Before I uttered a word my friend Julio, who was on my right, placed a hand on my right shoulder and said, "Now you see what we blacks have to deal with in Brazil, especially those of us in the black movement." I felt relieved, because his comment affirmed my suspicions about this scene. What "black" person would ever have the freedom to both construct and participate in such a dance? Brazilians are eroticized in the imagination of non-Brazilians. Academic types are not immune to such categorizing, whether conscious or unconscious. Who gets to do the eroticizing and who does not is key to understanding the role of racial and gendered gazes embedded in a matrix of power relations during such moments. When does one's "fieldwork" or site become the site of eros and voyeurism? This is a form of tourism most scholars and especially white scholars—Brazilian and foreign-born—rarely discuss or write about. Though there are certainly more anthropologically self-conscious scholars than the one noted above, I use this example to point to ways in which white scholars eroticize their relationships with black "subjects"—ways all too familiar to African-descended peoples. White scholars who participate in such dynamics outside the West have the option of creating a world for themselves based upon their desires. Few nonwhite scholars can create such a world in the field, in part out of the recognition that even under seemingly benign circumstances the power and politics of race and gender dynamics bleed into research sites. There are no pristine spaces where researchers and informants can operate "freely," unconstrained by the conditions and circumstances which created the relationship between first-world researcher and third-world informant in the first place.

This problematic extended into my own sites of research. During my first series of interviews with activists and various cultural workers, I made appointments with women at several organizations in Botafogo, Flamengo, and in Zona Norte. Women activists in Zona Norte, the least affluent and blackest part of the city, made me undergo an initial "screening" period of missed appointments or monosyllabic responses before opening up. I subsequently obtained invaluable insight into the distinctions between white feminist and black women's organizations, tensions between black women's activism and the predominantly male *movimento negro,* as well as uneasy alliances between heterosexual and lesbian black women advocates. Zona Sul and Centro organizations were another matter, however. Ensconced in a more affluent, spatially segregated and white part of the city, the women working in research, party-affiliated or religious-based organizations, were generally better educated and lighter skinned. People like Caetana Damasceno and Sonia Giacomini were quite genial and suffered through several versions of my improving Portuguese. Others, however, provided a decided chill when I attempted to make appointments or actually interview them. Skeptical eyes and clipped responses suggested something was awry. Equipped now with some experiential knowledge about these encounters, I immediately searched my mind for the possible disjunctures.

I came to suspect that the frostiness was actually an acknowledgment of the eroticization of the site of research. I both knew and had heard of other researchers from the United States and Europe whose extended stays in Brazil encompassed serial romances with Brazilian women. Isolation, human desire and need, and mutual attraction also guide amorous relations between researchers and informants, not just the political economy and the cultural nuances of first-third world relations. Moreover, the tensions between black male and female activists were palpable. Being married, I was at a remove from both the foreign and home-grown politics of desire—or so I thought. I had had discussions with several women anthropologists doing fieldwork in various parts of the country, whose stories told of being constantly propositioned by men who believed that a single or seemingly unattached foreign woman researcher in Brazil must be seeking more than just familiarity with a field site.

I decided to employ a new tactic. I rescheduled appointments with women activists who had either stood me up, acted distant, or been downright hostile, and brought along my wife and child, who accompanied me on the second installment of my fieldwork in 1989. In the presence of my wife and child, the interviewees were much more friendly, informative, and open. The three of us were invited to lunches, parties, and events I had never been invited to by the same people the previous year.

Aside from the obvious lessons of these second meetings, I also gained a practical knowledge of the implicit pressures placed on these women. The eroticization of black and brown Brazilian women has been analyzed by anthropologists like Angela Gilliam and Bella Feldman Bianco, and is deeply embedded in Brazilian history. From the institution of slavery, during which African female slaves were often prey to the sexual whims of slaveowners, to a culture industry internationally renowned for the icon of the *mulatta,* black and brown Brazilian women have constantly been depicted as sexually promiscuous, accessible, and *quente* (hot). This representation is part of Gilberto Freyre's foundational mythology of Brazilian civilization, in *Casa Grande e Senzala* and *Sobrados e Mocambos,* in which race relations are equated with sexual relations, and the erotic imagination of the Brazilian elite does not exist apart from their domination. How many foreign researchers, both male and female, first embarked for Brazil with this image in their minds? We will never know the answer to such a question, but I suspect that the women I eventually interviewed with wife and child in tow had seen many of those gazes before my eyes met theirs.

Diasporic Resonances: Here and Elsewhere

The representation of black men and women as objects of desire, leisure, dance, and prey has a long legacy in Latin America, as in other parts of the world. I lost count of the number of white Brazilians who looked at me with puzzlement when I declared my interest in studying Brazilian racial inequalities. "Racial inequalities? In Brazil? You must mean class inequalities," I was told more than once. This was brought home to me by white friends, particularly in Rio de Janeiro, several of whom looked upon me with a certain bemusement concerning my choice of research. "Why are you bothering, wasting your time studying something like racial discrimination, when you could be devoting your time to something your people are really good at, making music and art?" Earnest questions such as these from good friends, active participants in parties like PT, PSDB, and others were too painful and laborious for me to unpack, then or now. Never mind that I have not played a musical instrument in nearly thirty years, nor undertaken art lessons since I graduated from elementary school.

For some white Brazilians, even making music was not enough. It had to be a particular type of music. At a private dinner hosted by a prominent Brazilian anthropologist, the host bemoaned the fact that Brazilian music and culture were becoming more "Americanized." An example of this, she asserted, was the fascination black Brazilians in

Rio de Janeiro had for black popular music from the United States. "I might be saying this because I've had too much to drink, but this I believe is antimodern!" She proceeded to name several Afro-Brazilians guilty of this transgression. Silence immediately followed at a table of eight people, which included the anthropologists Richard and Sally Price. I asked her if black Brazilians were being antimodern because they had appropriated external musical idioms. Indeed, bricolage is a key aspect of modern cultures. Or was it the fact that they were appropriating "black" music that made them antimodern? " I know that you would probably disagree with me," she responded, "and maybe I am wrong, but I can't respond now." "I cannot think," I continued, "of any popular musical form coming out of Western Europe in the latter half of the twentieth century that did not adopt some form of blues, jazz, or R and B. Can you?" Silence. "Maybe it was my liquor talking, but this is how I feel." Richard Price in particular pressed the issue, while I sat back and pondered the implications of Afro-Brazilians being antimodern for liking a musical form that had already gained popularity in that most modern of places, Western Europe.

At another party, a well-known white movie director of films dealing with Afro-Brazilian themes announced that he knew the moment I walked into the room that I was not a black Brazilian, "because our blacks are weak; they are too busy keeping us strong." Although he acknowledged in a backhanded way the servile position of many *Brasileiros de cor* (Brazilians of color), it was an odd thing to say about one's countrymen and women. Were they all so deflated by the experience of racial slavery and their postemancipation privations that, to the last person, they all appeared weak and forlorn?

Over time, I came to recognize that foreign blacks in general and U.S. blacks in particular pose problems for white elites in Brazil. The laundromat incident involving my wife was similar to many recounted to me by foreign black researchers, tourists, professionals, and students working in Brazil who experienced first-hand the limits of Brazilian cordiality when attempting to enter predominantly white neighborhoods, stores, and nightclubs. In many instances, a foreign black was spared a beating, incarceration, or worse only by resorting to his or her primary language. The "foreignness" of their black status provides them with some liminality, yet it also provides a glimpse of what happens to black and brown Brazilians on a daily basis.

As in the encounter with the Brazilian filmmaker, I met many white Brazilians who seemed impelled to either acknowledge the existence of racial discrimination in Brazil or to contrast "angry" U.S. blacks with "our blacks." Not all African-Americans are angry, however. Most Afro-Brazilians I met were not content, as members of the white elite portrayed them. The exaggerated contrast, however, raised an issue that I call a burden of likeness, that is insufficiently discussed by blacks in the United States. As the most visibly successful African-descended community in the world, the iconography of "black America" is often used as a template for the rest of the black world. Invariably, black diaspora people in various parts of the world have developed, in the words of Afro-Canadian intellectual Rinaldo Walcott, ambivalent feelings of "attraction and revulsion" toward the iconography of the U.S. African-American experience.

This ambivalence stems from the crowding out of other black images on the global screen, and the often blatant representation by U.S. black politicians, business representatives, sports and entertainment figures of black Americans as the role model for the rest of the black world, complete with their consumption patterns, commodification and marketing of their own bodies, as well as their relatively successful struggles for civil rights. In my view, many U.S. blacks are unconscious of this very peculiar consequence of cultural imperialism. The resentment that ensues from the predominance of this imagery is inevitable. For the African-American researcher, this creates a hierarchical relationship within African diaspora studies which non—U.S. black scholars have begun to question.

Thus, all other African-descended populations, particularly those living in the developing world, are confronted with a question that encapsulates the attraction and revulsion alluded to by Walcott: "Why aren't we like them? Why be like them?" In Brazil, *Raça* (Race), the first nationally distributed magazine devoted to black and brown Brazilians, which was founded in 1996, clearly wants to be "white," to be "like them." The magazine reads and looks like a composite of *Ebony* and *Essence* magazines for blacks in the United States. Supporters of the magazine have argued that bourgeois implications aside, black Brazilians need positive images. I wonder what the *favelado* or *favelada* (resident of a poor or working-class community) thinks about the beautiful Afro-Brazilian models parading around in homes neither the models nor the *favelados* can ever buy, in outfits sold in stores they never even knew existed in Brazil.

"*Why* be like them?" This question recurs throughout the African diaspora, from Fela Kuti's James Brown-inflected music in Nigeria, the Black Consciousness movement in 1970s South Africa, to Paul Gilroy's writings on the Black Atlantic. Thus, African-American/Afro-Brazilian encounters in Brazil are framed in part by these two questions and their multiple responses. Complicating matters even further, however, is the actual distance between images of Michael Jordan, Janet Jackson, or Jesse Jackson, and the realities of residential segregation, interracial marriages, the Aryan Nation, integrated schools, and a panoply of other indicators of the health and malaise of U.S. race relations. The ready-made images of the African-American projected abroad are neither utopias nor dystopias but pictorial fragments of a reality that few blacks, U.S. or otherwise, can wholly grasp. The images of the United States that Afro-Brazilians align themselves with or against are simply that—images. Try explaining that to an Afro-Brazilian whose only chance of apprehending the United States is through a rap music video.

Conclusion

My experiences in Brazil taught me, among other things, that U.S. blacks like myself were sites of contestation over the nature of race relations in Brazil, vectors for the confluence of race, gender, and national identity. Many white Brazilians don't recognize and acknowledge the polarizations of race relations in their society and culture. Despite the public solidarity between members of black and white members of the Worker's Party, PSDB, and other organizations the white and Afro-Brazilian activists and intellectuals I met and befriended operated in two distinct spheres of the same world. Their bars, neighborhoods, and festive parties were rarely the same.

Afro-Brazilians inhabited several spheres of existence, which I attempted to straddle. By the end of my research experiences in Rio de Janeiro and São Paulo, I was treated like a close relative by many activists and others in the communities where I lived and worked, but I would never be mistaken for one of them, nor they me. Yet in negotiating these spaces and relationships in Rio de Janeiro and São Paulo, many of my activist friends discovered, much to their surprise, that African-Americans like myself are just as mixed up as everyone else.

NOTES

I would like to thank France Winddance Twine and Jonathan Warren for their editorial guidance and close reading of earlier versions of this chapter. I also thank Angela Gilliam and Onik'a Gilliam for their insightful suggestions.

1. The Zona Sul or South Zone is an affluent neighborhood in Rio where tourists, and middle- and upper-class white Brazilians frequent.

REFERENCES

Appadurai, Arjun. 1996. *Modernity at Large: Cultural Dimensions of Globalization.* Minneapolis: University of Minnesota Press.

Bell, Diane, Pat Caplan, and Wazir Jahan Karim. 1993. *Gendered Fields: Women, Men, and Ethnography.* New York: Routledge.

Fry, Peter. 1995–96. "O que a Cinderela Negra Tem a Dizer Sobre a Politica Racial no Brasil." *Revista USP* 28 (dez.–fev.): 122–35.

Gordon, Ted. 1998. *Disparate Diasporas.* Austin: University of Texas Press.

Hempel, C. 1952. "Typological Methods in the Natural and Social Sciences." In *Science, Language and Human Rights,* edited by the American Philosophical Association, vol. 1, pp. 65–86. Philadelphia: American Philosophical Association.

Okely, Judith, and Helen Callaway, eds. 1982. *Anthropology and Autobiography.* New York: Routledge.

Ramos, Guerreiro A. 1957. *Introdução Critica a Sociologia Brasileira.* Rio de Janeiro: Andes.

Sansone, Livio. 1996. "As Relaçoes Raciais em Casa Grande e Senzala: Revisitadas a Luz do Processo de Internacionalização e Globalização." In *Raça, Ciencia e Sociedade,* edited by Marcos Chor Maio and Ricardo Ventura Santos, pp. 207–18. Rio de Janeiro: Editora Fiocruz.

Stanfield, John H., II, and Dennis M. Rutledge, eds. 1993. *Race and Ethnicity in Research Methods.* Newbury Park, Calif.: Sage.

Taylor, Charles. 1985. *Philosophy and the Human Sciences* (Philosophical Papers, vol. 2). Cambridge: Cambridge University Press.

Whitehead, Tony Larry, and Mary Ellen Conaway, eds. 1986. *Self, Sex, and Gender in Cross-Cultural Fieldwork.* Urbana: University of Illinois Press.

Williams, Raymond. 1977. *Marxism and Literature.* New York: Oxford University Press.

Wolin, Sheldon S. 1969. "Political Theory as a Vocation," *American Political Science Review* 63, no. 4 (December): 1062–82.

Chapter 8

Violating Apartheid in the United States
On the Streets and in Academia

Philippe Bourgois

> What kind of a fuckin' moron do you think I am. You think I don't know what you're doin'? You think I'm stupid? You're babbling, you fuckin' drug addict. You're dirty white scum! Go buy your drugs in a white neighborhood! If you don't get the hell out of here right now, motherfucka', you're gonna hafta repeat your story in the precinct. You want me to take you in? Hunh? . . . Hunh? Answer me motherfucka'!

I had just made the mistake of trying to explain to two cruising police officers in East Harlem that I was an anthropologist studying poverty and marginalization. I tried to use my most polite voice and demeanor, but it was well past midnight at one of El Barrio's many crack sales corners in the mid-1980s, when U.S. politicians were busy launching yet another of their escalations in the War on Drugs. More importantly, I was the only white person (with the exception of the two policemen cursing me) anywhere in sight. As far as they—or anyone else in the primarily Puerto Rican neighborhood—were concerned, the only reason for a young white male to be on the streets in East Harlem after dark was either to purchase drugs or to arrest drug dealers.

I was new to the neighborhood and had underestimated the police's role in enforcing apartheid. Being humiliated and threatened with bodily harm by overweight, cursing, armed uniformed men with badges taught me fast, however. On that particular night I was reduced to staring at the ground mumbling, "Yes, sir" and shuffling away obediently when they ordered me to walk to the nearest bus stop and take the next transportation downtown. Behind me I heard: "If I see you around here later, white boy, ah'm'a take you in!"

I learned soon enough how to act appropriately in order to be able to continue living with my family in a tenement next to a bogus video arcade that sold crack while conducting the research for my book on inner-city social suffering. I was documenting the struggles for survival and meaning of a network of Puerto Rican crack dealers whom I had befriended (Bourgois 1995). By my second year on the street my adrenaline would no longer pump with panic when police officers pushed me against a wall and made me stand spread-eagled to be "patted down" for weapons and drugs. My accent proved to be a serious problem in these encounters because patrol officers in East Harlem are almost always white males from working-class backgrounds with heavy Irish- or Italian-American diction. In contrast to the Puerto Rican and African-American children on my block, who used to marvel at what they called my "television advertisement voice," the police officers assumed I was making fun of them, or putting on airs when I spoke politely to them in complete, upper-middle-class sentences. I learned that my only hope was to shorten my encounters with the patrol officers by staring at the ground, rapidly handing over my driver's license, and saying "yes-sir-officer" or "no-sir-officer" in minimalist, factual phrases. When I tried to sound sincere, friendly—or even polite—I risked offending them.

Conversely, when the police tried to be polite to me their actions only reinforced my sense of violating hidden apartheid laws. On one occasion a squad car overtook me as I was riding my bicycle to make sure I was not lost or insane: "You know where ya' going? This is Harlem!" Another time as I was sitting on my stoop at sunset to admire the spectacular colors that only New York City's summer smog can produce, a patrolman on the beat asked me, "What're you doing here?" I quickly showed him my driver's license with my address to prove I had a right to be loitering in public. He laughed incredulously, "You mean to tell me you live here! What'sa' matter with you?" I explained apologetically that the rent was inexpensive. Trying to be helpful he suggested I look for cheap rent in Queens, a multiethnic, working-class borough of mixed ethnicity near New York City's airports.

Racism and the Culture of Terror

It is not merely the police who enforce inner-city apartheid in the United States but also a racist "common sense" that persuades whites, and middle-class outsiders of all colors, that it is too dangerous for them to venture into poor African-American or Latino neighborhoods. For example, when I moved to East Harlem, virtually all my friends—whether white, black, or Latino/a—berated me for being crazy and irresponsible. Those who still visited me would often telephone me in advance to make sure I would meet them downstairs as they descended from their taxis. When I took taxis home from downtown Manhattan, drivers often raised their eyebrows when I gave them my address. Some flatly refused to take me, saying it was too dangerous. Indeed, most people still consider me crazy or at least irresponsible for having "forced" my wife and infant son to live for three and a half years with me in an East Harlem tenement. They often joke that my research sites are a product of a risk-craver's character flaw. In short, one is made to feel bizarre, stupid, loony, and perhaps even unethical—or at least irresponsible—when one insists on taking the inner city seriously enough to conduct participant-observation in it. It becomes worse if one engages the neighborhood respectfully enough to actually enjoy and learn from living and studying on the streets.

Most people in the United States are somehow convinced that they will be ripped limb from limb by savagely enraged local residents if they set foot in Harlem. While everyday danger is certainly real in El Barrio, the vast majority of the 110,599 people—51 percent Latino/Puerto Rican, 39 percent African-American, and 10 percent "other"—who lived in the neighborhood, according to the 1990 census, are not mugged with any regularity—if ever. Ironically, the few whites residing in the neighborhood are probably safer than their African-American and Puerto Rican neighbors since, as the opening vignette demonstrated, most would-be muggers assume whites are either police officers or drug addicts—or both—and hesitate before assaulting them. Caesar, the primary lookout at the Game Room crackhouse, was the first person to explain this to me:

> Felipe, people think you're a *fed* [federal agent] if anything. But that's good; it makes them stay away from you.

Think about it: If you was selling shit on the street and you see a white guy coming by, you wouldn't really want to bother with him.

But then again, some people also think, "He's white and he's in the neighborhood, so he must be crazy." If they didn't, they'd just come up to you and crack you in the face and take your wallet.

You're lucky. Look at me, I'm Puerto Rican. If I was to walk into Bensonhurst,[1] they would figure, "We could beat the shit out of this dude." They might think that I got to be crazy or something but they will test me or kick my ass.

During all the years I spent on the streets of El Barrio walking around at all hours of the night, I was only mugged once—and that was at 2:00 A.M. in a store where everyone else was also robbed at the same time. My wife, who is Costa Rican, was never mugged and she circulated freely throughout the neighborhood—although she was cautious after dark. During these years at least half a dozen of our friends living downtown in supposedly safer neighborhoods were mugged. I do not mean to overstate the safety of El Barrio; my seventy-year-old Filipino landlord was mugged in the hallway of our apartment building in broad daylight while walking out of his ground-floor apartment. Everyone in the neighborhood is conscious of the real possibility of assault and grows eyes on the backs of their heads—but that is a reality to a large extent for hundreds of thousands of New Yorkers throughout the city's many diverse neighborhoods. Even the toughest drug dealers in the network I studied would ask a friend to accompany them for protection when they were carrying money or drugs after dark.

Violence cannot be reduced to its statistical expression which would show that the vast majority of the murders and beatings in any given inner-city neighborhood are confined to a small subgroup of individuals directly involved in substance abuse and the underground economy, or who are obviously vulnerable, such as frail, elderly persons. The violence of street culture pervades daily life in El Barrio and shapes mainstream society's perception of the ghetto in a manner completely disproportionate to its objective danger. Part of the reason is that even when violent incidents do not physically threaten bystanders, they are highly visible and traumatic. For example, during my first thirteen months of residence in El Barrio I witnessed a slew of violent incidents:

- A deadly shotgun shooting outside my apartment window of a drug-dealing woman (who also happened to be the mother of a three-year-old child).
- A bombing and a machine gunning of a numbers joint by rival factions of the local "mafia"—once again, within view of my window.
- A shoot-out and police car chase in front of a pizza parlor where I happened to be eating a snack with my wife.
- The aftermath of the fire-bombing of a heroin house by an unpaid supplier around the block from where I lived.
- Half a dozen screaming, clothes-ripping fights.

None of these particular incidents came close to threatening me physically, but their traumatic nature and prominent public visibility contributed to the sense of an omnipresent threatening reality which extended far beyond the statistical possibility of becoming a victim.[2] To analyze the very different contexts of South America and Nazi Germany, Michael Taussig coined the term "culture of terror" to convey the dominating effect of widespread violence on a vulnerable society (1987). In contemporary Spanish Harlem one of the consequences of the "culture of terror" dynamic is to silence the peaceful working-class majority of the population who reside in the neighborhood. They isolate themselves from the community and grow to hate those who participate in street culture—sometimes internalizing racist stereotypes in the process. A profound ideological dynamic mandates that one distrust one's neighbors. Loic Wacquant has referred to this in the context of the South Side of Chicago as the "depacification of everyday life" caused by public and private sector infrastructural breakdown (1993). John Devine refers to this in the context of the institutional abandonment of large lower-tier public schools in New York City as the street's "culture of violence" (1996). Dozens of political and intellectual leaders who were forged on Harlem's streets, including most notably Malcolm X and Piri Thomas, have powerfully evoked this phenomenon in their autobiographies (Malcom X 1964; Thomas 1967; see also Canada 1995).

It is difficult to write constructively about and against the culture of violence because mainstream society uses the images of terror and mayhem to dehumanize both victims and perpetrators. In the United States savage images of the inner city justify an unwillingness to confront segregation, economic marginalization, and public sector breakdown (Di Leonardo 1998). This politically demobilizing and socially segregating experience of violence in the U.S. inner city is especially insidious because, unlike the brutality civilians experience under repressive war-torn regimes like those of Central America in the 1980s (cf. Green 1994; Jenkins 1991; Martin-Baro 1990; Pedelty 1995; Argueta 1983; Binford 1996) or Mozambique since decolonization (Nordstrom 1997), the terror is not purposefully and systematically perpetuated by armies and death squads for the explicit purpose of political control. Instead, in the United States, this "peace-time violence" or "invisible genocide"(Scheper-Hughes 1996) emerges confusedly and inconsistently from the politicoeconomic logics of a restructuring economy, compounded by a public sector retreat from the welfare state and the rise of a prison industrial complex. Consequently, in many ways street violence in the United States is even more politically demobilizing and demoralizing than the physically more terrifying and brutal political violence of repressive regimes. Worse yet, a historically entrenched racialized logic legitimizes confining this violence spatially to inner cities where generations of vulnerable youths lead lives of poverty, underemployment, long-term incarceration, or premature death.

Denying the Culture of Violence

I had a professional and personal imperative to deny or "normalize" the culture of terror during the years I lived in El Barrio. Many local residents employ this strategy. They readjust their daily routines to accommodate the shock of everyday brutality in order to maintain their own sense of sanity and safety. In order to be successful in my street ethnography I had to be relaxed and enjoy myself on the street. I had to feel comfortable while hanging out with friends and engaging in relaxed conversation. I had to genuinely enjoy myself in order to put in the long hours on the street that my ethnography required. This was not difficult during daylight hours or even during the early evening when El Barrio streets are often warm and appealing. There are children running every which way, playing tag and squealing with delight; one's neighbors are out taking a stroll and often pause to strike up a friendly conversation; a loudspeaker pulses salsa music from a tenth-story housing project window so that everyone on the street below can step in tune for free.

In short, there is a sense of community in the neighborhood despite the violence. In fact, most residents even know the nicknames of their more hostile or suspicious neighbors. Having grown up in Manhattan's silk stocking district, the northern end of which lies just seven blocks downtown from El Barrio's southern border at East 96th Street, I always appreciated the shared sense of public space that echoes through Spanish Harlem's streets on warm sunny days. In the safe building where I grew up downtown, my neighbors did not have nicknames, and when one shared the elevator with them, they usually did not even nod in acknowledgment of one's existence.[3]

When I now visit East Harlem at night almost a decade since I moved away from New York City, I can feel at an emotional level how apartheid institutionalizes itself hegemonically through its myth/truth of the culture of terror: I find myself afraid. I wonder if my academic friends might indeed be right—am I an irresponsible risk craver, am I too old to be doing this? I resist the temptation to hail a taxi and succumb to U.S. apartheid's insidious logic of conformity through fear. I remember that I really do want to meet up with my old friends from the crack scene and that I belong and like it here. I stop on a dark block, stare at a shattered lamppost and remind myself that I spent over four years walking these streets at all hours of the night and virtually nothing ever happened to me. It is not mayhem here. The levels of violence are nowhere near as overwhelming as we are made to think they are. Often, to underscore my point I will stop in front of a housing project entrance and wait to see a young child skip between buildings. If I am unlucky, instead I will see young men having an argument. The fact of the matter, however, is that most people are just living normal, vulnerable lives in El Barrio. Inner-city streets do not propagate contagious plagues.[4] One is not brave, stupid, or crazy to walk through the inner city in search of friends or of community, irrespective of one's ethnicity, class—and more arguably—of one's gender and age.

It was easy to normalize life on the street. During my residence, I deeply enjoyed the friendly public space that the working-class majority in El Barrio were often able to project during daylight hours—and often even after dark. It was the dealers themselves, however, who frequently shattered my sense of optimism and insisted that I respect the violent minority who really controlled the streets when push came to shove—especially after dark. Indeed, in the interest of debunking the veil of projected fear that slanders East Harlem and enforces its class and ethnic segregation in the minds of most outsiders, one should not glorify the neighborhood and depict it as a stable, supportive working-class community. That is not the case, and most upwardly mobile residents move out when they can afford to do so. In one particular instance toward the end of my stay I had commented to Caesar, the lookout at the Game Room crackhouse, that the block felt safe. His outraged comical response was particularly interesting, in that it traced the full ambiguous cycle of the culture of terror by demonstrating the instrumental brutality of the people who were supposed to be protecting us. Both the criminals and the police played by the rules of the culture of terror, once again leaving little room for coherent political resistance:

> *Caesar:* "Yo Pops [waving Primo, the crackhouse manager, over], listen to this. [turning to me] Felipe thinks the block is chill.
>
> Well let me tell you Felipe, what happened earlier today, because all day it was wild on this block. I didn't even have to watch HBO today. I just had to look out the window and I had a full array of murder and beat down and everything. There was even a fire. I saw an assortment of all kinds of crap out there.
>
> It all started when two crackheads—an older man and a black dude—yoked this girl. They beat her down and took her jewelry. Punched her in the eye; just cold bashed her. She was screaming and the old guy kicked her some more. It was in the daytime like around two.
>
> Then the cops came and caught the muggers and beat them down. There was at least twenty cops stomping out them two niggas because they resisted.
>
> And they should never have attempted that shit because they got the beat-down of their lives. The cops had a circus with the black kid's face. Hell yeah! They were trying to kill that kid. That's why they needed two ambulances.
>
> Homeboy got hurt! Both of them was in stretchers bleeding hard. It wasn't even a body there. It was just a blob of blood that was left over. The cops had pleasure in doing it.
>
> It was not a normal beat-down like: throw-you-up-on-a-car extra hard. I'm talking about 'take your turn, buddy [grinning];

hold 'em right here [punching] and BOOM and BOOM.' And this guy goes BOOM [pretending to fall unconscious].

Even *'buela* [grandma] saw it from the window next to me. And she was yelling and someone else was yelling, 'Abuse! Abuse! Police brutality!'

If I woulda' had a little video camera I woulda' sent it to Al Sharpton.[5] Because it was a black dude that they did that beat-down to. Coulda' caused a major political scandal and Sharpton woulda' been right up here with that wack perm he's got."

Philippe: "How does it make you feel to see the cops doing that?"

Caesar: "I was feeling really sorry for myself because I was thinking about getting hit. I could feel the pain they was feeling 'cause I know what it is to be beat down by cops. They don't let up; they be trying to kill you, man! They do it with pleasure [grinning].

That's stress management right there. That's release of tension. That's my-wife-treated-me-dirty-you'll-pay. That's terrorism with a badge. That's what that is.

The cops look forward to that. They get up in the morning and go, 'Yeah, Ah'm'a gonna kick some minority ass today.' [Rubbing his hands together and licking his lips.]

I could tell that attitude, because I would be the same if I was a police officer. 'Cause you take the badge for granted. The badge gets to your head. You know what I'm saying? Makes you feel like you're invincible; like you could do whatever you goddamn well please.

I would have the same attitude. I'm going to hurt somebody today. I don't care if he's white or Puerto Rican. And I'm going to have pleasure in doing it. I'm full into it. And I would be a happy married man because I wouldn't fight with my wife.

I don't even know why they have human police officers. They should just put animals out there patrolling the streets. Word up! 'Cause they're worse than animals. It's like they're animals with a mind."

Internalizing Institutional Violence

Although we obviously worried occasionally about the danger of police brutality, it was not one of our primary daily concerns. There was always a strong undercurrent of anxiety over the risk of arrest at the crackhouse, but ironically we were considerably less worried about being brutalized by the police when they raided compared to what we risked at the hands of our fellow inmates in the holding pen. Until the late 1990s, judges in Manhattan virtually never sent anyone to jail for selling or buying small quantities of a drug the first time they were arrested. A hand-to-hand sale of crack to an undercover officer usually resulted in a two-to-four-year suspended felony sentence. The problem in an arrest, however, was that one usually had to wait in a municipal jail holding pen for forty-eight to seventy-two hours before being arraigned by the judge in the special Narcotics Court (Glaberson 1990).

Our fate in these overcrowded "bull pens" was a frequent subject of anxious discussion and a forum for the assertion of threatened masculinity. I captured one of these violently masculinist jousts on my tape recorder. Caesar's nondrug-using cousin, Eddie, was reminding all of us in the Game Room that we risked being sodomized in jail if the police picked us up in a sweep that night. Eddie's father was African-American, and Caesar made sure that he racialized his retort as well as demonstrated his superior technical knowledge of the likelihood of sexual assault in a New York City holding pen.

> *Eddie:* "Caesar, don't you come crying to me when they take that ass a' yours downtown and bust your cherry [laughter]."
>
> *Caesar* [businesslike]: "Unnh-uhh! They don't rape niggas in the bull pen no more 'cause a' AIDS. You don't even get raped on Rikers [New York City's biggest municipal jail] no more.
>
> You get raped when you go Upstate where they got them big, black, brick-Georgia, Georgia-Tech Bulldog, Black Muslim ham hocks that been in the slammer twenty years.
>
> They be runnin' that little ass a' yours [jumping to within an eighth of an inch of Eddie's face]. Because they bigger than you. They been lifting weights. They big and they take your shit [spinning around into my face]. And they take your arm like this [twisting my arm] and they put it down and they dog it [spinning around and seizing Eddie in a full nelson]. And they jerk it around [pumping his crotch against Eddie's rear]. And you like: [switching roles to grab at his head and pull his hair, shrieking] 'AHHUUHH.'

[Swinging around again into Primo's face] And they're taking
that ass and they make you a fag. You gotta be like a lamb and
wash drawers and shit, and socks.

And people out on the street [swinging his face around yet
again to within an eighth of an inch of my nose] be recognizing
YOU!"

I was especially sensitive to Caesar's violently masculinist harangue
that night because the New York City police had just deployed their
new elite Tactical Narcotic Teams—appropriately nicknamed TNT—in
El Barrio.[6] TNT was founded in 1989 to assuage popular outrage during the height of the national just-say-no-to-drugs hysteria. TNT's specific directive was to bust the small, street-level dealer rather than the
wholesale supplier. A week earlier, at 2:00 A.M., TNT had arrived in U-
Haul trucks to block off both ends of a notorious crack-copping block
a few streets down from the Game Room crackhouse. They rounded up
everyone loitering on the sidewalk and even dragged people out of private apartments from the few still-inhabited tenements located on the
block.

The night of Caesar and Eddie's jousting over jailhouse rape I had
forgotten my driver's license. Not carrying a picture identification is a
sure guarantee for inciting police wrath. The recording from this session ends with my voice cursing Caesar through cackles of nervous
background laughter:

Philippe: "Outta my face Caesar! What the fuck's the matter with
you! You a fucking pervert, or what?

Primo, I'm outta here. You guys have made me *petro* [para-
noid]. I'll be right back though, I'm just going upstairs to get
my I.D."

Making Friends with the Crack Dealers

Before I lived in the neighborhood, I thought access to drug scenes was
going to be difficult. When I walked through the neighborhood it felt
as if my white skin signaled the terminal stage of a contagious disease
sowing havoc in its path. Busy street corners emptied amidst a hail of

whistles whenever I approached, as nervous drug dealers scattered in front of me, certain that I was an undercover narcotics agent.

I slowly lost my pariah status once I moved into the neighborhood full-time. By a stroke of good luck, I was suffering from a serious case of procrastination in finishing my doctoral dissertation on ethnic divisions in the Central American labor movement (Bourgois 1989). This turned me into a wonderfully relaxed, talkative neighbor. I much preferred to be sitting on my tenement stoop chitchatting with whoever might be available than returning upstairs to undertake the final edit on my dissertation. In short, I became a friendly, familiar, and unthreatening public figure on my street—the "white boy on the block."

Once the Game Room crackhouse opened two doors down from my stoop in late 1985, I overeagerly precipitated a disastrous first attempt to access it. I asked my crack-addicted neighbor to introduce me to Primo, the crackhouse manager, who was later to become my best friend on the scene—and who remains a close friend as I write this ten years later. He shyly giggled and turned his back on me, as if to hide his face, asking my neighbor, loud enough for me to hear, "What precinct did you pick him up at?" Again, time healed this faux pas. I let the crackhouse scene introduce itself to me on its own terms. In fact, I could not avoid it. I had to pass the crackhouse anytime I went anywhere: to the subway; to the supermarket; or just out for a stroll.

Within a few weeks, Primo was inviting me to drink an occasional beer with the bevy of friends, lookouts, and addicts congregating in front of his fake video arcade. None of them had ever been tête-à-tête with a friendly white before, so it was with a sense of relief that they saw that I hung out with them out of genuine interest rather than to obtain drugs or engage in some other act of *perdicion*. The only whites they had ever seen at such close quarters had been school principals, policemen, parole officers, and angry bosses. Even their school teachers and social workers were largely African-American and Puerto Rican. Despite his obvious fear, Primo could not hide his curiosity. As he confided to me several months later, he had always wanted a chance to "conversate" with an actual live representative of mainstream, "drug-free," white America.

Over the next few weeks, I regularly spent a few hours at the Game Room crackhouse chatting with Primo and whoever else was on duty that shift—either Little Benzie or Caesar. To my surprise, I became an exotic object of prestige; the crackhouse habitués actually wanted to be seen in public with me. I had unwittingly stepped into a field of racist power relations where my presence intimidated people. I had triggered within Primo a wave of internalized racism whereby he enthusiastically presented himself as superior to "the '*sinverguenza mamao* [shameless scum]' all around us here." He kept trying to differentiate himself "from all these illiterate Puerto Ricans" who "work in *factorias*." I was especially embarrassed when he began letting me know how good he thought it was for the development of his mind to be talking with me. At the same time, however, he still thought I might be an undercover police officer. Almost a month after I met him, he said, "I don't care if tomorrow you come and arrest me, I want to talk to you. You're good people." It was not until three years later that Primo would casually describe me to others as "the white nigga' who always be hangin' with me." As a matter of fact, I still remember the night when I first graduated to "honorary nigga'" status. Primo had imbibed more alcohol than usual, and I had walked him up to his girlfriend's high-rise project apartment to make sure he would not get mugged in the stairway, because the elevators were broken as usual.[7] Upon our safe arrival, swaying in the doorway, he grabbed me by the shoulders to thank me: "You're a good nigga', Felipe. You're a good nigga'. See you tomorrow."

Gender Bending

It was not until five years later at 2:00 A.M. in the stairwell of Primo's mother's high-rise project where Primo and Benzie had gone to sniff a "speedball" (combination of heroin and cocaine) during New Year's week that they told me what their first impressions of me at the Game Room had really been. Primo had ripped open a $10 glassine envelope of heroin and dipped his house key into the white powder in order to lift a dab to his left nostril. He sniffed deeply, repeating the motion deftly two more times to his right nostril before sighing and reaching out for me to hand him the forty-ounce bottle of Ole English malt liquor that I was swigging from. Benzie, meanwhile, was crushing the contents of a $15 vial of cocaine inside a folded dollar bill by rolling it between his thumbs and forefingers. This gets rid of any clumps and crystals and makes it easier to sniff. He then dipped a folded cardboard matchbook cover into the inch-long pile of white powder and sniffed dryly twice before laying it down gently in the corner of the stair he was sitting on:

> *Primo:* "When I first met you, Felipe, I was wondering who the hell you were, but, of course, I received you good because you sounded interesting; so, of course, I received you good [reaching for the cocaine]. *Te recibí como amigo, con respeto* [I welcomed you as a friend, with respect]."
>
> *Benzie* [interrupting and handing me the malt liquor bottle]: "Felipe, I'm going to tell you the honest truth—and he knows it. [pointing to Primo] The first time I met you I thought that you was in a different way. . . . But I would really rather not tell you [sniffing from the heroin packet with Primo's key]."
>
> *Philippe* [drinking]: "It's alright don't worry; you can tell me. I won't get angry."
>
> *Benzié:* "Yeah . . . well . . . [turns to Primo to avoid eye contact with me, and sniffs again] yeah, you remember? I used to tell you, you know, the way he used to talk. The way he used to be. That I thought maybe . . . you know, . . . How you call it? That some people are bisexual. Even though you had a wife, I thought you was like . . . dirty.
>
> It was really 'cause of the way you talk and 'cause of the way you act. You always asking a lot of questions, and a lot a gay people be like that—you know, trying to find out the way you are.
>
> But then after a while, when I got to know you [grabbing the bottle from me], I saw the way you was hanging; and I got to know you better; but still, I always had that thought in my head, "Man, but, but this nigga's a faggot. [drinking]"
>
> *Primo* [cutting Benzie short]: "Damn, shut up man! You're going to give Felipe a *complejo* [complex]. [Putting his arm over my shoulder] It was just 'cause you was white. He was thinking, '*Quien es este blanquito?*' [Who is this white boy?]"
>
> *Philippe:* "So was it my accent? My voice? The way I move my body?"
>
> *Benzie:* "Yeah, like your accent . . ."
>
> *Primo* [interrupting]: "I told him you were an anfropologist [*sic*], and that the way you speak is just like intelligent talk. I mean you just speak your way. And maybe, we don't understand a few words, but it's alright.

> But when you talk Spanish, then you really be sounding differ-
> ent. Then you really be sounding different. You know, when you
> talk Spanish, you sound like an Español [Spaniard].
>
> Even my mother thought you was gay, but that was because she
> was only talking to you through the phone [gunshots]. One day
> she asks me [in Spanish], 'Who's this little white boy who's always
> calling here? Is he a *pato* [faggot] or something? [*Quien es este
> blanquito que siempre llama aqui? Es pato o algo asi?*]'
>
> And I said [once again in Spanish], 'No! What are you talking
> about? He is a professor. He speaks Spanish and English and
> French. [*No! De que tu hablas? El es profesor. Habla español, in-
> gles, y frances.*]'"

My femininity on the streets of El Barrio is yet another testimony to Bourdieu's insights about class and culture being inscribed on our bodies in
ways of which we are completely oblivious (Bourdieu 1977). I may have
felt some kind of vain personal pique at having been misidentified sexually at a time in my life when I fancied myself to be at least minimally
streetwise. I had purposefully, publicly participated in the standard com-
ing-of-age patriarchal rituals in order to appear less threatening: that is, I
had got married and had a baby. By the time my son was old enough to
be baptized in the local church, I was close enough to several of the dealers to invite them to the party at my mother's apartment downtown.

Children: The Truly Vulnerable

These rituals, however, may have been more for my benefit than theirs.
Indeed, raising my newborn son, Emiliano, in El Barrio helped open me
up both practically and theoretically to the centrality of the social suffering of children under U.S. apartheid. It focused my attention on the
structuring of gender power relations and the centrality of intimate and
domestic violence in the lives of the vulnerable. I began to hear more
clearly the omnipresent underlying wail of crying babies that competed
with the salsa and rap music pulsing from my neighbors' windows.

At the same time, I am convinced El Barrio has special energy and
love for children. I learned this with my own newborn Emiliano in my
arms generating countless blessings and constant cooing. I even learned
to appreciate my local supermarket's inefficiency and decrepitude, for

every time I passed it by on the sidewalk at least three of the four teenage cashiers ran from their machines to tap on the display window and threw kisses and grimaces at my appreciatively giggling baby. Downtown society's industrialized taylorist logic would have long since obliged the manager to fire those affectionate wannabe mothers. When I took Emiliano to white parties downtown I noticed that he was disappointed with the adults. He expected a more appreciatively physical reaction from them. Very few of my white friends and acquaintances even knew how to hold my baby comfortably; none of them grabbed him spontaneously out of my arms for a cuddle and a blessing the way my acquaintances regularly did on the street uptown. In fact, some of my downtown friends even asked me to leave my son at home with a baby-sitter when they invited me to their homes.

My love affair with street life's intergenerational affection and integration began to sour when my son's first words at sixteen months of age turned out to be "tops, tops, tops." I had been trying to access a new and particularly active crack-copping corner, and had been taking him along with me to allay the suspicions of the sellers that I might be an undercover cop.[8] That corner had four competing "spots," each selling $3 vials. The sellers on duty shouted or hissed at their prospective clients to advertise their particular brands, delineated by the color of the plastic stoppers on their vials: "Greytop, greytop, greytop! Pinktop, Pinktop, Pinktop! Blacktop, etc." A few weeks later, I found myself in the midst of an angry crowd surrounding two white police officers who had just killed an African-American man high on angel dust. It was only when the crowd had begun chanting "Open season on the black man! Murderers! Murderers!" that I noticed that the only other whites present were the two "killer cops" frantically shouting into their walkie-talkies for help.[9] Emiliano, perched on my shoulders, caused the tense crowd to burst into laughter by clapping his hands gleefully in time with the angry chanting.

As a parent, I was learning the lesson faced by all the working mothers and fathers on my block. Either I had to abandon public space and double-lock my child in my cramped tenement apartment and assume a hostile attitude toward street culture, or I would have to accept the fact that my child would witness drugs and violence on a daily basis. My perspective on the future of the children living around me further soured when Iris, the mother of ten-year-old Angel and eight-year-old Manny, my two favorite shiny-eyed street friends, fell apart on crack and became pregnant. My wife and I stopped dropping by at their apartment unannounced after finding them one evening sitting in the dark (because the electricity bill had not been paid), scraping the last corners of peanut butter out of an empty jar. Their mother had passed out on the bed after the previous night's crack "mission."

I began organizing biweekly trips for them, and whoever else happened to be hanging out on the block, to cross New York's invisible apartheid barriers to visit museums and other world renowned bourgeois havens such as the FAO Schwartz toy store and Trump Tower. They loved the Andy Warhol exhibit at the Museum of Modern Art, and Angel even assured me that the Frick Museum's collection of Dutch Masters was "not boring at all." In contrast, they were not impressed by the Whitney Museum's "alternative" multimedia rap/break dance/graffiti/skate board extravaganza.

The full force of the racial and class boundaries confining the children of El Barrio became glaringly clear on these outings. In the museums, for example, we were usually flanked by guards with hissing walkie-talkies. Often I was eyed quizzically as if I might be some kind of pedophile, parading my prey. Angel was particularly upset at the Joan Miro exhibit at the Guggenheim when he asked one of the guards—who himself was Puerto Rican—why he was being followed so closely, and was told, "to make sure you don't lift your leg."

The hardest dynamic to face now when I return to El Barrio for visits is precisely the especially painful vulnerability of street children. I have lost the defense mechanisms that allow people engaged with street culture to "normalize" violence against children. For example, I still cannot forget the expression in the terrified, helpless eyes of the five-year-old boy who was watching his mother argue with a cocaine dealer at 2:00 A.M. in the stairwell of a tenement where Primo and I had taken shelter from a thundershower, on my second night back in the neighborhood after my first yearlong hiatus. Primo shrugged when I tried to discuss the plight of the child with him, "Yeah, Felipe, I know, I hate seeing that shit too. It's wack."

Disrespecting Hierarchy and Vulnerability

My most serious faux pas in carving out a legitimate relationship at the crackhouse occurred when I inadvertently disrespected Primo's boss, Ray, the owner of the franchise of crackhouses that I was studying. I had asked him to read aloud to the wannabes in his coterie outside one of his crackhouses the caption on a newspaper photo describing my research. An embarrassing silence engulfed us when it became clear to everyone that Ray could not read the caption. He was functionally illiterate.

In revenge, Ray declared me a persona non grata and reminded me that people in his neighborhood "sometimes get found in the garbage with their heart ripped out and their bodies chopped up into little pieces. You understand what I'm saying?" He further confirmed my marginality by announcing to his employees that he had dreamed that I was "Some kind of agent—like an FBI or CIA agent—no it was more like you was from Mars or something, that you was sent here to spy on us." I took these warnings seriously, both because of the salience of the meaning of dreams in Nuyorican culture and also because Ray had a reputation for gratuitous violence and murder.

Time passed, and Ray eventually forgave me. Indeed, he began greeting me once again with his usual question, "How's that book comin' Felipe? Finished yet?" thereby communicating to everyone within earshot that I had his formal permission to be prying into his personal business. By the time I left New York, my relationship with Ray had once again become problematic. This time, however, it was because he trusted me too much. He expected me to serve as his cultural broker to the outside world, demanding that I help him launder his money. He was no longer ashamed to admit to me that he was helpless outside the cocoon of El Barrio's streets and needed basic help for the simple acts of obtaining a "picture ID" that would allow him to apply for a driver's license. Scared lest I offend the man once again, I usually concocted excuses to avoid becoming a facilitator to his money-laundering schemes of buying tax-defaulted and drug-bust confiscated buildings at police auctions.

Participant-Observation Methods and Theory under U.S. Apartheid

I have addressed only a few of the many potential pitfalls I encountered while violating apartheid. Ultimately, however, the research was feasible because all humans everywhere respond well to respectful interaction. We all appreciate having our life stories taken seriously. The urge to convey meaning transcends the barriers of institutionalized social inequality. I am convinced, consequently, that it was only because of my long-term physical presence in the neighborhood that I was allowed to overcome—even if clumsily and contradictorily—the racial, class, and gender boundaries that keep most academics off inner-city streets.

Methodologically, it is only by establishing lasting relationships based on mutual respect that one can begin to ask provocative personal questions, and can expect to engage in substantive conversations about the complex experience of extreme social marginalization in the United States. Perhaps this is why the experience of poverty and social marginalization is so poorly understood. The traditional, quantitative survey methodologies of upper-middle-class sociologists or criminologists collected via hit-and-run parachute visits behind apartheid lines tend to collect fabrications. Few people on the embattled margins of society trust outsiders when they ask invasive personal questions, especially concerning money, drugs, and alcohol. In fact, nobody—whether rich or poor—likes to answer such indiscrete incriminating queries.

Historically, inner-city poverty research has consequently been more successful at reflecting the biases of an investigator's society than at analyzing the experience of poverty or documenting race and class apartheid. The state of research into poverty and social marginalization in any given country emerges almost as a litmus test to gauge contemporary social attitudes toward inequality and social welfare. This is particularly true in the United States, where discussions of poverty almost immediately become polarized around moralistic value judgments about individual self-worth, and frequently degenerate into stereotyped conceptions of race. In the final analysis, most people in the United States, rich and poor alike, believe in the Horatio Alger myth of going from rags to riches. They are also intensely moralistic about, and often racialize, issues related to wealth and class. Perhaps this deeply rooted judgmental and racist ideology stems from their puritanical and Calvinist heritage which, together with the legacy of a history of genocide, slavery, and colonial conquest, has fueled U.S. capitalism for so many centuries. Even progressive leftist academics in the United States secretly worry that the poor may actually deserve their fate. As a result they often feel compelled to portray the inner city in an artificially positive manner that is not only unrealistic, but is also theoretically and analytically flawed.

The ideological context of inner-city poverty research in the United States is probably best epitomized by the best-selling books of the anthropologist Oscar Lewis in the 1960s. He collected thousands of pages of life history interviews with an extended family of Puerto Ricans who had migrated to East Harlem and the South Bronx in search of employment. Some thirty years later, his culture of poverty theory remains at the center of contemporary polemics about the inner city in the United States. Although he was a social democrat in favor of expanding government poverty programs, his theoretical analysis offers a psychologically reductionist—almost a blame-the-victim—explanation for the transgenerational persistence of poverty. At some level it sounded the death knell for the Great Society dreams of the Johnson administration and helped disabuse the hope of the early 1960s that poverty in America could be eradicated. If anything, his theory resonates more than ever with the campaigns for individual responsibility and family values that have been so celebrated by politicians in U.S. national elections at the end of the twentieth century. In a 1966 *Scientific American* article Lewis wrote:

> By the time slum children are six or seven, they have usually absorbed the basic attitudes and values of their subculture. Thereafter they are psychologically unready to take full advantage of changing conditions or improving opportunities that may develop in their lifetime.
> . . . It is much more difficult to undo the culture of poverty than to cure poverty itself.

In their anger and frustration over the way Lewis's family-based and Freudian-influenced focus on impoverished Puerto Rican immigrants confirms conservative American biases, liberal social scientists have often fallen into the trap of glorifying the poor and of denying any empirical evidence of personal self-destruction. When I moved into the same inner-city neighborhood where the Puerto Rican families that Lewis studied had lived in over thirty years ago, I was determined to avoid his failure to examine structural inequality, and to document the way oppression is painfully internalized in the day-to-day lives of the persistently poor. Striving to develop a political economy perspective that takes culture and gender seriously, and which recognizes the link between individual actions and social-structural determination, I focused on how an oppositional street culture of resistance to exploitation and social marginalization is contradictorily self-destructive to its participants. In fact, street dealers, addicts, and criminals become the local agents administering the destruction of their surrounding community.

Beyond the Identity Politics of Being Worthy

The dearth of ethnographic research on devastating urban poverty, especially in the 1970s and 1980s, is related to the fear of succumbing to a pornography of violence that reinforces popular racist stereotypes. Most ethnographers offer sympathetic readings of the culture or people they study. Indeed, cultural relativism is a fundamental anthropological tenet: cultures are never good nor bad; they simply have an internal logic. In fact, however, the experience of structurally imposed social suffering is usually hideous; it destroys human integrity, and ethnographers never want to make the people they study look ugly. This failure to confront social suffering is unfortunate because, as Kleinman argues, suffering constitutes "everything that really matters" (1997). As noted, the imperative to sanitize the vulnerable is particularly strong in the United States because of the survival-of-the-fittest, blame-the-victim theories of individual action that dominate popular "common sense."

Consequently, a detailed examination of social marginalization encounters serious problems with the politics of representation. I worried that the life stories and events presented in my book would be misread as negative stereotypes of Puerto Ricans, or as a hostile portrait of the poor. I struggled over these issues for several years because I agree with those social scientists who criticize the inferiorizing narratives that have predominated in much of the academic and popular literature on poverty in the United States (Benmayor, Torruellas, and Juarbe 1992; Rodriguez 1995). At the same time, however, countering traditional, moralistic biases and middle-class hostility toward the poor should not come at the cost of sanitizing the suffering and destruction that exists on inner-city streets. Out of a righteous or "politically sensitive" fear of giving the poor a bad image, I refuse to ignore or minimize the social misery I witnessed, because that would make me complicit with oppression.[10]

In order to document and denounce U.S. apartheid, I had to confront the contradictions of the politics of representation of social marginalization in the United States by presenting brutal events, relatively uncensored as I experienced them, or as they were narrated to me, by the perpetrators themselves. In the process, I tried to build an alternative, critical understanding of the U.S. inner city by organizing my central arguments, and by presenting the lives and conversations of the crack dealers, in a manner that emphasizes the interface between structural oppression and individual action. I also strategically introduced the human and historically entrenched vulnerability of the main characters in the opening chapters. I developed the historical and political economy context first and portrayed the characters as victims of social-structural oppression and interpersonal abuse before subsequently confronting the reader in later chapters with the fuller horrors of these very characters as perpetrators of violence and abuse against their own loved ones and against their immediate community. Building on cultural production theory and drawing from feminism, I hoped to restore the agency of culture, the autonomy of individuals, and the centrality of gender and the domestic sphere to a political economy understanding of the experience of persistent poverty and social marginalization in the urban United States.

Political economy analysis is not a panacea to compensate for individualistic, racist, or otherwise judgmental interpretations of social marginalization. Reductionist structuralist interpretations often obscure the fact that humans are active agents of their own history, rather than passive victims. Ethnographic method allows the "pawns" of larger structural forces to emerge as real human beings who shape their own futures. Nevertheless, when I was writing up my material I often caught myself falling back on a rigidly structuralist perspective in order to shield myself from the painful details of how real people hurt themselves and their loved ones in their struggle for survival in daily life. As I noted just above, this analytical and political problem can be understood in the context of the theoretical debate over structure versus agency, that is, the relationship between individual responsibility and social-structural constraints. Through the cultural practices of opposition, individuals shape the oppression that larger forces impose on them (Bourdieu 1977; Foley 1990; Fordham 1988; Macleod 1987; Willis 1977).

The difficulty of relating individual action to political economy, combined with the personally and politically motivated timidity of ethnographers in the United States through the 1970s and 1980s, has obfuscated our understanding of the mechanisms and experiences of oppression. I cannot pretend to be able to resolve the structure versus agency debate; nor can I confidently assuage my own righteous fear that hostile readers will misconstrue my ethnography as "giving the poor a bad name." Nevertheless, I have felt it imperative from a personal and ethical perspective, as well as from an analytic and theoretical one, to expose the horrors I witnessed among the people I befriended, with only a minimal censoring of gory details.[11] The depth and overwhelming pain and terror of the experience of poverty and racism in the United States need to be talked about openly and confronted squarely, even if that makes us uncomfortable. I tried to document the range of strategies that the urban poor devise to escape or circumvent the structures of segregation and marginalization that entrap them, including those that result in self-inflicted suffering. We must go beyond righteous dichotomizations in our politics. We should jettison the notion of worthy versus unworthy victims; we do not need to sanitize culture in order to celebrate it. We certainly do not need to portray the cultures of structurally vulnerable communities as middle-class visions of working-class redemption. Suffering and oppression are much more complicated and important than our sterile political slogans and seductive academic theories can convey. Individuals and processes are neither all good nor all bad. Most important, no matter their quirks, failures, and agonies communities, cultures, and individuals have a right to an existence free from structurally imposed suffering—even if that is utopian.

Academic Violence

I wrote this essay in the hope that "anthropological writing can be a site of resistance" (Scheper-Hughes 1992: 25), and in the conviction that social scientists should, and can, "face power" (Wolfe 1990). At the same time, as I have stated several times, I continue to worry about the political implications of exposing the minute details of the lives of the poor and powerless to the U.S. public. Under an ethnographic microscope everyone has warts and anyone can be made to look like a monster. Furthermore, as Laura Nader stated succinctly in the early 1970s, "Don't study the poor and powerless because everything you say about them will be used against them" (Nader 1972).

I do not know if it was possible for me to present the story of my three and a half years' residence in El Barrio without falling prey to a pornography of violence, or a racist voyeurism—ultimately the problem and the responsibility also lies in the eyes of the beholder, as the academic reaction to the book since its publication has confirmed. Despite the academic awards it has won in both anthropology and sociology the book has also generated pointedly negative political polemics. Reviewers either hate it or love it. Somewhat predictably—but still disappointingly—middle-class cultural nationalists fall into the trap of the right-wing racialized debates that hegemonize U.S. thinking. They fixate on what they interpret to be unworthy images of Puerto Ricans. My fieldwork, however, was never meant to be "about the Puerto Rican community"; and it certainly is not about "Puerto Ricanness." Happily, most reviewers understand the book to be a denunciation of U.S. apartheid rooted in a historical analysis of politicoeconomic restructuring and the reconstitution of gendered power relations. Nevertheless, the more vitriolic political polemics in academic venues tell me that the book serves as a Rorschach test rather than as grist for intellectual or political debate.[12] Unfortunately, while academics hiss and spit at one another over their differing theoretical interpretations of poverty and oppression in the United States, income inequality widens, corporate profits continue to reach new heights, and new generations of inner-city youth are sent to prison in rising numbers.

NOTES

This paper was written with support from the National Institute on Drug Abuse (grant # R01-DA10164). I also want to thank the following institutions for their generous financial support while I conducted fieldwork in East Harlem: the Harry Frank Guggenheim Foundation, the Russell Sage Foundation, the Social Science Research Council, the Ford Foundation, the Wenner-Gren Foundation for Anthropological Research, the United States Bureau of the Census, and the National Institute on Drug Abuse (grant # R03-DA06413-01). I thank Harold Otto and

Ann Magruder for their transcription, typing, and office coordinating. I thank Cambridge University Press for allowing me to excerpt and revise passages from *In Search of Respect: Selling Crack in El Barrio.*

1. Bensonhurst is a working-class Italian-American neighborhood in the Bronx. On August 23, 1989, a group of young white men in the neighborhood killed Yusuf Hawkins, a sixteen-year-old African-American who had come to Bensonhurst to buy a used car advertised in the local newspapers. They thought he was dating an Italian-American woman who lived on the block (*New York Times*, August 25, 1989: A1, B2).

2. In one case, a stray bullet ricocheted off the curb next to us while we lounged in front of the Game Room. I hesitated to include this particular incident in my book for fear of oversensationalizing my experience of neighborhood violence in a self-celebratory macho manner. In fact, we did not feel we were in imminent danger of getting shot although the crackhouse where I spent most of my time was held up three times in four years. The transcriptions of my tape recordings are frequently punctuated by gunshots. In my original round of editing I was so close to the material that I did not transcribe the sound of gunshots, treating it as static interference or traffic noise.

3. My childhood census tract was listed as the richest in all of New York City in the 1990 census. Its average household income ($249,556) was more than eleven times higher than the average household income (just over $21,000) of my census tracts in El Barrio (*New York Times*, March 20, 1994: A6). The Census of Population and Housing of the official U.S. Census provides a lower figure of $147,567 for the median household income in this silk stocking census tract, number 150.02.

4. Of course, deadly diseases do strike inner-city residents at a greater rate than elsewhere (Wallace 1988).

5. Al Sharpton is an African-American, inner-city Reverend in New York City who caught the attention of the media for his flamboyant denunciations of racism and his community-level mobilizations in the 1990s.

6. The TNT strategy was declared to be a failure and discontinued in early 1994 (*New York Times*, November 16, 1998: A1, B5).

7. That particular year, the neighboring housing projects where Primo's girlfriend, Maria, lived had the highest murder rates of all the Housing Authority Projects in Manhattan.

8. It may indeed appear somewhat mercenary or irresponsible of me to have taken my son with me as a normalizing prop to crack spots. The fact of the matter, however, is that every parent living on that particular block had to carry their babies through the same crack sales point every time they took them out for a walk. Besides, like most new fathers, I loved strolling the streets with my baby in my arms. It was fun. Not only did it feel normal to be with him, but

it felt healthy, loving, and sharing. Ten years later, urban inner-city fieldwork strolls across apartheid-like demarcations in San Francisco are still something we both enjoy sharing together.

9. I found out the next day in the *New York Times* that the victim was forty-four years old (*New York Times,* November 16, 1989: B2).

10. As Nancy Scheper-Hughes (1992: 172) notes in her ethnography of a Brazilian shantytown:

> For anthropologists to deny, because it implies a privileged position (i.e., the power of the outsider to name an ill or a wrong) and because it is not pretty, the extent to which dominated people come to play the role . . . of their own executioners is to collaborate with the relations of power and silence that allow the destruction to continue.

11. In fact, I did exclude a number of conversations and observations that I thought projected an overly negative portrayal of the crack dealers and their families out of context or might appear gratuitously offensive. (For example, in this draft I cut short Caesar's harangue on jailhouse rape. A verbatim transcript of the tape would have continued for several additional graphic, rhyming, obscene, and violently depressing pages.) Much of my "censuring" occurred around descriptions of sexual activities. In several cases, I felt the passages might be considered straightforward pornography. I also wanted to avoid excessively invading the privacy of the major characters in the book. I discussed these issues at length with all of them. Only one person actually asked me to delete some material from the epilogue, which of course I did. Selection, editing, and censorship have tremendous political, ethical, and personal ramifications that ethnographers must continually struggle over, without ever being confident of resolving.

12. For example, while one academic is able to dismiss *In Search of Respect: Selling Crack in El Barrio* (Bourgois 1995) as a "yellow journalism study" devoid of "historical political economic analysis" (Di Leonardo 1998: 394), a *New York Times* (right-wing) cultural critic manages to accuse it of being "ultra-leftist because it identifies 'class exploitation, racial discrimination and of course, sexist oppression' as the underlying cause of everything (Bernstein 1995)." In the same contradictory vein, an anthropological society awarded this "yellow journalism study" a commendation for the humanistic quality of its writing (*Anthropology Newsletter* 1996; see also 1997).

REFERENCES

Anthropology Newsletter. 1996 (November). "Prizes and Awards." 10.
———. 1997 (May). "Prizes and Awards." 24.

Argueta, Manlio. 1983. *One Day of Life.* New York: Vintage Books.

Benmayor, Rina, Rosa Torruellas, and Anna Juarbe. 1992. "Responses to Poverty among Puerto Rican Women: Identity, Community, and Cultural Citizenship." New York: Centro de Estudios Puertorriqueños, Hunter College. Report to the Joint Committee for Public Policy Research on Contemporary Hispanic Issues of the Inter-University Program for Latino Research and the Social Science Research Council.

Bernstein, Richard. 1995. "Entering Young Drug Dealers' Minds." *New York Times,* December 27: B6.

Binford, Leigh. 1996. *The El Mozote Massacre, Anthropology, and Human Rights.* Tucson: University of Arizona Press.

Bourdieu, Pierre. 1977. *Outline of a Theory of Practice.* New York: Cambridge University Press. Originally published in 1972.

Bourgois, Philippe. 1989. *Ethnicity at Work: Divided Labor on a Central American Banana Plantation.* Baltimore: Johns Hopkins University Press.

———. 1995. *In Search of Respect: Selling Crack in El Barrio.* Cambridge: Cambridge University Press.

Canada, Geoffrey. 1995. *Fist, Stick, Knife, Gun: A Personal History of Violence in America.* Boston: Beacon Press.

Devine, John. 1996. *The New Panopticon: The Construction of Violence in Inner City High Schools.* Chicago: University of Chicago Press.

Di Leonardo, Micaela. 1998. *Exotics at Home: Anthropologies, Others, American Modernity.* Women in Culture and Society. Chicago: University of Chicago Press.

Foley, Douglas E. 1990. *Learning Capitalist Culture: Deep in the Heart of Tejas.* Philadelphia: University of Pennsylvania Press.

Fordham, Signithia. 1988. "Racelessness as a Factor in Black Students' School Success: Pragmatic Strategy or Pyrrhic Victory?" *Harvard Educational Review* 53: 257–93.

Glaberson, William. 1990. "Trapped in the Terror of New York's Holding Pens." *New York Times,* March 23: A1, B4.

Green, Linda. 1994. "Fear as a Way of Life." *Cultural Anthropology* 9 (2): 227–56.

Jenkins, Janis Hunter. 1991. "The State Construction of Affect: Political Ethos and Mental Health among Salvadoran Refugees." *Culture, Medicine, and Psychiatry* 15 (2): 139–65.

Kleinman, Arthur. 1995. *Writing at the Margin: Discourse between Anthropology and Medicine.* Berkeley: University of California Press.

———. 1997. "Social Suffering: Everything That Really Matters." Colloquium Presented to the Anthropology Department, University of California, Berkeley, November 3.

MacLeod, Jay. 1987. *Ain't No Makin' It: Leveled Aspirations in a Low-Income Neighborhood.* Boulder: Westview Press.

Malcolm X. 1964. *The Autobiography of Malcolm X.* New York: Grove Press.

Martin-Baro, Ignacio. 1990. "De la Guerra Sucia a la Guerra Psicologica." *Revista de Psicologia de El Salvador* 31: 109–22.

Nader, Laura. 1972. "Urban Anthropologist Perspectives Gained from Studying Up." In *Reinventing Anthropology,* edited by Dell Hymes, pp. 284–311. New York: Pantheon.

Nordstrom, Carolyn. 1997. *A Different Kind of War Story* (Ethnography of Political Violence). Philadelphia: University of Pennsylvania Press.

Pedelty, Mark. 1995. *War Stories: The Culture of Foreign Correspondents.* New York: Routledge.

Rodriguez, Clara E. 1995. "Puerto Ricans in Historical and Social Science Research." In *Handbook of Research on Multicultural Education,* edited by James A. Banks. New York: Macmillan.

Scheper-Hughes, Nancy. 1992. *Death without Weeping: The Violence of Everyday Life in Brazil.* Berkeley: University of California Press.

———. 1996. "Small Wars and Invisible Genocides." *Social Science and Medicine* 43 (5): 889–900.

Taussig, Michael. 1987. *Shamanism, Colonialism, and the Wild Man: A Study in Terror and Healing.* Chicago: University of Chicago Press.

Thomas, Piri. 1967. *Down These Mean Streets.* New York: Knopf.

Wacquant, Loic. 1993. "Décivilisation et démonisation: la mutation du ghetto noir americain." In *L'Amerique des francais,* edited by Christine Faure and Tom Bishop, pp. 103–25. Paris: Editions Français Bourin.

Wallace, Roderick. 1988. "A Synergism of Plagues: 'Planned Shrinkage,' Contagious Housing Destruction, and 'AIDS in the Bronx.'" *Environmental Research* 47: 1–33.

Willis, Paul. 1977. *Learning to Labor: How Working Class Kids Get Working Class Jobs.* Aldershot, England: Gower.

Wolfe, Eric. 1990. "Distinguished Lecture: Facing Power—Old Insights, New Questions." *American Anthropologist* 92 (3): 586–96.

Chapter 9

Race and Peeing on Sixth Avenue

Mitchell Duneier

There are few topics about which there is less frank talk than race and racism. On Sixth Avenue, one of them was peeing. On a fall afternoon, I sat in my office on the eighth floor of the Social Science Building at the University of Wisconsin-Madison. I had stolen a few minutes between office hours and the upcoming noon department meeting to finish listening to one of the many tapes I had made while working as a vendor of scavenged written matter with unhoused and rehoused black men during the previous summer in New York City's Greenwich Village.[1] As I listened to the tape, I squirmed in my seat, for I had been putting off peeing ("holding it in") so I could get to the end of the tape before the start of the noon meeting.

I came across a dialogue between two unhoused men—Mudrick telling Keith that the Assistant Manager kicked him out of McDonald's for not being a "customer" when he tried to use the bathroom. A comparison I did not plan to make was suddenly evident: Mudrick is an unhoused vendor. He works on the street. I am a professor. I work in an office building. The unhoused vendor, a fifty-seven-year-old black man, has just relied on the goodwill of a teenage black boy with the title "Assistant Manager" to let him use the bathroom. I, by contrast, use the bathroom of the social science building whenever I please.

We are told by the methods literature to ask questions that will enable us to dialogue with theory, that are important in the real world, or make some contribution to the literature. What we are not told is *how* to overcome blinders that may derive from differences between ourselves and the people we write about. These blinders influence the conception of questions, and the determination that certain topics should be noticed in the first place.

On my way to the faculty meeting I stopped in the eighth floor men's room. As I stood in front of the urinal, I thought of Mudrick's not having the same opportunity on the sidewalk. Where *did* Mudrick pee? My mind wandered to Sixth Avenue and here is the image I saw: Unhoused black men—Mudrick, Keith, Ron, and others—their backs to me, standing urinating against the wall of the elite Washington Square Court condominium or in a large trash container rented by the Gap. It was a scene I had observed often during my years working as a vendor, but one which had never registered as important enough to jot on a note pad, or think about twice. It was so much part of my taken-for-granted reality that it did not bear note. I had probably assumed that the men who were peeing against the side of the Washington Square Court condiminium were just lazy, and no different, by the way, from all my upper-middle-class male friends who do the same thing when they are in the middle of the golf course and are too lazy to go back to the clubhouse to take a piss. This is the kind of male behavior I have taken for granted throughout my life. And the things we take for granted often do not end up in our field jottings.

On the tape I had just listened to, I was confronted with a single conversation that posed a challenge to my taken-for-granted assumptions. Mudrick had been *excluded* from the McDonald's bathroom. As an unhoused man he was not peeing against the condominium out of the same kind of laziness I had observed in my upper-middle-class white friends on the golf course.

Racial Insights, Class Locations

But why, if I had been working out on the street every day and night with these men, had I not *understood* this to be a problem? How was it that while working with the housed and rehoused vendors I had not noticed this basic aspect of their lives, let alone conceived of it as a research issue?

As an upper-middle-class white male, I had skin and class privileges that the men I was working with did not have. As I thought back to the previous summer on these blocks, I thought of the hundreds of times I had crossed the street and darted to the back of Pizzeria Uno without once wondering if anyone would deny me entrance. Though we were occupying the same physical space and engaging in common activities out on the street, my experience of urinating (and, I would later learn, of defecating), had been radically different from that of the men I worked with. This is part of the reason I did not perceive it as a research topic. The fact that I *did* finally consider it, that I did ultimately recognize a research issue, came from a constellation of lucky circumstances, one of which being that while listening to the tape in my office far away I happened to have been squirming in my seat, holding it in, which made me particularly sensitive to the issue of peeing when I heard that five-second snippet of tape that might have otherwise run by unnoticed.

Now here is a question. What if I had not belonged to a more privileged social position than my subjects? What if, instead, I was poor and black and similarly excluded? I would surely have understood this to be an aspect of daily life, but would I have understood it to be a topic? I don't know the answer, but one possibility is that being excluded from public bathrooms is so taken for granted on the street that it is rarely discussed. I never heard discussions about it during the previous summer, and the discussion I *did* hear on the tape was hardly a discussion, more like a reference to an incident that did not deserve elaboration. I do not believe that someone from the same social position as the vendors would necessarily have seen exclusion from bathrooms as a research topic, any more than my colleagues at the university would see the circumstances of bathroom use on the eighth floor of the social science building as an interesting research issue.

I suspect that a black male professional researcher might have had less difficulty than these men gaining access to local public bathrooms, but I cannot be certain. Researching race usually entails researching class and it is often difficult for researchers to know if they are being treated differently from the people they write about due to skin, class, gender privileges, or by some interaction between them. Despite the social differences between us, it is possible that I would have arrived at an understanding of this situation if the men had talked about it. They did not. I remain uncertain as to how to interpret their silence. Did they simply find this to be an unremarkable aspect of their struggles as unhoused men, since this form of exclusion was so routine? Or did that want to protect me (and themselves) from further humiliation and embarrassment by not discussing my own racial and class privileges as a white upper-class academic? I have routinely noted that people who experience race and class discrimination tend to be quite sensitive toward the feelings of those who do not share their experiences. In fact, in my experience neither blacks nor whites in the United States talk honestly about race in the other's presence.

Further Uncertainties: Rapport and Acceptance

When one of the differences that separates me from the people I write about is race, there can be much uncertainty as to whether I am hearing what I need to hear or know what I think I know. (Of course, this also applies to issues of class and gender.)

Consider an event that occurred one time when I appeared on Sixth Avenue at approximately 6:00 A.M. for my first day of work as a vendor.[2] Within minutes of my arrival that first day, I knew that it would be difficult for me to gain the trust of the men. Not only was I separated from them by racial privilege, but the social class, religious, ethnic, and educational gulf between me and them was significant. How could I expect them to trust me?

The men were wondering the same thing. One conversation captured on my tape recorder illustrates this. I had been interviewing one of the men, who had been holding my tape recorder, when I got called away.

While listening to the tapes a few months later, I came across the ensuing conversation. The participants have asked me to conceal their identities here.

> "What you think he's doing to benefit you?" X asked.
> "A regular black person who's got something on the ball should do this, I would think," said Y.
> "He's not doing anything to benefit us, Y."
> "I'm not saying it's to benefit us," said Y. "It's for focus."
> "No. It's more for them, the white people."
> "You think so?" said Y.

"Yeah. My conversations with him just now, I already figured it out. It's mostly for them. They want to know, why there's so much homeless people into selling books. . . . I told him because Giuliani came in and he said nobody could panhandle no more. Then the re-cycling law came in. People voted on it."

"Case in point," said Y. "You see, I knew he had to talk to you. I can't tell him a lot of things cause I'm not a talker."

"I told him, in California, there's people doing the same thing that we're doing. They doing it on a much more higher level. They are white people. You understand?"

"Yeah."

"They have yard sales."

"Yeah."

"They put the shit right out there in their yard. He knows. Some of them make a million dollars a year. But what they put in their yard, these are people that put sculptures. They put expensive vases. These are peoples that drives in their cars. All week long, all they do is shop."

"Looking for stuff." said Y. "Like we go hunting, they go shopping."

"Right. Very expensive stuff. They bring it and they put it in their yard and sell it. And they do it every weekend. Every Saturday. Every Sunday. So they making thousands. He's not questioning them: How come they can do it? He's questioning us! He want to know how did the homeless people get to do it. That's his whole main concern. Not really trying to help us. He's trying to figure out, how did the home-less people get a lock on something that he consider *lucrative*."

"Good point," said Y.

"You gotta remember, he's a Jew, you know. They used to taking over. They used to taking over no matter where they go. When they went to Israel. When they went to Germany. Why do you think in World War II they got punished so much? Because they owned the whole of Germany. So when the regular white people took over, came to power, they said, 'We tired of these Jews running everything.'"

"But throughout time, the Jewish people have always been busi-ness people."

"But they love to take over."

Y laughed.

"Of course" X laughed, hysterically. "That's what he's doing his research on, now. He's trying to figure out how did these guys got it. How come we didn't get it?"

Y laughed.

X continued laughing, hysterically, unable to finish his next sentence.

"I don't think so," said Y.

"But he's not interested in trying to help us out."

"I'm not saying that, X. I'm saying he's trying to focus on the point."

"I told him that, too," said X. "Everyone he talk to, they're gonna talk to him on the level like he's gonna help them against the police or something like that. They're gonna look to him to advocate their rights."

"No. I don't think that, either. I think it's more or less to state the truth about what's going on. So people can understand that people like you and I are not criminals. We're not horrible people. Just like what you said, what happens if we couldn't do this? What would you do if you couldn't sell books right now?"

Hearing those stereotypical, ignorant, and possibly anti-Jewish words many months after I had been on the street, brought it home to me that—conventional wisdom to the contrary—participant observers need not be fully accepted or trusted in order to learn many things. I had no idea that X harbored any suspicions toward me, yet I had gone about my work on the blocks throughout the summer that preceded my listening to this tape. In this sense, fieldwork is very much like life itself. We may *feel* fully trusted and accepted by colleagues and "friends," but full acceptance is difficult to measure by objective standards and a rarity in any case. If we cannot expect such acceptance in our everyday lives, it is probably unrealistic to make it the standard for successful fieldwork.

At the same time, participant observers like myself who do cross-race fieldwork should be aware that there are a range of things members who belong to different racial groups may not say in the presence of someone they consider a racial outsider. For blacks in the United States, it has been necessary as a survival mechanism to "wear the mask," to quote the black poet Paul Laurence Dunbar, who wrote:

We wear the mask that grins and lies,
It hides our cheeks and shades our
eyes,—
This debt we pay to human guile;
With torn and bleeding hearts we smile,
And mouth with myriad subtleties. (Dunbar 1967: 167)[3]

Dunbar's words are no less relevant today, and it would have been a methodological error for me, a white researcher, to assume that apparent rapport is real trust, or that the poor blacks I was writing about would always feel comfortable taking off the mask in my presence. I assume that the tone and content changes when whites are in the room.

Indeed, there are a range of things that I might have never heard, simply because I am a white man. For example, if a vendor had a negative experience dealing with a white customer, it is likely that he would not have made an antiwhite or anti-Semitic statement in my presence. But the fact that such utterances never occurred in my presence does not mean that they did not occur at all. My particular job as a social scientist is to look for answers to research questions based on the data a white, upper-middle-class Jewish scholar can be expected to collect, and to avoid research questions that I cannot possibly answer reliably, given the influence of my social characteristics on what I can expect to see and hear. Although it is impossible to know all the questions that I can or cannot expect to answer, I try to avoid research questions that *assume* I will be privy to openness from blacks, especially about whites.

This does not mean that I don't sometimes find out about things I hadn't expected to. I learned how to do fieldwork from Howard S. Becker, and one of the things he taught me is that most social processes have a structure that comes close to insuring that a certain set of situations will arise over time. In practice these situations require people to do or say certain things because there are other things going on that require them to do that, things that are more influential than the social condition of a fieldworker being present. Most of the things in a vendor's day—from setting up his magazines, to going on "hunts" for magazines, to urinating—are structured. This is why investigators like myself can sometimes learn about a social world even though we did not have the rapport we thought we had, and although we occupy social positions quite distinct from the persons we write about.

As my research came to its conclusion, some of the vendors allowed me to work on their sidewalk because they understood the purpose of my research the way I did, others wanted to have me around as a source of small change and loans,[4] while others may have decided they would tolerate my presence because they were accustomed to tolerating lots of things they did not trust on the sidewalk. However, it would be naive for me to think that I knew what they thought, or that they trusted or accepted me fully. And most importantly for the purposes of the present discussion, I recognize that I will never be certain how the details of their lives were not visible to me due to my social position.

Access to Racist Statements

While I may be disadvantaged when conducting cross-class and cross-racial research in public, my access to specific forms of information about how racism operates is facilitated by my position as an upper-class white male researcher. For instance, I was able to gain access to uncensored antiblack sentiments. After I had completed my research, I began having discussions about my findings with Nolan Zail, an architect from Australia on the frontiers of designing innovative housing alternatives for unhoused persons in New York City. One of the issues we discussed concerned the difficulty some unhoused men had in moving their magazines and personal belongings around, as well as the complaint made by Business Improvement Districts and police officers that the presence of these vendors was unsightly and frustrating because their merchandise and belongings were strewn on the pavement below their tables. I asked Zail whether he could design a vending cart which could address some of these concerns.

Here was a potential opportunity for us to use what we knew to make a small if practical contribution to improve conditions of Sixth Avenue. Surely this was not the same as helping to transform the larger structural conditions which brought about these problems, but it might make a difference in the day-to-day lives of some of the men, one of whom was Ishmael Walker. First, though, it was necessary to find out if Ishmael wanted such a cart, and how he would feel about such an effort on his behalf. I could not ignore the fact that both Zail and I are white, and that Ishmael had described being treated in patronizing ways by many whites throughout his life.

Zail suggested that we meet with Ishmael to try to establish what kind of functional characteristics he was looking for in a vending cart. There on the sidewalk, Zail spent time with Ishmael trying to understand how his table functions within his business and life routine as an unhoused vendor. He told Ishmael that he would be happy to assist him with the design and development of the cart.

Ishmael responded by describing a number of needs surrounding his desire to display written matter in a way that his experience as a vendor had taught him would maximize sales. He described his need for sufficient storage space to safely hold his merchandise and personal belongings. He also said that it would be useful if the design could make provision for a separate lightweight carriage which he could use for his hunts and that could be attached to the vending cart.

Zail designed a cart and presented drawings to Ishmael on several occasions to get his further input and reaction, after which he modified the designs to incorporate these further suggestions. In one of these later meetings, Ishmael expressed his desire to pay back the costs of manufacturing the cart with installment payments. The issue of money had not yet come up (I knew it would in due time), and we agreed that this would be a good way to do it. In the meantime, I received permission from Ishmael to try to raise the money to initially pay for the manufacture of the cart through donations.

When Ishmael was satisfied with the design of the potential product, Zail and I scheduled an appointment with one of the largest manufacturers of steel and aluminum food carts to ask him to fabricate the metal vending cart. The manufacturer was already making a food cart pretty similar to the one we would ask him to make for us. His reaction to our ideas, and the difficulty we had getting the cart built, became another kind of "data" for me, showing how much prejudice there is against the destitute and unhoused.

"Okay, let's see what you got," he said, as we began the meeting.

"This is an example of what we have in mind," I said, as Zail placed the architectural drawings in front of him.

"Did you show this to X?" [X was a powerful man in New York real estate who the manufacturer asserted was an enemy of sidewalk vending.]

"No," I replied.

"Well then, forget about it!" he said.

"He doesn't have any say about what goes on in Greenwich Village," I said.

"Mitch, please! They own everything that's happening. The real estate board controls New York City. They *are* the real estate board. You're gonna show them this? Are you kidding? They want to get rid of these people!"

"Part of their argument for getting rid of these guys is that it looks so bad," I responded.

"It's not a question that we can't make something," he said. "It's the opposition. If we go out there with one of these carts, they would crucify us. They would nail me to the cross."

"Nail you?"

"Look! You know what started all this? Really simple. They want to get all the Niggers off the street. They told me: 'We want them off. They're bad for business!' *You* want to put them on, *Mitch*! Why you making so much trouble, Mitch? You're spitting in their face with this!"

"What we are saying," Zail interjected, "is that this is what you can do to improve the image. . . . It's actually not too dissimilar from the cart you have there."

"So how does this help the homeless?"

"Well, for several reasons," Zail continued. "One, is that it allows storage. Two is display. It can be displayed in a professional manner, rather than strewn all over. Now he can actually display it neatly. In a sense it's a more professional way and more aesthetically pleasing."

"All we're asking is for you to make *one* of these for us on an experimental basis," I said. If it worked for Ishmael, we would likely order more."

"I'll make anything you want," the manufacturer replied. "If that's what you're telling me to do. But there is nothing that will change their appearance!"

"It will increase the aesthetic of this type of vending," I said.

"What about him, the homeless person?" he asked.

We seemed destined to go around in circles.

A few weeks later, Zail called to confirm a subsequent meeting with the manufacturer, but he said he had changed his mind. He wouldn't have any part of our project. He didn't want to do anything to make the "homeless" vendors look more like the food vendors who constituted the real market for his carts. He said he was also concerned about antagonizing the real estate interests of the city, who he said were already trying to eliminate food vendors on public sidewalks. (In fact, one year later Mayor Giuliani tried to eliminate food vendors from hundreds of locations in lower Manhattan and Midtown, but changed his mind in response to a public outpouring of support for the food vendors.)

It stands to reason that the white food-cart manufacturer felt comfortable employing racist language in our presence because he viewed Zail and me as racial insiders. This final insight is not, of course, new to researchers. When Drake and Cayton wrote about the attitudes of white tavern owners in their classic study, *Black Metropolis* (1945), they used quotations culled from interviews conducted by white research assistants. Like the research assistants whose data became integral to *Black Metropolis,* it is unlikely that we would have ever been privy to such data had we been black. It is likely that the white cart manufacturer would have been less willing to openly express his attitudes in the presence of a U.S. black researcher. This is consistent with a pattern that I have witnessed in my everyday life whereby the conversations among whites change in response to the presence or absence of black people.

NOTES

I would like to thank France Winddance Twine and Jonathan Warren for their insightful editorial guidance and Hakim Hason for many helpful conversations.

1. Manhattan's Greenwich Village is an urban space characterized by extremes of wealth and poverty as well as marked ethnic and racial hierarchies. My knowledge of the Village is based on extensive ethnographic fieldwork, primarily on three adjacent blocks along Sixth Avenue, from Eighth Street and Greenwich Avenue to Washington Place, over the period September 1992 to October 1998, with daily observation from September 1992 to June 1993 and complete immersion during the summer months of 1996 and 1997 (for more details, see Duneier 1999). Taking advantage of a New York ordinance that makes special allowance for the street sale of printed matter, the vendors sell books (mainly used) and magazines from tables they set up on the public sidewalks.

2. A full account of the circumstances which led me to meet these men and to begin working on the street can be found in the methodological appendix to my book *Sidewalk* (1999).

3. I thank Aldon Morris for bringing Paul Laurence Dunbar's poem to my attention.

4. See *Sidewalk* (Duneier 1999) for a detailed discussion of this issue.

REFERENCES

Drake, St. Clair, and Horace Cayton. 1945. *Black Metropolis*. New York: Harcourt, Brace, and World.

Dunbar, Paul Laurence. 1967. "We Wear the Mask." In *Lyrics of Lowly Life* (Seacaucus, N.J.: Citadel Press, 1997.

Duneier, Mitchell. 1999. *Sidewalk*. New York: Farrar, Straus, and Giroux.

Chapter 10

Women in Prison
Researching Race in Three National Contexts

Kum-Kum Bhavnani and Angela Y. Davis

Women in prison comprise an enormous, invisible, and silenced population. This chapter draws on research based on interviews with over one hundred imprisoned women in the United States, the Netherlands, and Cuba. Our collaborative research contests their multiple marginalizations, not the least of which is racism, that render them invisible and silent. We also question the ubiquitous status of prisoners (particularly women prisoners of color) as objects of research. In our study, women prisoners' insights about the conditions of their imprisonment have been used to raise new questions, which in turn have informed the ultimate direction of our work.[1]

We are interested in the ways in which presently and formerly incarcerated women can help explain the increasing reliance on public forms of punishment for women who historically have been punished largely within private spheres. We are also interested in the extent to which counterdiscourses forged by antiracist social movements inform imprisoned women's ability to explicitly theorize the role of racism in imprisonment practices. As women researchers of color—one South Asian and the other African-American—who have been involved in antiracist movements in Britain and the United States for many years, our own perspectives are informed both by our experiences as activists in different national contexts and by our commitment to link our academic research to strategies for radical social change. Our study thus begins with the assumption that the overutilization of imprisonment to address a range of social problems—which would more appropriately be dealt with by nonpunitive institutions—constitutes a major contemporary crisis. This means that our work is linked to efforts to transform public policy and to activist strategies that emphasize the importance of including imprisoned women in a new public discourse of resistance to imprisonment rather than to more conventional research agendas to generate knowledge *about* a subjugated group.

In conceptualizing this study of women's imprisonment and our role as researchers, we considered our own racialized backgrounds within the political contexts defining our activist histories. We were—and continue to be—concerned with the possibility of forging feminist alliances across racial boundaries. Whereas Kum-Kum Bhavnani was involved during the seventies and eighties in labor, feminist, and prison activism in Britain at a time when the category "black" was politically defined as embracing people of African, Asian, and Middle Eastern descent, Angela Davis was active during the same era in a number of campaigns informed by the category "women of color," which addressed political issues affecting Native American, Latina, African-American, and Asian American women. The issues addressed were thus not racially exclusive. In imagining the groups of imprisoned women we would interview, we did not establish goals for specific racial *groups* but rather considered the general racialization of imprisonment *practices,* which have a disproportionate impact on women of color and poor white women. We were much more interested in the women's critical perspectives about racialized and gendered prison systems and the way they might help demystify the role of the state than in learning about *individuals* and their relationship to the racial groups with which they identified. The democratic framework in which we attempted to formulate this project is a reflection of our own attempt to render the boundaries between research and activism more permeable.

We chose the three countries where we conducted our interviews for specific reasons. We are most familiar with the penal system in the United States and are concerned with the gendered character of the emergent prison industrial complex, which has resulted in the proliferation of women's prisons and an attendant intensification of penal repression. Within the United States, the number of prisoners per capita far exceeds that of any other capitalist country.[2] The Netherlands, which is experiencing a significant increase in the number of prisoners for the first time in its history, has one of the lowest per capita rates of incarceration, as well as a history of progressive penal reform.[3] As far as Western capitalist countries go, it is at the other end of the spectrum. Finally, we chose Cuba so that we might ascertain the differences, if any, between penal regimes for women in capitalist countries and penal regimes under socialism. While our study of imprisoned women in the United States began with the premise that race played a pivotal role in determining who goes to prison and how long a convicted woman remains behind bars, we set out to discover the significance of race in the other two national settings as well.

It is worth noting that Angela Davis's history as a political prisoner during the early seventies and as an internationally known political activist both obstructed and facilitated our research. We attribute the fact that we were unable to gain access to the California Institution for Women (CIW) to her reputation as a former prisoner and prison activist. As we indicate below, we changed the venue of our U.S. interviews to the San Francisco County Jail because the warden at CIW never granted us permission to enter the prison. On the other hand, the director of the women's prison in the Netherlands was herself a prison activist and was aware of Angela's history as a former political prisoner and of her work on prisoners' rights. This clearly facilitated our ability to conduct research in the prison she supervised. Our access to women's prisons in Cuba was directly related to Angela's historical connections with the Association of Cuban Women, an organization that had played a major role in organizing the Cuban campaign for her freedom.

While Angela's experiences and history as a former political prisoner facilitated our access to prisons in the Netherlands and in Cuba, it also sometimes led to a tendency on the part of the prison staffs to treat Angela as the primary researcher, which contradicted the egalitarian way we had structured our research relationship. We made it clear that in our collaborative project, we both claimed equal status as coinvestigators. But in spite of tactful reminders, Kum-Kum's name was frequently misspelled and in official documents was listed after Angela's, even though our own practice was to list our names in alphabetical order. On the other hand, the prisoners we interviewed seemed far more sophisticated than their keepers. Even though many of them knew of Angela—one even had a child named after her—they always treated us as equals and never indicated a preference for being interviewed by one of us over the other. Collaborative research relationships rarely unfold without complications. In our case, the assumption of a hierarchal relationship by the prison administrations could have negatively affected our research relationship. However, we talked openly about the impact this behavior might have on our work, thus struggling to preserve our own collaborative spirit.

Explanations for the sparsity of literature on imprisoned women usually point to the relatively small percentage of women in prison compared to their male counterparts. It is true that in most countries women constitute between 5 and 10 percent of imprisoned populations.

> On average only one out of every twenty prisoners is a woman. Women constitute roughly 50 percent of the population of any country, yet provide only 5 per cent of its prisoners. . . . This is not specific to any one country or region, but is reflected all over the world. There are variations. In Spain, the proportion of women in prison is 10 per cent, in the United States over 6 percent, in France 4 per cent, in Russia 3 per cent and in Morocco it is 2 percent. But nowhere in the world do women make up more than one in ten of the whole [prison] population.[4]

What is rarely taken into consideration, however, is the fact that modes of punishment are both racialized and gendered in ways that indicate a historical continuum linking women's imprisonment with incarceration in mental institutions and with modes of private punishment such as domestic violence.[5] In the context of a developing global prison industrial complex, the relatively small percentages of imprisoned women are now rising. In the United States, the rate of increase in women's incarceration has surpassed the rate of increase in men's.[6] As international women's movements contest patriarchal structures and ideologies, a new consciousness of women's rights in "private" settings has begun to subvert old attitudes of acquiescence toward misogynist violence. However, even as the private punishment of women becomes less hidden from view and less taken for granted, the state-inflicted punishment of women still remains relatively invisible. In the United States and Europe, as well as in countries in which people of European descent are most dominant, women of color are disproportionately targeted by contemporary modes of public punishment. Thus the hyperinvisibility of women's prisons reflects a larger contemporary tendency to incarcerate structures of racism within those institutions that function in public discourse as sites where expendable populations and problems are deposited and hidden away.

According to Mary Helen Washington, "the class, gender, and racial politics of prisons in this country conspire to make most of us feel, not only separate from the world of prison but indifferent to it, untouched and unconcerned."[7] Racialized socioeconomic patterns are camouflaged by representational practices that criminalize poor women and men of color, thereby justifying their imprisonment and allowing the racist structures that affect access to employment, health care, education, and housing to go unrecognized. It may not be entirely fortuitous that California, the first state to abolish affirmative action, also has the largest prison population in the country. It is therefore important to view prisons as productive sites for research on racism and an important opportunity to challenge conservative claims regarding the "end of racism."

In the United States, the current shift from a social welfare state to one prioritizing social control[8] has helped to generate the conditions for an emergent prison industrial complex and has caused the numbers of imprisoned women to rise even more strikingly than those of their male counterparts.[9] As government policies in Canada, in many parts of Europe, and in some African and Latin American countries reveal a similar shift toward larger penal systems, the practice of imprisonment disproportionately affects people of color—not only in the United States but on an international level.[10] In the Netherlands, for example, the imprisoned population has begun to increase significantly for the first time in that country's history, due largely to the influx of black and immigrant men and women who can be found disproportionately in the prisons. While our research on and with imprisoned women in the United States, the Netherlands, and Cuba is largely concerned with the ways women prisoners think about alternatives to incarceration, our study also tries to highlight the gendering of racism in imprisonment practices and in general attempts to address the intersections of class, race, gender, and sexuality as they are perceived and theorized by the women with whom we spoke and as we ourselves attempt to theorize these intersections. In this sense, our project attempts to address issues that exceed both conventional research agendas and activist strategies that treat prisoners—and especially women prisoners—as objects of knowledge or as simply the beneficiaries of liberatory movements.

Collaboration and Access

Having previously met each other through political and intellectual work, in the early 1990s we began to explore the possibility of long-term collaborative research that would allow us to productively draw from our respective training in the humanities and social sciences. In 1993, we were awarded resident research fellowships at the University of California Humanities Research Institute (UCHRI) in connection with its Minority Discourse Initiative which that year called upon fellows to think critically about the normalization of certain social science discourses in relation to public policy. It was in this context that we decided to conduct a series of interview with women prisoners in California. Since the UCHRI is housed on the Irvine campus in Southern California, we planned to interview prisoners at the California Institute for Women (CIW), located in Frontera, a relatively short distance from Irvine.

As activists, we were not unaware of the general difficulties of access to prisons. Nevertheless, we assumed that a legitimate and compelling scholarly project would be accepted by the California Department of Corrections (CDC). However, our instincts as scholars did not adequately reflect our sophistication as political activists, for, despite prompt submission of our application, the CDC never granted us permission to enter the prison. After submitting all the necessary documents to the CDC authorities in charge of approving research proposals, we were led to believe that the approval of our project by the warden at CIW was simply a formality. As we made final preparations for our move to Irvine and for our visits to CIW, we waited to hear from the warden. In further communications with the research department of CDC, we were advised to be patient with the department's slow-moving bureaucracy. However, once we arrived in Irvine and still had not received word from CIW, it became obvious to us that more might be at issue than bureaucratic sluggishness. After numerous messages left at the warden's office went unanswered, the director of the Humanities Research Institute intervened for us, under the assumption that his messages would not be so easily disregarded. While he was never allowed to speak with the warden, he was told by an unidentified official in an off-the-record communication that "Angela Davis would never be allowed inside the California Institute for Women." The warden, the official indicated, felt that she had things under control in the prison and would not allow Angela Davis to come in and "rock the boat." We received the official denial of our request after the proposed research period would already have begun.

Because we were determined to pursue our project with imprisoned women, we decided to investigate the possibility of another interview site. Since Angela had previously taught at the San Francisco County Jail, we decided to submit our project proposal to Michael Morcum, the director of the County Jail system's program facility, who had previously served a sentence in San Quentin and was active during the 1970s in the formation of the California Prisoners' Union. The fact that an access permit came through in a matter of days caused us to think in more complex terms about the ways in which individual administrators are interpolated within the correctional system. Ironically, we had applied for the UCHRI fellowship in Irvine because CIW was in the vicinity and had both moved to Irvine to conduct the interviews. Now we would be required to make numerous research trips to the San Francisco Bay Area during the course of our residence in Southern California. Despite these initial difficulties, we soon recognized that given the San Francisco Program Facility's pioneering efforts to minimize racism within the jail, which we discuss later in this essay, the interviews would be extremely productive.

We interviewed thirty-five of the approximately one hundred women at the San Francisco County Jail's Program Facility. In this section of the County Jail, located in San Bruno, California, male and female inmates were required to participate in "programs"—that is, in educational classes, cultural programs, Alcoholic or Narcotic Anonymous sessions, and organic gardening classes. Men were housed in four dormitories and women in the remaining two. Our interview pool was comprised of women who volunteered to participate after attending a session during which we described our project. In our introductory statements, we described our activist and academic histories, our desire to use a "grounded theory" approach and generally democratic research methods, as well as our hopes that this work would ultimately help to transform public discourses and policies around women in prison. We explained that we were not interested in the women's legal cases and therefore would not ask them to explain to us why they were in jail. Rather, we wanted them to offer their own perspectives about women's imprisonment and about alternatives to incarceration.

As with the other two sites of our study, we first asked for volunteers to participate in focus groups, to help us think about the kinds of questions that would be most productive. That far more women volunteered than we expected may have been a result of our decision not to construct them as research subjects whose criminal histories we wanted to probe. As at the other two sites, women who had not initially volunteered later attempted to join the project as news about the interviews traveled. While we were able to accommodate some of them, we never succeeded in talking to all the women who volunteered. In San Francisco, our interview pool, like the overall jail population, was comprised of an African-American majority, but also Latinas, white women, and one Asian American. However, in the individual interviews, we did not ask different questions based on the assumed racial identities of these women.

While the U.S. component of the research presented huge access problems, we gained entrance to the prison in the Netherlands—Amerswiel Prison for Women—with relative ease. The director, Bernadette van Dam, was herself a well-known advocate of the rights of imprisoned women and, unlike the warden at CIW, welcomed scholarly work designed to make a difference in the lives of women in prison. Angela had visited this prison the previous year and had interviewed the director, as well as several prisoners. When we formally submitted a request to the Dutch Ministry of Justice to conduct interviews at Amerswiel, both the prison director and the Ministry of Justice immediately approved our proposal. While we spent most of our 1996 visit to the Netherlands in Amerswiel, we did have the opportunity to visit two other women's prisons—in Breda and Sevenum—as well as the men's prison in Breda.

Amerswiel Prison is located in the town of Heerhugowaard, thirty miles outside Amsterdam. At the time of our interviews, the prison consisted of four residential units—the Short Term, Long Term, Individual Guidance, and Drug Rehabilitation Units—housing seventy-nine women altogether. With one exception, our interviewees were women in the Short and Long Term Units, which housed twenty-seven and twenty-six women respectively. Approximately half of the women imprisoned in Amerswiel were women of color—of Surinamese, South American, and Asian descent. Our interview pool, consisting of volunteers, comprised approximately the same percentage of women of color.

While our own racial and national backgrounds were sometimes noted by the women we interviewed, it was our status as researchers and prison activists that most interested the women who raised questions about our research project. Virtually all the women we interviewed were aware of the prison director's international advocacy on behalf of women in prison, especially with respect to the rights of imprisoned mothers. In fact, some of the women criticized Bernadette van Dam for devoting more time to public campaigns around imprisoned women than to the women under her direct supervision. They pointed out that they saw more of her on television than in person. In general, however, most of the women expressed their appreciation for her public advocacy. Because of their awareness of the director's work as a prison activist, the prisoners tended to locate our work within a similar political framework. However, when we presented our work to the two groups from which the volunteer pool was selected, we did not attempt to conceal our own leanings toward prison abolitionism. While we were explicit about our interest in the racialization of the prison regime in general and in the awareness of racism exhibited by the prisoners, we raised no specific questions about particular racial groups. In our own discussions about interview strategies, "racial matching" was never really an issue. Therefore both of us conducted interviews with black, Asian, South American, and white Dutch prisoners. Since almost all the prisoners were fluent in English, all our interviews, except those with women from Colombia, were conducted in English. We talked with the Colombian women with the aid of a Spanish-English translator.

The organization of the Cuban component of our research was much more complicated, not only because of the general communication difficulties related to the U.S. embargo on Cuba, but also because we were required to obtain a research license from the U.S. State Department in order to legitimately travel to Cuba. Our Cuban sponsor, the Association of Cuban Women, acted as the intermediary to allow us to gain clearance to visit women's prisons there.

Initially, both of us had planned to make the trip to Cuba. However, just as we had scheduled the trip, Kum-Kum, who had been attempting for some time to adopt, was informed that a baby was available for adoption. Consequently, she faced the dilemma, encountered by many women (and some men), of negotiating a balance between her domestic desires and her research passions. Ultimately she decided that she did not want to be separated from her small baby at such a critical stage in the baby's development and decided to forgo the trip. We decided that Angela should go on with the project, accompanied by one of her students, Isabel Velez, whose bilingual skills would allow her to serve as translator. Since we had previously used a translator in the Dutch prison for interviews with women from South America, we felt a translator would be able to help us again.

Angela and Isabel conducted forty-five interviews at women's prisons in three Cuban provinces—Pinar del Rio, Havana, and Camagüey. At the time of the interviews, there were seventy women in the prison in Pinar del Rio, six hundred in Havana, and one hundred and sixty-three in Camagüey. In accordance with the overall conceptualization of our project, our concerns focused less on the racial identities of our interviewees than on the way in which they perceived and characterized the racial dynamics of the prison regimes. However, it was inevitable that questions about racial identification should arise, especially since racial categories in Cuba are far more fluid than in the United States. Some people with whom we talked indicated that their official identity cards listed them as "white," although they would describe themselves as *mulatta* or *jabao* (the color of a fruit). In fact, many of the women who counted as "white" by Cuban standards, would be characterized as "women of color" by U.S. standards. Therefore, our questions regarding the proportion of women of color in the prison and differential treatment based on race could never be simply answered. As a result, the Cuban component of our project raised by far more the most complicated questions regarding race.

Ethical Dilemmas

In the three sets of interviews we conducted, many of the women expressed their appreciation for what they considered to be better conditions of imprisonment than they imagined to exist elsewhere. At the same time they were emphatic that although they had abundant educational and vocational opportunities, they were still in prison and they had been deprived of their most precious possession, their liberty. That a significant number of the women we interviewed made positive comments about the conditions of their confinement, along with the critiques they proposed, was in part related to the way we chose the sites of our research. In each instance, we had developed relationships either with the authorities directly in charge of the prison or, as in Cuba, had previous relationships with organizations that intervened for us. These relationships were based on our own respect for the comparatively progressive penal methods employed in each of the sites. However, our own prison politics are best described as abolitionist,[11] and at no time did we attempt to conceal our political leanings from the authorities. As a result, the space we negotiated for our research was fraught with contradictions. Like the women prisoners who constantly pointed out—in the Netherlands, for example—that despite the creature comforts they enjoyed, they were still in prison, or—in California—that regardless of the prison's antiracist and antihomophobic policies, they were still in prison, or—in Cuba—that regardless of their prospects of reintegrating themselves into society, they were still in prison, we too continually reminded ourselves that the purpose of our research was to point to the possibility of handling much behavior legally constructed as "crime" without resorting to imprisonment.

As we have reflected on our research, our one overarching dilemma with its methodological and ethical dimensions has been precisely this: how do we balance our abolitionist perspective with our role as scholars and as human beings who clearly recognize that the prisons in which we worked did indeed provide relatively liveable conditions for the women who inhabited them? As we conducted our field research, we talked at length about how we might best draw on the progressive aspects of the penal settings and regimes we were studying and simultaneously negotiate a relationship between our ultimate political aims and the need to affirm the importance of humane conditions of confinement for women and men in prison. A constant theme of our discussions was how we might be able to forge a productive research and activist agenda out of the tension between our ultimate goal of prison abolition and our recognition that penal reform is also essential, if only to improve the daily lives of the millions who have been removed from the free world. Given the historical tendency of reform movements to strengthen prison institutions and discourses,[11] we were especially concerned about how to locate our work within a larger long-term political project of opposing the prison industrial complex and of arresting the proliferation of prisons.

Even as we recognized the power circuits that flowed through the research process and through the prison systems we were studying, we tried to forge collaborative relationships in our conversations with the prisoners. By not withholding information about our political motives and goals and by not treating the women as individuals whom we expected to generate knowledge about themselves to be later collectivized by the researchers, we hoped to demonstrate the possibility of more democratic approaches to research. Just as we did not want to address them as representatives of their respective racial groups, nor did we want to treat them as somehow representing a class of prisoners who could benefit from but not act as agents in an emancipatory political project. When it proved difficult for our interviewees to imagine social landscapes in which prisons were not prominent features, we did not assume that it was any easier for us, despite our adherence to abolitionism. As researchers and as prisoners, we struggled with the same overwhelming ideological constraints.

A related dilemma was whether to interview the administrative and custodial staff in the prisons we studied. Because we did not want to convey the impression to our primary interviewees that we were approaching them with preconceptions and biases acquired from the administrators and guards, we initially decided against interviewing prison personnel. Although we did not naively assume that it was possible to obtain ideas from the prisoners that were "pure" and unmediated, we did feel that this was the best way to achieve our goal of involving imprisoned women in a larger conversation about the radical transformation of punishment systems. However, early on in the actual interview process, we realized that we needed certain information that could only be provided by the administrators and guards. As a result, we decided that while we would talk with prison officials, these interviews would take place only after we had completed our interviews with the prisoners.

We did not treat this methodological decision as a satisfactory solution to our quandary, but rather recognized that practical decisions sometimes highlight the artificiality and abstractness of theoretical research frameworks. Seemingly contradictory on-the-ground decisions can open up new paths of inquiry. Moreover, this decision led us to acknowledge that just as we had tried to avoid essentializing the women we interviewed in relation to their racial backgrounds and their status as prisoners, civilian and uniformed prison personnel were also more than representatives of the state. Ironically, this particular decision to interview prison personnel yielded some interesting results, especially with respect to the official contract that prisoners at the San Francisco County Jail Program Facility were required to sign, agreeing to adhere to the announced antiracist, antisexist, and antihomophobic policies of the jail.

Researching Racism

Throughout the world, prisons are predictably the most consistently multiracial and multicultural locations,[12] making them not only important sites for negative inquiry but also productive sites for positive multicultural, multiracial alliance building. Of course, race is understood differently in different national contexts. Based on the long history of antiracist social movements in the United States, racism in this country is often understood to refer to institutional and individual discrimination against black, Latino, Native American, and Asian-American people. In Europe, *racism* is viewed as synonomous with *xenophobia.* Thus in the Netherlands, which often prides itself—though not always justifiably—as being the least racist country in Europe, responses to our questions about racism tended to focus on attitudes toward foreigners, rather than on racism by white Dutch people against nonwhite Dutch citizens.

In the Program Facility at the San Francisco County Jail, specific efforts were undertaken to minimize racism, sexism, and homophobia in the operation of the jail. In fact, according to the director, each prisoner was required to sign the following contract upon being booked into the Program Facility in which she or he agreed not to engage in racist, sexist, or homophobic behavior:

> I understand that I am required to treat others and myself with respect and dignity. I understand that racism, sexism, anti-gay/lesbian remarks, glorification of substance abuse or criminal behavior and any other form of anti-social behavior will result in loss of privileges, extra work duty or removal from the program facility.[13]

This clause in the contract provided jail personnel with the leverage to avoid a more complicated discussion of racism, as jail rules barred prisoners from exhibiting perceptibly racist behavior. Because antiracism was constructed as a jail rule implemented by guards and administrators, it was linked to the regimes of power and surveillance and attributed to the prisoners as subjects of prison authority. Discussions with the jail personnel who thought of themselves as progressive revealed that they were proud of their pioneering roles as overseers charged with identifying potential violations of the antiracist, antisexist, and antihomophobic rule. In a sense, this pattern was a microcosmic reflection of the larger contemporary proclivity to relegate the process of minimizing racism to the U.S. legal sphere—which constitutes the subject as a rational, free *individual*—and to use legal prohibitions as evidence of the decline of racism in civil society.[14]

However, many of the prisoners we interviewed—both women of color and white—noticed a disparity between the official policy and the treatment they received, thus proposing astute political analyses regarding the persistence of racism within a putatively antiracist framework. One woman said that some guards treated prisoners differently based on their racial backgrounds. Her observations regarding the racism of deputies contested the relegation of racist behavior to the prisoners.[15] She described incidents in which she and other black women were severely limited in the amount of time they were allowed to use the telephone, whereas the deputies allowed a white prisoner to stay on the pay phone for several hours. She said that she and a group of her black friends had consciously monitored certain deputies' practices of allowing white prisoners to spend much more time on the telephone than prisoners of color. This was an obvious example of everyday strategies of resistance to racism within the jail.

Given the shifting definitions of racism referred to above, we were not entirely surprised that the questions we asked women prisoners about the impact of racism within the prison setting did not always travel well from one research site to another. Since our questions were informed by popular and scholarly discourses on race in the United States, they were most easily understood by and most directly answered by prisoners, guards, and administrators alike at the jail in San Francisco. One interviewee in the Netherlands indicated that there was little overt discussion of racism in the prison, but that she was planning to raise this issue with the prison authorities in the near future.[16] Responses by a substantial number of our interviewees in the Netherlands helped us understand the implicit xenophobia that informed attitudes and behavior toward prisoners from South America. A Colombian woman said: "There's a lot of racism here. If you're Colombian, black or from another country they don't give you anything. . . . There's nothing for [Dutch] people . . . in jail, and less if they are Colombian."[17] Another South American woman also criticized the xenophobic attitudes of the custodial personnel when she told us about her skin rash that had gone untreated: "It's not normal that my skin is like this and I've got a rash. It's already twenty days [that I have been] asking for the doctor. If I'd been Dutch, the doctor would have shown up immediately."[18]

A white Dutch woman was critical of the general tendency on the part of the Dutch to represent themselves as egalitarian:

> I always feel attracted to other cultures. But I didn't catch it by birth, because my mother and father are totally white, and they were very . . . yeah, I think my father was a racist, in a way that he doesn't speak it aloud, but in his thinking, like I've seen with many Dutch, they say, "I am not a racist," but if you see their behavior, you can see that their behavior has racist elements.[19]

She also pointed to the pattern among prison guards and administrators of infantilizing prisoners from South America: "So if they deal with the Spanish women, they deal with them like they're not grown-up people. Like they're dealing with children, you know? And I am very much irritated by that type of approach. I hate it. I really hate it."[20] She also indicated that there was a pattern of belittling non-Dutch-speaking prisoners, and particularly women whose cultural and language practices involved gesticulating with their hands. Our interviews in the Dutch prison thus revealed that women of color were not the only prisoners who had thought about the workings of racism. In fact, one white Dutch woman, expressing her solidarity with the women from South America, indicated that she was attempting to learn Spanish in order to communicate with her coprisoners.[21]

In Cuba, the prisoners' reluctance to engage in discussions about race seemed to be linked to the way in which popular discourses on race and racism are overdetermined by the particular history of racism in the United States and by Cuban solidarity with antiracist activists in black, Puerto Rican, and Native American movements. They talked with ease about such figures as Martin Luther King and Malcolm X, and although most of the prisoners were too young to have experienced the Cuban solidarity campaign which developed around Angela's case during the early seventies, many of them had learned about her history as well. Because our questions about race and racism were generally understood within a U.S. context, all the interviewees insisted that racism was neither an issue in the prison nor in society at large. When we asked one woman whether she felt there was a way to talk about race that was enlightening and not indicative of discrimination, she answered, " Yes, you can talk about it in order to unify instead of separate or discriminate. The more unity there is between people, white and black, there would be a better world, more unified."[22] She also felt that people in the United States might learn important lessons from Cuba in the quest for racial equality.

The administrators' observations about the role of race in the prison context both reflected and diverged from prisoners' comments. In Cuba, for example, the prison directors and guards, like the prisoners themselves, tended to interpret questions referring to race as questions about racial discrimination. In San Francisco, questions about race and racism led administrators to refer us to the contract each prisoners was required to sign upon entering the program facility. However, the Sheriff of San Francisco, who is in charge of the county jail system, initiated discussion about the disproportionately high numbers of black and brown prisoners in his jails. He indicated that his responsibility as sheriff required a special sensitivity toward prisoners of color as he instituted social programs for inmates.

Just as administrators of the Program Facility in San Francisco tended to interpret questions about racism as synonomous with race relations among the prisoners, so in the Netherlands, the director of Amerswiel Prison responded to our questions about racism by focusing on relations between prisoners, especially between white Dutch women and women from South America. Further, her comments suggested to us that the enforced equality of prison—where each one is equally deprived of certain rights and liberties, regardless of race—makes it an interesting test of the limits of liberal thinking around racism.

Conclusion

Many of the contradictions we confronted—our knowledge that prisoners were ubiquitous subjects of research, the discrepancies between official policy and everyday practice, the fact that denials of entry arrived too late to matter, that assurances of equality could proliferate, and that equality was imagined as the morally correct action of each free individual toward the other backed up by the force of a state that would never be analyzed as a subject—were about the nature of a liberal system and the limits of a research methodology that would fail to address its own hegemonic context first and last. The prisoner from the Netherlands told us she was learning Spanish in order to communicate with her fellow prisoners is a far better example of how to create a just society than a state like California that abolishes affirmative action and bilingual education, while building more prisons to hold those populations who cannot fail to be endlessly misapprehended by the system. Thus, the "results" of our research exceed the scope of most research agendas that can be imagined around prisoners, including even those that might be significant, like gathering information about health care in prison, family relations and social welfare, and even racism.

The prison was our best research site not because conditions are so bad there but because the segmentation of the prison system away from our consciousness allows the liberal state to manage its population. To attempt to solve the problem of racism without considering the most degraded of its subjects would be contrary to any analytic agenda. Still, the information garnered in this process would also outstrip its intended uses, since learning the language of those with whom you seek to build community is not only a means toward bettering conditions in prison but toward their betterment in the free world outside.

NOTES

1. See Kum-Kum Bhavnani, *Talking Politics: A Psychological Framing for Views from Youth in Britain* (Cambridge: Cambridge University Press, 1991). See especially chapter 3.

2. Elliot Currie, *Crime and Punishment in America* (New York: Henry Holt, 1998), p. 16.

3. Willen de Haan, *The Politics of Redress, Crime, Punishment and Penal Abolition* (London: Unwin, Hyman, 1990), p. 37. See also Willen de Haan, "Abolitionism and the Politics of 'Bad Conscience,'" in *Abolitionism: Toward a Non-Repressive Approach to Crime,* edited by Herman Bianchi and Rene van Swaaningen (Amsterdam: Free University Press, 1986), p. 158.

4. Vivien Stern, *A Sin against the Future: Imprisonment in the World* (London: Penguin Books, 1998), p. 138.

5. See Angela Y. Davis, "Public Imprisonment, Private Violence: Reflections on the Hidden Punishment of Women," *New England Journal on Criminal and Civil Confinement* 24, no. 2 (summer 1998): 339–49.

6. Since 1980, the U.S. imprisoned female population has increased by 275 percent, while the male population has increased by 160 percent. Marc Mauer and Tracy Huling, *Young Black Men and the Criminal Justice System: Five Years Later* (Washington, D.C.: The Sentencing Project, 1995).

7. Mary Helen Washington, "Prison Studies as Part of American Studies," *American Studies Newsletter* 22, no. 1 (March 1999): 1.

8. See Katherine Beckett, *Making Crime Pay: Law and Order in Contemporary American Politics* (New York: Oxford University Press, 1997).

9. Mauer and Huling, *Young Black Men and the Criminal Justice System*.

10.

All around the world the same pattern can be seen. Prisons contain higher proportions than would be expected of people from groups that suffer from racism and discrimination. How does this disproportion happen? There are many reasons, often related to blatant discrimination in the wider society, and crude racism by the law enforcement agencies. Sometimes the disproportion arises from policies which concentrate minorities in poor areas and restrict their opportunities. Often the criminal justice processes tend to discriminate against minorities, sometimes in very subtle ways. . . . The cumulative effect of all this discrimination is the disproportionate number of minorities in the prisons of the world. (Stern, *A Sin against the Future,* p. 117)

11. Ruth Wilson Gilmore, "Globalization and U.S. Prison Growth: From Military Keynesianism to Post-Keynesian Militarism," *Race and Class* 40, nos. 2/3 (1998–99): 171–88. See also Michel Foucault, *Discipline and Punish: The Birth of the Prison,* translated by Alan Sheridan (New York: Vintage, 1979). Originally published in English in 1977.

12. In Australia, for example, although aboriginal people constitute only 1 to 2 percent of the general population, they comprise 30 percent of the imprisoned population. Stern, *A Sin against the Future.*

13. From the contract drawn up by the San Francisco Sheriff's Department.

14. See Kimberlé Crenshaw, Neil Gotanda, Gary Peller, and Kendall Thomas, eds. *Critical Race Theory: The Key Writings That Formed the Movement* (New York: New Press, 1995).

15. Interview at San Francisco County Jail, Program Facility, November 1993.

16. Interview at Amerswiel Prison for Women, April 1996.

17. Interview at Amerswiel Prison for Women, April 1996.

18. Interview at Amerswiel Prison for Women, April 1996.

19. Interview at Sevenum Prison, April 1996.
20. Ibid.
21. Interview at Amerswiel Prison for Women, April 1996.
22. Interview at the Prison for Women in Havana, June 1997.

Afterword
Racism and the Research Process

Howard S. Becker

This volume concerns itself with the problems introduced into the research process by the fact that the people doing the research and those whose lives are, for lack of a better term, "being made social science of" are identified (in the United States and most other countries) by race—by themselves, by each other, and by the eventual readers of the research. These problems are not easily summarized, let alone solved, and I propose to deal with just a few that seem to me especially salient.

Let's begin with what seems a mundane (though by no means minor) problem that many of the authors report. You, the researcher, are doing your field work, interviewing someone or participating in a social event or occasion as an observer, and someone says something blatantly racist. Since you likely regard yourself as a political liberal or radical (most social scientists do) and certainly not a racist, this poses an immediate practical problem. What do you *do*? Do you voice disapproval, and thus risk alienating the very people on whose goodwill and cooperation your research in some measure depends? Do you swallow your convictions and keep quiet, and thus give implicit support to racism by allowing its public expression to go unchallenged? What if the people who are voicing the racist ideas and sentiments are themselves members of subordinate groups, perhaps the very victims of racism themselves? Bangladeshis, we're told, speak bitterly and rudely about blacks, and some blacks speak in a racist way about Jews (though, in the case reported here, not in the actual presence of the Jewish fieldworker). And some white people, of course, are forever saying terrible things about members of all the other groups. And if you do hear this material because you are a member of the very oppressed group whose members uttered it, do you then report that you heard it (adding to the burdens of an oppressed group the problems of being labeled racist), and risk being charged with ethnic disloyalty and with betraying friends who have helped you?

Some of the authors in this volume speak of these problems woefully, resentfully, resignedly; a few are even optimistic, believing that they have found a way out. Everyone would like to find The Right Solution, both instrumentally (in terms of successfully completing the fieldwork) and politically and morally (that is, preserving one's self-respect by not permitting one's silence to suggest complicity).

Nothing I have read here looks like that kind of solution and there is, it seems to me, an obvious reason for this: no simple solution exists to be discovered. My personal impulse would be to keep quiet, that there will be better occasions and more effective ways to fight racism than getting into an argument with someone from whom you want information. But that might not be such a good idea either, if the people you're working with are, say, members of the radical right who, if they catch you supressing facts about yourself that eventually come out, might decide you are a dangerous infiltrator who needs to be dealt with radically. It will be easier, of course, if they're people with whom you feel some common ground.

Alain Touraine, Michel Wieviorka, and their colleagues have pioneered the use of a method they call intervention, which is one kind of solution (see the description in, for instance, Wieviorka 1993: 299–310). They interviewed members of a group—to take an example, members of the Italian Red Brigades, who had fled Italy and were living in Paris—at length, in groups, over some period of time, in repeated sessions. The members spoke repeatedly and critically about workers, capitalists, politicians, police, and others. Finally, Wieviorka said he was going to bring members of those groups to confront the accusations the members were making. And he did. The ensuing dialogue, in which he was primarily a bystander—albeit occasionally also a provocateur—challenged the stereotyped commentary of the members, surely more effectively than would have been the case had Wieviorka done it himself.

But that solution is seldom available in the looser, less controlled situations in the field our authors describe. They mostly work in the world as it is, not as they have remade it for their research. They don't get to invite people to talk to one another, though they get to be there when and if members of different groups do talk to each other.

What's involved here is balancing multiple, but conflicting, goods. To speak in the simplest terms, racism is bad, so opposing it publicly is good; but understanding a racist situation so that it can be dealt with effectively is also a good thing, though it might require you to keep quiet in order to learn more about what you are trying to change. Getting information that allows you to do your research is a good thing, but getting punished when your duplicity is discovered is certainly a bad thing. And so on.

Another problem arises when researchers want to maximize the political effectiveness of their research, a goal often summarized as doing "activist research." Many social scientists would like their work to have practical results, to be useful in a good cause, in this case to be of real use in the fight against racism. They speak of "antiracist research." But few social scientists have succeeded in having much impact on public policy and political action, although we often claim credit for having done so. When there has been an effect that might reasonably be attributed to social science research, the results are like as not the exact opposite of what the researchers intended. So the many social scientists—Erving Goffman, Thomas Szasz, Michel Foucault, and others—who wrote about the evils of mental hospitals were surely describing real abuses. And their writings may have played a role in the closing down of many hospitals and the freeing of many people from that kind of incarceration. It's more likely that their work was part of a general shift in public discussion and thinking, what Herbert Blumer called a "cultural drift," that cannot be traced to anything as specific as the work of any social scientist or group of them. And it's almost surely true that one of the first major implementations of this policy, the closing of state hospitals in California, was due mainly to then-Governor Ronald Reagan's realization that state expenditures could be dramatically cut this way. In any event, the results of what was called "deinstitutionalization" did not measure up to the hopes that had been entertained. Instead, many people see this social-science-inspired action as one of the likely causes of the "homeless problem."

When we are honest with ourselves, we realize that, for the most part, we don't have much effect on anything. Several generations of social scientists, beginning with Alfred Lindesmith (1947), have done research whose clear message was that the legal prohibition of drugs has no good effects and many harmful ones, one of them being the racially selective application of the laws. Some people have been convinced by such arguments, among them many law-enforcement officials in the United States and elsewhere, and many mayors of cities in the United States. But the effect on public policy and on the racial consequences of the laws has been negligible, even though this is a case in which the evidence is quite one-sided. (It is unlikely that the philanthropist George Soros was so influenced. His Open Society Foundation has sponsored the Lindesmith Center, which has actively supported, financially and otherwise, initiatives proposing real changes in the drug laws in several U.S. states. Naming the center after a pioneer in this field of research probably testifies to some kind of influence's having occurred. But the influence is, to say the least, indirect.)

Here again some judgment has to be exercised. Is there any way to know that the results of my work will have an effect and, if so, one I and people for whose good I want to work will be happy with? And if I can't know that, is it smart to pursue that goal?

Still another problem suggested by but not central to this volume stems from the variable meaning of race. Although we all talk from time to time as though it were obvious that some people are black and some are white and some are Latino and some are Asian, and so on, you can never tell for sure. People who are white in one context are black in another. As the authors further attest, to say that someone is black or white or Asian does not tell you much about that person anyway. These groups, far from being monolithic, are internally differentiated by class, gender, and along a variety of other axes.

To say that you can't be sure what race someone is misstates the problem. It is not as though you could tell if you only had more information. Race gets attributed to actors and acted on by them from moment to moment in the course of the interactions they are involved in. It operates when the participants invoke it and is ignored, in favor of other distinctions, when they think it less relevant. This is a lesson taught by pragmatists and symbolic interactionists—interaction is built up from moment to moment. The outcome of a sequence of interaction in unpredictable. We can't foretell its ending from what we know of the people and the situation as it begins. Whether the people involved will be identified, by themselves or others, as members of this or that racial group is just not predictable by us or them across contexts. That we can often make a pretty good guess doesn't make racial identity any less problematic.

Which is not to say that race doesn't have consequences when people don't deliberately invoke it or when they aren't even, in some sense, conscious of it. Several chapters in this book explain just how people fail to invoke it when being racially conscious would be inconvenient or unpleasant. But much of the discussion centers on the problems that arise when people *are* aware of racial positions, their own and that of the people they are doing fieldwork with.

One such problem is the question of so-called "racial matching" in the field. Everett Hughes used to say that the great barriers to communication in almost any society (and certainly in the ones anthropologists and sociologists mainly concern themselves with these days) were age, sex, class, and race. These are the lines across which people find it hard to trust one another, hard to understand one another, and hard to believe that the other understands them. Hughes didn't mean to suggest that people can't communicate across these lines, only that there are difficulties that presumably don't arise when the people involved are just alike in all these ways (which does not mean, either, that there are no difficulties when people are alike in these respects.)

Wittgenstein wrote, in *Philosophical Investigations* (Wittgenstein 1973: 223), "If a lion could talk, we could not understand him." He meant, I think, that the lion's way of life was so different from ours that there would be nothing to talk about, no feature of life that would be of mutual interest or mutually intelligible. I always wanted to make an addition to his remark, so that it read, "If a lion could talk, we could not understand him, *at first.*" That is, if we interacted with the lion over some period of time, we would have something in common, if only our interaction. We and the lion might not understand our interaction in the same way, but our ideas and observations wouldn't be totally unintelligible to one another either. We'd have something to talk about. And might well find ways of reaching some kind of agreement on what things were, how they worked, what had been done, what should be done—all that. As the interaction proceeded, presumably things would continue to come up about which we and the lion might have misunderstandings, and those misunderstandings might or might not be resolved.

So it can't be taken for granted that problems of communication arise automatically from people's differing along the major social axes.

Neither can it be taken for granted that, once solved, they are solved permanently. These are things that fieldworkers, and everyone else who is reflective about social life, know. But we sometimes ignore their implications when we start to theorize and deliver general pronouncements. One crucial implication is that there is no general rule that tells us when people who differ in these ways will be able to understand one another and when they won't. It's possible that coexisting over some period of time will lead to some kind of (certainly not total) understanding, but that's certainly not guaranteed, since the parties may have good reason to conceal things from each other.

A difficult problem that arises from racial differences in the field has to do with researchers' responsibilities to the people they write about. Many people who study race relations are concerned that their research do no harm to the people they work with or to causes they sympathize with. They are concerned, more specifically, that their work not give aid or comfort, however unintentionally, to the forces of racism, intolerance, and oppression. So they try to make sure that their work is at least not racist in its approach, analysis, and consequences.

But that is not so easy. How can authors be sure that their work won't be misconstrued or misused? How can they know that they haven't, in fact, done something that will allow that kind of misuse, that their work doesn't suffer from some flaw that they haven't detected? We have learned, over the years, that what was at one time standard practice has later turned out to have unsuspected racist or sexist overtones and implications. Practices and ideas that seem progressive in one era are likely to seem reactionary or at least partially wrong headed decades down the road. Survey researchers routinely "solved" the problem of measuring social class by asking the occupation of an interviewee's father; many still do, as though the mother had nothing to do with it. The people who do this now may not be sexist themselves, just lazy, but their work could reasonably be argued to be sexist. The people who did it fifty years ago were—well, what were they? It's hard to say they were sexist; they didn't yet know there was a problem.

And that is a general problem: how can we avoid the mistakes we aren't aware of, because no one has yet called them to public attention?

The risks here are subtle and multiple. We can encourage racism inadvertently by listening to its expression in silence. We can use categories that embody assumptions that accept racial distinctions and generalizations that are unwarranted by any evidence. We can do work whose findings will be used to harm the interests of people who we think have already suffered enough harm. This volume calls our attention to just such difficulties.

Doing research is always risky, personally, emotionally, ideologically, and politically, just because we never know for sure just what results our work will have.

The authors in this book have run these risks, thoughtfully and courageously. They have done their best and have told us, in the kind of detail that will help the rest of us do our research in ways that, in the words of the documentary photographer Lewis Hine, show us what needs to be appreciated and what needs to be changed.

REFERENCES

Blumer, Herbert. 1969. *Symbolic Interactionism.* Englewood Cliffs, N.J.: Prentice Hall.

Foucault, Michel. 1965. *Madness and Civilization.* New York: Random House.

Lindesmith, Alfred. 1947. *Opiate Addiction.* Bloomington, Ind.: Principia Press.

Szasz, Thomas. 1961. *The Myth of Mental Illness.* New York: P. B. Hoechler.

Wieviorka, Michel. 1993. *The Making of Terrorism.* Chicago: University of Chicago Press.

Wittgenstein, Ludwig. 1973. *Philosophical Investigations: The English Text of the Third Edition.* New York: Prentice Hall.

Bibliography

Abu-Lughod, Lila. 1986. *Veiled Sentiments: Honor and Poetry in a Bedouin Society.* Berkeley: University of California Press.

———. 1991. "Writing against Culture." In *Recapturing Anthropology: Working in the Present,* edited by Richard G. Fox, pp. 137–62. Santa Fe, N.M.: School of American Research Press.

———. 1993. *Writing Women's Words: Bedouin Stories.* Berkeley: University of California Press.

Adler, Patricia, and Peter Adler. 1995. "The Demography of Ethnography." *Qualitative Sociology* 24 (1): 3–29.

Agar, Michael. 1980. *The Professional Stranger.* New York: Academic Press.

Aguilar, John L. 1981. "Insider Research: An Ethnography of a Debate." In *Anthropologists at Home in North America: Methods and Issues in the Study of One's Own Society,* edited by Donald A. Messerschmidt. Cambridge: Cambridge University Press.

Allen, Theodore. 1994. *The Invention of the White Race.* New York: Verso.

Almaguer, Tomas. 1994. *Racial Fault Lines: The Historical Origins of White Supremacy in California.* Berkeley: University of California Press.

Altorki, Saraya. 1988. "At Home in the Field." In *Arab Women in the Field: Studying Your Own,* edited by Soraya Altorki and Camillia Fauzi El-Solh, pp. 49–68. Syracuse: Syracuse University Press.

Anderson, Margaret L. 1993. "Studying across Difference: Race, Class, and Gender in Qualitative Research." In *Race and Ethnicity in Research Methods,* edited by John Stanfield II and Dennis M. Rutledge. Newbury Park, Calif.: Sage.

Andrews, George Reid. 1991. *Blacks and Whites in São Paulo, 1888–1988.* Madison: University of Wisconsin Press.

Anthropology Newsletter. 1996 (November). "Prizes and Awards." 10.

———. 1997 (May). "Prizes and Awards." 24.

Appadurai, Arjun. 1996. *Modernity at Large: Cultural Dimensions of Globalization.* Minneapolis: University of Minnesota Press.

Argueta, Manlio. 1983. *One Day of Life.* New York: Vintage Books.

Banerjee, Sumanta. 1989. "Marginalization of Women's Popular Culture in

Nineteenth Century Bengal." In *Recasting Women: Essays in Colonial History,* edited by Kumkum Sangari and Sudesh Vaid. New Delhi: Kali for Women.

Barkun, Michael. 1994. *Religion and the Racist Right: The Origins of the Christian Identity Movement.* Chapel Hill: University of North Carolina Press.

Baumgartner, M. P. 1988. *The Moral Order of a Suburb.* New York: Oxford University Press.

Beatty, Paul. 1996. "Taken out of Context." *Granta* 53 (spring): 167–94.

Becker, Howard S. 1970. *Sociological Work: Methods and Substance.* New Brunswick, N.J.: Transaction Books.

Beckett, Katherine. 1997. *Making Crime Pay: Law and Order in Contemporary American Politics.* New York: Oxford University Press.

Bell, Diane, Pat Caplan, and Wazir Jahan Karim. 1993. *Gendered Fields: Women, Men, and Ethnography.* New York: Routledge.

Benmayor, Rina, Rosa Torruellas, and Anna Juarbe. 1992. "Responses to Poverty among Puerto Rican Women: Identity, Community, and Cultural Citizenship." New York: Centro de Estudios Puertorriqueños, Hunter College. Report to the Joint Committee for Public Policy Research on Contemporary Hispanic Issues of the Inter-University Program for Latino Research and the Social Science Research Council.

Beoku-Betts, Josephine. 1994. "When Black Is Not Enough: Doing Field Research among Gullah Women." *NWSA Journal* 6 (3): 413–33.

Bernstein, Richard. 1995. "Entering Young Drug Dealers' Minds." *New York Times,* December 27: B6.

Bhavnani, Kum-Kum. 1991. *Talking Politics: A Psychological Framing for Views from Youth in Britain.* Cambridge: Cambridge University Press.

Binford, Leigh. 1996. *The El Mozote Massacre, Anthropology, and Human Rights.* Tucson: University of Arizona Press.

Blauner, Robert. 1972. *Racial Oppression in America.* Berkeley: University of California Press.

Blauner, Robert, and David Wellman. 1998. "Toward the Decolonization of Social Research." In *The Death of White Sociology: Essays on Race and Culture,* edited by Joyce Ladner. Baltimore: Black Classic Press. Originally published in 1973.

Blee, Kathleen M. 1991. *Women of the Klan: Racism and Gender in the 1920s.* Berkeley: University of California Press.

———. 1996. "Becoming a Racist: Women in Contemporary Ku Klux Klan and Neo-Nazi Groups." *Gender & Society* 10 (6): 680–702.

———. 1998a. "Reading Racism: Women in the Modern Hate Movement." In *No Middle Ground: Women and Radical Protest,* edited by Kathleen M. Blee, 180–98. New York: New York University Press.

———. 1998b. "White-Knuckle Research: Emotional Dynamics in Fieldwork with Racist Activists." *Qualitative Sociology* 21 (4): 381–99.

Blumer, Herbert. 1969. *Symbolic Interactionism*. Englewood Cliffs, N.J.: Prentice Hall.

Bolles, A. Lynn. 1985. "Of Mules and Yankee Girls: Struggling with Stereotypes in the Field." *Anthropology and Humanism Quarterly* 10 (4): 114–19.

Bonacich, Edna. 1972. "A Theory of Ethnic Antagonism: The Split Labor Market." *American Sociological Review* 37: 547–59.

———. 1973. "A Theory of Middleman Minorities." *American Sociological Review* 38: 583–94.

———. 1980. "Class Approaches to Ethnicity and Race." *Insurgent Sociologist* 10 (2): 9–23.

Bonnett, Alastair. 1996. "Anti-Racism and the Critique of 'White' Identities.'" In *New Community: The Journal of the European Research Centre on Migration and Ethnic Relations* 22 (10): 97–110.

———. 1997. "Constructions of Whiteness in European and American Anti-Racism." In *Debating Cultural Hybridity: Multi-Cultural Identities and the Politics of Anti-Racism,* edited by Pnina Werbner and Tariq Modood, pp. 173–92. London: Zed Books.

Bourdieu, Pierre. 1977. *Outline of a Theory of Practice*. New York: Cambridge University Press. Originally published in 1972.

———. 1984. *Distinction: A Social Critique of the Judgment of Taste,* translated by Richard Nice. Cambridge: Harvard University Press.

Bourgois, Philippe. 1989. *Ethnicity at Work: Divided Labor on a Central American Banana Plantation*. Baltimore: Johns Hopkins University Press.

———. 1995. *In Search of Respect: Selling Crack in El Barrio*. Cambridge: Cambridge University Press.

Breines, Wini. 1992. *Young, White, and Miserable: Growing Up Female in the Fifties*. Boston: Beacon Press.

Brown, Jacqueline. 1998. "Black Liverpool, Black America, and the Gendering of Diasporic Space." *Cultural Anthropology* 13 (3): 291–325.

Brown, Peggy. 1994. "On LI, Race Looms Large." *Newsday,* May 20.

Burdick, John. 1998a. "The Lost Constituency of Brazil's Black Movements." *Latin American Perspectives* 25 (1): 136–55.

———. 1998b. *Blessed Anastácia: Women, Race, and Popular Christianity in Brazil*. New York: Routledge.

Canada, Geoffrey. 1995. *Fist, Stick, Knife, Gun: A Personal History of Violence in America*. Boston: Beacon Press.

Carroll, Rebecca. 1997. *Sugar in the Raw: Voices of Young Black Girls in America*. New York: Crown Trade Paperbacks.

Carter, Donald Martin. 1997. *States of Grace: Senegalese in Italy and the New European Immigration*. Minneapolis: University of Minnesota Press.

Chan, Sucheng. 1991a. *Asian Americans: An Interpretive History.* Boston: Twayne Publishers.

———. 1991b. *Asian Californians.* San Francisco: MTL/Boyd & Fraser.

Chang, Edward T., and Russell Leong, eds. 1994. *Los Angeles—Struggles toward Multiethnic Community.* Seattle: University of Washington Press.

Chatterjee, Partha. 1989. "The Nationalist Resolution of the Women's Question." In *Recasting Women: Essays in Colonial History,* edited by Kumkum Sangari and Sudesh Vaid. New Delhi: Kali for Women.

Chin, Frank, Jeffery Chan, Lawson F. Inada, and Shawn Wong, eds. 1974. *An Anthology of Asian American Writers.* Washington, D.C.: Howard University Press.

Clifford, James, and George Marcus, eds. 1986. *Writing Culture: The Poetics and Politics of Ethnography.* Berkeley: University of California Press.

Collins, Patricia Hill. 1990. *Black Feminist Thought: Knowledge, Consciousness, and the Politics of Empowerment.* New York: Routledge.

———. 1991. "Learning from the Outsider Within: The Sociological Significance of Black Feminist Thought." In *Beyond Methodology: Feminist Scholarship as Lived Research,* edited by Mary Margaret Fonow and Judith A. Cook, pp. 35–59. Bloomington: Indiana University Press.

Currie, Elliot. 1998. *Crime and Punishment in America.* New York: Henry Holt.

Davis, Angela Y. 1998. "Public Imprisonment, Private Violence: Reflections on the Hidden Punishment of Women." *New England Journal on Crime and Civil Confinement* 24 (2): 339–49.

Davis, James F. 1993. *Who Is Black? One Nation's Definition.* University Park: Pennsylvania State University Press.

D'Amico-Samuels, Deborah. 1991. "Undoing Fieldwork: Personal, Political, Theoretical, and Methodological Implications." In *Decolonizing Anthropology: Moving Further toward an Anthropology for Liberation,* edited by Faye Harrison, pp. 68–87. Washington, D.C.: American Anthropological Association.

Degler, Carl. 1971. *Neither Black nor White: Slavery and Race Relations in Brazil and the United States.* New York: Macmillan.

De Haan, Willen. 1986. "Abolitionism and the Politics of 'Bad Conscience.'" In *Abolitionism: Toward a Non-Repressive Approach to Crime,* edited by Herman Bianchi and Rene van Swaaningen. Amsterdam: Free University Press.

———. 1990. *The Politics of Redress, Crime, Punishment and Penal Abolition.* London: Unwin, Hyman.

Denzin, Norman. 1989. *The Research Act: A Theoretical Introduction to Sociological Methods.* Englewood Cliffs, N.J.: Prentice Hall.

Denzin, Norman, and Yvonna S. Lincoln, eds. 1994. *Handbook of Qualitative Research.* Thousand Oaks, Calif.: Sage.

DeVault, Marjorie. 1995. "Ethnicity and Expertise: Racial-Ethnic Knowledge in Sociological Research." *Gender & Society* 9 (5): 612–31.

Devine, John. 1996. *The New Panopticon: The Construction of Violence in Inner City High Schools.* Chicago: University of Chicago Press.

Di Leonardo, Micaela. 1998. *Exotics at Home: Anthropologies, Others, American Modernity* (Women in Culture and Society). Chicago: University of Chicago Press.

Doane, Ashley W., Jr. 1995. "Dominant Group Ethnic Identity in the United States: The Role of 'Hidden' Ethnicity in Intergroup Relations." *Sociological Quarterly* 38 (3): 375–97.

Drake, St. Clair, and Horace Cayton. 1945. *Black Metropolis: A Study of Negro Life in a Northern City.* New York: Harcourt, Brace, and World.

Dunbar, Paul Laurence. 1967. "We Wear the Mask." In *Lyrics of Lowly Life.* Seacaucus, N.J.: Citadel Press.

Duneier, Mitchell. 1999. *Sidewalk.* New York: Farrar, Straus and Giroux.

Dyer, Richard. 1988. White. *Screen* 29 (fall): 44–64.

———. 1997. *White.* New York: Routledge.

Edwards, Rosalind. 1990. "Connecting Method and Epistemology: A White Woman Interviewing Black Women." *Women's Studies International Forum* 13 (5): 477–90.

Ellis, Carolyn. 1995. "Emotional and Ethical Quagmires in Returning to the Field." *Journal of Contemporary Ethnography* 24 (1): 68–98.

Espiritu, Yen Le. 1997. *Asian American Women and Men.* Thousand Oaks, Calif.: Sage.

Essed, Philomena. 1991. *Understanding Everyday Racism: An Interdisciplinary Theory* (Sage Series on Race and Ethnic Relations, volume 2). Newbury Park, Calif.: Sage.

———. 1994. "Contradictory Positions, Ambivalent Perceptions: A Case Study of a Black Woman Entrepreneur." *Feminism and Psychology* (special issue entitled *Shifting Identities, Shifting Racisms*): 99–118.

Fabian, Johannes. 1983. *Time and the Other: How Anthropology Makes Its Object.* New York: Columbia University Press.

Facio, Elisa. 1993. "Ethnography as Personal Experience." In *Race and Ethnicity in Research Methods,* edited by John H. Stanfield II and Rutledge Denis. Newbury Park, Calif.: Sage.

Fanon, Frantz. 1967. *The Wretched of the Earth.* Harmondsworth, England: Penguin.

Feagin, Joe R., and Melvin P. Sikes. 1994. *Living with Racism: The Black Middle-Class Experience.* Boston: Beacon Press.

Figueira, Vera Moreira. 1990. "O Preconceito Racial na Escola." *Estudos Afro Asiáticos* 18: 63–72.

Fine, Gary Alan. 1993. "Ten Lies of Ethnography: Moral Dilemmas of Field Research." *Journal of Contemporary Ethnography* 22 (3): 267–94.

Fisher, Maxine P. 1980. *The Indians of New York City: A Study of Immigrants from India.* New Delhi: Heritage Publishers.

Flagg, Barbara. 1997. "Transparently White Subjective Decision Making." In *Critical White Studies: Looking behind the Mirror,* edited by Richard Delgado and Jean Stefancic, pp. 220–26. Philadelphia: Temple University Press.

Foley, Douglas E. 1990. *Learning Capitalist Culture: Deep in the Heart of Tejas.* Philadelphia: University of Pennsylvania Press.

———. 1995. *The Heartland Chronicles.* Philadelphia: University of Pennsylvania Press.

Fordham, Signithia. 1988. "Racelessness as a Factor in Black Students' School Success: Pragmatic Strategy or Pyrrhic Victory?" *Harvard Educational Review* 53: 257–93.

Foucault, Michel. 1965. *Madness and Civilization.* New York: Random House.

Fox, Richard. 1991. *Recapturing Anthropology: Working in the Present.* Santa Fe, N.M.: School of American Research Press.

Frankenberg, Ruth. 1993. *White Women, Race Matters: The Social Construction of Whiteness.* Minneapolis: University of Minnesota Press.

———. 1997. *Dis-Placing Whiteness: Essays in Social and Cultural Criticism.* Durham: Duke University Press.

Fry, Peter. 1995–96. "O que a Cinderela Negra Tem a Dizer Sobre a Politica Racial no Brasil." *Revista USP* 28 (dez.–fev.): 122–35.

Gallagher, Charles. 1995. "White Reconstruction in the University." *Socialist Review* 94 (1/2): 165–88.

———. 1997a. "Redefining Racial Privilege in the United States." *Transformations* 8 (1): 28–39.

———. 1997b. "White Racial Formation: Into the Twenty-First Century." In *Critical White Studies: Looking Behind the Mirror,* edited by Richard Delgado and Jean Stefancic. Philadelphia: Temple University Press.

Gilliam, Angela. 1970."From Roxbury to Rio and Back in a Hurry." *Journal of Black Poetry* 1: 8–12.

Gilmore, Ruth Wilson. 1998–99. "Globalization and U.S. Prison Growth: From Military Keynesianism to Post Keynesian Militarism." *Race and Class* 40 (2/3): 171–88.

Giroux, Henry. 1997a. *Channel Surfing: Race Talk and the Destruction of Today's Youth.* New York: St. Martin's Press.

———. 1997b. "Racial Politics and the Pedagogy of Whiteness." In *Whiteness: A Critical Reader,* edited by Mike Hill, pp. 294–315. New York: New York University Press.

———. 1997c. "White Squall: Resistance and the Pedagogy of Whiteness." *Cultural Studies* 11 (3): 376–89.

Glaberson, William. 1990. "Trapped in the Terror of New York's Holding Pens." *New York Times,* March 23: A1, B4.

Glazer, Nathan, and Daniel P. Moynihan. 1963. Beyond the Melting Pot. Cambridge: M.I.T. Press.

Goffman, Erving. 1959. *The Presentation of Self in Everyday Life.* New York: Anchor Books.

Golde, Peggy, ed. 1970. *Women in the Field: Anthropological Experiences.* Berkeley: University of California Press.

Gordon, Milton. 1964. *Assimilation in American Life: The Role of Race, Religion, and National Origins.* New York: Oxford University Press.

Gordon, Ted. 1998. *Disparate Diasporas.* Austin: University of Texas Press.

Green, Linda. 1994. "Fear as a Way of Life." *Cultural Anthropology* 9 (2): 227–56.

Guimarães, Antonio Sérgio Alfredo. 1995. "Racism and Anti-Racism in Brazil: A Postmodern Perspective." In *Racism and Anti-Racism in World Perspective,* edited by Benjamin Bowser, pp. 108–226. Newbury Park, Calif.: Sage.

Gutierrez, David G. 1995. *Walls and Mirrors: Mexican Americans, Mexican Immigrants, and the Politics of Ethnicity.* Berkeley: University of California Press.

Gwaltney, John L. 1976. "Going Home Again—Some Reflections of a Native Anthropologist." *Phylon* 30: 236–42.

———. 1980. *Drylongso: A Self-Portrait of Black America.* New York: Random House.

Hall, Stuart. 1981. "The Whites of Their Eyes: Racist Ideologies and the Media." In *Silver Linings: Some Strategies for the Eighties,* edited by G. Bridges and R. Brunt. London: Lawrence and Wishart.

Hamm, Mark S. 1993. *American Skinheads: The Criminology and Control of Hate Crimes.* New York: Praeger.

Hanchard, Michael G. 1994. *Orpheus and Power: The Movimento Negro of Rio de Janeiro and São Paulo, 1945–1988.* Princeton: Princeton University Press.

Harper, Dean. 1994. "What Problems Do You Confront? An Approach to Doing Qualitative Research." *Qualitative Sociology* 17 (10): 89–95.

Harris, Marvin. 1952. "Race Relations in Minas Velhas: A Community in the Mountain Region of Central Brazil." In *Race and Class in Rural Brazil,* edited by Charles Wagley, pp. 47–81. Paris: UNESCO.

———. 1956. *Town and Country in Brazil.* New York: Columbia University Press.

Harrison, Faye. 1991. "Ethnography as Politics." In *Decolonizing Anthropology: Moving towards an Anthropology for Liberation,* edited by Faye Harrison, pp. 88–109. Washington, D.C.: Association of Black Anthropologists/American Anthropological Association.

Hartigan, John, Jr. 1997a. "Establishing the Fact of Whiteness." *American Anthropologist* 88 (3): 495–505.

———. 1997b. "Locating White Detroit." In *Displacing Whiteness: Essays in Social and Cultural Criticism,* edited by Ruth Frankenberg. Durham: Duke University Press.

Hartman, Heidi. 1981. "The Unhappy Marriage of Marxism and Feminism: Towards a More Progressive Union." In *Women and Revolution,* edited by Lydia Sargent. London: Pluto.

Hatchett, Shirley, and Howard Schuman. 1975–76. "White Respondents and Race-of-Interviewer Effects." *Public Opinion Quarterly* 39 (4): 523–28.

Hempel, C. 1952. "Typological Methods in the Natural and Social Sciences." In *Science, Language, and Human Rights,* edited by the American Philosophical Association, vol. 1, pp. 65–86. Philadelphia: American Philosophical Association.

Hochschild, Jennifer L. 1995. *Facing Up to the American Dream.* Princeton: Princeton University Press.

hooks, bell. 1981. *Ain't I a Woman: Black Women and Feminism.* Boston: South End Press.

———. 1990. *Yearning: Race, Gender, and Cultural Politics.* Boston: South End Press.

———. 1992. "Representing Whiteness in the Black Imagination." In *Cultural Studies,* edited by Lawrence Grossberg, Cary Nelson, and Paula Treichler. New York: Routledge.

Hurtado, Aída. 1994. "Does Similarity Breed Respect? Interviewer Evaluations of Mexican-Descent Respondents in a Bilingual Survey." *Public Opinion Quarterly* 58: 77–95.

Hutchinson, Harry W. 1952. "Race Relations in a Rural Community of the Bahian Recôncavo." In *Race and Class in Rural Brazil,* edited by Charles Wagley, pp. 16–46. Paris: UNESCO.

———. 1957. *Village and Plantation Life in Northeastern Brazil.* Seattle: University of Washington Press.

Hyman, Herbert, et. al. 1954. *Interviewing in Social Research.* Chicago: University of Chicago Press.

Ignatiev, Noel. 1995. *How the Irish Became White.* New York: Routledge.

Ignatiev, Noel, and John Garvey, eds. 1996. *Race Traitor.* New York: Routledge.

Islam, Naheed. 1993. "In the Belly of the Multicultural Beast I Am Named South Asian." In *Our Feet Walk The Sky: Women of the South Asian Diaspora,* edited by the Women of South Asian Descent Collective. San Francisco: Aunt Lute.

———. In press. "Race Markers Transgressors: Mapping a Racial Kaleidoscope within an (Im)migrant Landscape." In *American Encounters,* edited by Rajini Srikanth, Roshni Rustomji-Kerns, and Leny Strobel. Boston: Rowan and Littlefield.

Jackson, Kenneth T. 1985. *Crabgrass Frontier: The Suburbanization of the United States*. New York: Oxford University Press.

Jayawardena, Kumari. 1995. *The White Woman's Other Burden: Western Women and South Asia during British Rule*. New York: Routledge.

Jeansonne, Glen. 1996. *Women of the Far Right: The Mother's Movement and World War II*. Chicago: University of Chicago Press.

Jenkins, Janis Hunter. 1991. "The State Construction of Affect: Political Ethos and Mental Health among Salvadoran Refugees." *Culture, Medicine, and Psychiatry* 15 (2): 139–65.

Jensen, Joan M. 1988. *Passage from India: Asian Indian Immigrants in North America*. New Haven: Yale University Press.

Jibou, Robert M. 1988. *Ethnicity and Assimilation: Blacks, Chinese, Filipinos, Japanese, Koreans, Mexicans, Vietnamese, and Whites*. Albany: State University of New York Press.

John, Mary E. 1989. "Postcolonial Feminists in the Western Intellectual Field: Anthropologists and Native Informants?" *Inscriptions* 5: 49–73.

Jones, Delmos. 1982. "Towards a Native Anthropology." In *Anthropology for the Eighties: Introductory Readings*, edited by Johnetta B. Cole, pp. 471–82. New York: Free Press. Originally published in 1970.

Jordon, Winthrop D. 1977. *White over Black: American Attitudes towards the Negro, 1550–1812*. New York: Norton.

Kelly, Barbara. 1993. *Expanding the American Dream: Building and Rebuilding Levittown*. Albany: State University of New York Press.

Kenny, Lorraine Delia. In press. *Daughters of Suburbia: Growing Up White, Middle Class, and Female*. New Brunswick: Rutgers University Press.

Kim, Choong Soon. 1977. *An Asian Anthropologist in the South: Field Experiences with Blacks, Indians and Whites*. Knoxville: University of Tennessee Press.

Kim, Elaine H. 1982. *Asian American Literature: An Introduction to the Writings and Their Social Context*. Philadelphia: Temple University Press.

Kleinman, Arthur. 1995. *Writing at the Margin: Discourse between Anthropology and Medicine*. Berkeley: University of California Press.

———. 1997. "Social Suffering: Everything That Really Matters." Colloquium Presented to the Anthropology Department, University of California, Berkeley, November 3.

Kondo, Dorinne K. 1986. "Dissolution and Reconstruction of Self: Implications for Anthropological Epistemology." In *Cultural Anthropology* 1 (1): 74–88.

———. 1990. *Crafting Selves: Power, Gender, and Discourses of Identity in a Japanese Workplace*. Chicago: University of Chicago Press.

Kottak, Conrad Phillip. 1990. *Prime-Time Society: An Anthropological Analysis of Television and Culture.* Belmont, Calif.: Wadsworth.

Kulick, Don, and Margaret Willson. 1995. *Taboo: Sex, Identity and Erotic Subjectivity in Anthropological Fieldwork.* London: Routledge.

Kumar, Nita. 1992. *Friends, Brothers, and Informants: Fieldwork Memoirs of Banaras.* Berkeley: University of California Press.

Ladner, Joyce. 1998. *The Death of White Sociology: Essays in Race and Culture.* Baltimore: Black Classic Press. Originally published in 1973.

Lewin, Ellen, and William Leap. 1996. *Out in the Field: Reflections of Lesbian and Gay Anthropologists.* Urbana: University of Illinois Press.

Liddle, Joanna, and Rama Joshi. 1986. *Daughters of Independence: Gender, Caste and Class in India.* New Brunswick: Rutgers University Press.

Light, Ivan, and Edna Bonacich. 1988. *Immigrant Entrepreneurs: Koreans in Los Angeles.* Berkeley: University of California Press.

Límon, José E. 1991. "Representation, Ethnicity, and the Precursory Ethnography: Notes of a Native Anthropologist." In *Recapturing Anthropology: Working in the Present,* edited by Richard Fox. Santa Fe, N.M.: School of American Research (Advanced Seminar Series).

———. 1994. *Dancing with the Devil: Society and Cultural Poetics in Mexican-American South Texas.* Madison: University of Wisconsin Press.

Lindesmith, Alfred. 1947. Opiate Addiction. Bloomington, Ind.: Principia Press.

Lipsitz, George. 1995. "The Possessive Investment in Whiteness: Racialized Social Democracy and the 'White' Problem in American Studies." *American Quarterly* 47 (3): 369–87.

Loewen, James W. 1971. *The Mississippi Chinese: Between Black and White.* Prospect Heights, Ill.: Waveland Press.

Lofland, John, and Lyn H. Lofland. 1984. *A Guide to Qualitative Observations and Analysis,* 2d ed. Belmont, Calif.: Wadsworth.

López, Ian F. Haney. 1996. *White by Law: The Legal Construction of Race.* New York: New York University Press.

Lowe, Lisa. 1996. *Immigrant Acts: Asian American Cultural Politics.* Durham: Duke University Press.

MacLeod, Jay. 1987. *Ain't No Makin' It: Leveled Aspirations in a Low-Income Neighborhood.* Boulder, Colo.: Westview Press.

Malcolm X. 1964. *The Autobiography of Malcolm X.* New York: Grove Press.

Marable, Manning. 1993. "Beyond Racial Identity Politics: Towards a Liberation Theory for Multicultural Democracy." *Race and Class* (1): 113–30.

Marcus, George E. 1998. *Ethnography through Thick and Thin.* Princeton: Princeton University Press.

Marcus, George, and Michael M. Fischer, eds. 1986. *Anthropology as Cultural Critique: An Experimental Moment in the Human Sciences.* Chicago: University of Chicago Press.

Martin-Baro, Ignacio. 1990. "De la Guerra Sucia a la Guerra Psicologica." *Revista de Psicologia de El Salvador* 31: 109–22.

Mauer, Marc, and Tracy Huling. 1995. *Young Black Men and the Criminal Justice System: Five Years Later.* Washington, D.C.: The Sentencing Project.

Maykovich, Minado Kurokawa. 1977. "The Difficulties of a Minority Researcher in Minority Communities." *Journal of Social Issues* 33 (4): 108–19.

Maynard, Mary, and June Purvis, eds. 1994. *Researching Women's Lives from a Feminist Perspective.* London: Taylor and Francis.

Mazumdar, Sucheta. 1989. "Race and Racism: South Asians in the United States." In *Frontiers of Asian American Studies.* Pullman: Washington State University Press.

McGinty, Derek. 1997. "Race Issues in Brazil." In *The Derek McGinty Show,* December 19. American Public Radio: Washington, D.C.

McIntosh, Peggy. 1992. "White Privilege and Male Privilege: A Personal Account of Coming to See Correspondences through Work in Women's Studies." In *Race, Class and Gender: An Anthology,* edited by Patricia Hill Collins. Belmont, Calif.: Wadsworth.

Melendy, H. Brett. 1981. *Asians in America: Fillipinos, Koreans, and East Indians.* New York: Hippocrene Press.

Memmi, Albert. 1991. *The Colonizer and the Colonized.* Expanded edition. Introduction by Jean Paul Sartre. Boston: Beacon Press. Originally published by Orion Press in 1965.

Merton, Robert. 1972. "Insiders and Outsiders: A Chapter in the Sociology of Knowledge." *American Journal of Sociology* 78 (July): 9–47.

Messerschmidt, Donald. 1981. *Anthropologists at Home in North America: Methods and Issues in the Study of One's Own Society.* Cambridge: Cambridge University Press.

Michalowski, Raymond J. 1996. "Ethnography and Anxiety: Field Work and Reflexivity in the Vortex of U.S.–Cuban Relations." *Qualitative Sociology* 19 (1): 59–82.

Min, Pyong Gap. 1996. *Caught in the Middle: Korean Merchants in America's Multiethnic Cities.* Berkeley: University of California Press.

Morrison, Toni. 1992. *Playing in the Dark: Whiteness in the Literary Imagination.* New York: Vintage Books.

Nader, Laura. 1972. "Urban Anthropologist Perspectives Gained from Studying Up." In *Reinventing Anthropology,* edited by Dell Hymes, pp. 284–311. New York: Pantheon.

———. 1988. "Up the Anthropologist—Perspectives Gained from Studying Up." In *Anthropology for the Nineties: Introductory Readings,* edited by Johnetta B. Cole. New York: Free Press.

Naples, Nancy. 1996. "A Feminist Revisiting of the Insider/Outsider Debate:

The 'Outsider Phenomenon' in Rural Iowa." *Qualitative Sociology* 19 (1): 83–106.

Narayan, Kirin. 1993. "How Native Is a 'Native' Anthropologist?" *American Anthropologist* 95: 671–86.

Nascimento, Abdias. 1989. *Brazil: Mixture or Massacre: Essays in the Genocide of a Black People.* Dover, Mass.: Majority Press. Originally published in 1979.

Nordstrom, Carolyn. 1997. *A Different Kind of War Story* (Ethnography of Political Violence). Philadelphia: University of Pennsylvania Press.

O'Connell Davidson, Julia. 1995. "British Sex Tourists in Thailand." In *(Hetero)sexual Politics,* edited by M. Maynard and J. Purvis. London: Taylor and Francis.

Ogbu, John. 1995. "Cultural Problems of Minority Education: Their Interpretations and Consequences—Part 2: Case Studies." *Urban Review* 27 (4): 271–97.

Okely, Judith, and Helen Callaway, eds. 1982. *Anthropology and Autobiography.* New York: Routledge.

Okihiro, Gary Y. 1994. *Margins and Mainstreams: Asians in American History and Culture.* Seattle: University of Washington Press.

Omi, Michael, and Howard Winant. 1986. *Racial Formation in the United States: From the 1960s to the 1990s.* New York: Routledge. Originally published in 1986.

Ong, Paul, Edna Bonacich, and Lucie Cheng. 1994. *The New Asian Immigration in Los Angeles and Global Restructuring.* Philadelphia: Temple University Press.

Ortner, Sherry B. 1991. "Reading America: Preliminary Notes on Class and Culture." In *Recapturing Anthropology: Working in the Present,* edited by Richard G. Fox. Santa Fe, N.M.: School of American Research Press.

Park, Kyeyoung. 1997. *The Korean American Dream: Immigrants and Small Business in New York City.* Ithaca: Cornell University Press.

Park, Robert E. 1950. *Race and Culture.* Glencoe, Ill.: Free Press.

Patai, Daphne. 1988. *Brazilian Women Speak: Contemporary Life Stories.* New Brunswick: Rutgers University Press.

Pedelty, Mark. 1995. *War Stories: The Culture of Foreign Correspondents.* New York: Routledge.

Phoenix, Ann. 1994. "Practising Feminist Research: The Intersection of Gender and 'Race' in the Research Process." In *Researching Women's Lives from a Feminist Perspective,* edited by Mary Maynard and June Purvis. London: Taylor and Francis.

Portes, Alejandro, and Ruben G. Rumbaut. 1990. *Immigrant America: A Portrait.* Berkeley: University of California Press.

Powdermaker, Hortense. 1939. *After Freedom: A Cultural Study in the Deep South.* New York: Atheneum.

Quesada, James. In press. "From Central American Warriors to San Francisco Day Laborers: Suffering and Exhaustion in a Trans-National Context." In *Transforming Anthropology.*

Ramos, Guerreiro A. 1957. *Introdução Crítica a Sociologia Brasileira.* Rio de Janeiro: Andes.

Reichmann, Rebecca. 1995. "Brazil's Denial of Race." *NACLA Report on the Americas* 28 (6) 35–44.

Reinharz, Shulamit. 1992. *Feminist Methods in Social Research.* New York: Oxford University Press.

Rhodes, Penny J. 1994. "Race-of-Interviewer Effects: A Brief Comment." *Sociology: The Journal of the British Sociological Association* 28 (2): 547–58.

Rodríguez, Clara E. 1991. *Puerto Ricans: Born in the U.S.A.* Boulder, Colo.: Westview Press. Originally published in 1989.

———. 1995. "Puerto Ricans in Historical and Social Science Research." In *Handbook of Research on Multicultural Education,* edited by James A. Banks. New York: Macmillan.

Roediger, David. 1991. *The Wages of Whiteness: Race and the Making of the American Working Class.* New York: Verso.

———. 1994. *Toward the Abolition of Whiteness: Essays on Race, Politics and the Working Class.* New York: Verso.

Root, Maria P. 1992. *Racially Mixed People in America.* Newbury Park, Calif.: Sage.

Roy, Beth. 1998. "Goody Two-Shoes and the Hell-Raisers: Women's Activism, Women's Reputations in Little Rock." In *No Middle Ground: Women and Radical Protest,* edited by Kathleen M. Blee, pp. 96–132. New York: New York University Press.

Sansone, Livio. 1996. "As Relações Raciais em Casa Grande e Senzala: Revisitadas a Luz do Processo de Internacionalização e Globalização." In *Raça, Ciencia e Sociedade,* edited by Marcos Chor Maio and Ricardo Ventura Santos, pp. 207–18. Rio de Janeiro: Editora Fiocruz.

Schemo, Diana Jean. 1994. "Facing Big-City Problems: L.I. Suburbs Try to Adapt." *New York Times,* March 16.

Scheper-Hughes, Nancy. 1992. *Death without Weeping: The Violence of Everyday Life in Brazil.* Berkeley: University of California Press.

———. 1996. "Small Wars and Invisible Genocides." *Social Science and Medicine* 43 (5): 889–900.

Schneider, David M. 1980. *American Kinship: A Cultural Account.* Chicago: University of Chicago Press. Originally published in 1968.

Schuman, Howard, and Jean M. Converse. 1971. "The Effects of Black and

White Interviewers on Black Responses in 1968." *Public Opinion Quarterly* 35 (1): 44–68.

Schutte, Gerhard. 1991. "Racial Oppression and Social Research: Field Work under Racial Conflict in South Africa." *Qualitative Sociology* 14 (2): 127–46.

Segrest, Mab. 1994. *Memoir of a Race Traitor.* Boston: South End Press.

Sherriff, Robin. 1997. Untitled. Ph.D. diss., City University of New York.

Simpson, Amelia. 1993. *Xuxa: The Mega-Marketing of Gender, Race and Modernity.* Philadelphia: Temple University Press.

Simpson, Jennifer S. 1996. "Easy Talk, White Talk, Back Talk: Some Reflections on the Meanings of Our Words." *Journal of Contemporary Ethnography* 25 (3): 372–89.

Skeggs, Beverly. 1994. "Situating the Production of Feminist Ethnography." In *Researching Women's Lives from a Feminist Perspective,* edited by Mary Maynard and June Purvis. London: Taylor and Francis.

Skidmore, Thomas E. 1993. *Black into White: Race and Nationality in Brazilian Thought.* Durham: Duke University Press. Originally published in 1974.

Smith, Dorothy. 1987. "Women's Perspective as a Radical Critique of Sociology." In *Feminism and Methodology: Social Science Issues,* edited by Sandra Harding. Bloomington: Indiana University Press.

Sniderman, Paul M., and Thomas Piazza. 1993. *The Scar of Race.* Cambridge: Harvard University Press.

Stanfield, John H., II. 1994. "Ethnic Modeling in Qualitative Research." In *Handbook of Qualitative Research,* edited by Norman Denzin and Yvonna S. Lincoln. Thousand Oaks, Calif.: Sage.

Stanfield, John H., II, and Dennis M. Rutledge, eds. 1993. *Race and Ethnicity in Research Methods.* Newbury Park, Calif.: Sage.

Stern, Vivian. 1998. *A Sin against the Future: Imprisonment in the World.* London: Penguin Books.

Stoler, Ann Laura. 1991. "Carnal Knowledge and Imperial Power: Gender, Race, and Morality in Colonial Asia." In *Gender at the Crossroads of Knowledge: Feminist Anthropology in a Postmodern Era,* edited by Micaela di Leonardo. Berkeley: University of California Press.

Szasz, Thomas. 1961. *The Myth of Mental Illness.* New York: P. B. Hoechler.

Takaki, Ronald, ed. 1987. *From Different Shores: Perspectives on Race and Ethnicity in America.* New York: Oxford University Press.

———. 1989. *Strangers from a Different Shore: A History of Asian Americans.* Boston: Little Brown.

Tamale, Sylvia R. 1996. "The Outsider Looks In: Constructing Knowledge about American Collegiate Racism." *Qualitative Sociology* 19 (4): 471–95.

Tatum, Beverly. 1997. *Why Are All the Black Kids Sitting Together in the Cafeteria?* New York: Basic Books.

Taussig, Michael. 1987. *Shamanism, Colonialism, and the Wild Man: A Study in Terror and Healing.* Chicago: University of Chicago Press.

Taylor, Charles. 1985. *Philosophy and the Human Sciences* (Philosophical Papers, vol. 2). Cambridge: Cambridge University Press.

Telles, Eduardo, and E. Murguia. 1990. "Phenotypic Discrimination and Income Differences among Mexican Americans." *Social Science Quarterly* 71 (4): 682–93.

Thomas, Piri. 1967. *Down These Mean Streets.* New York: Knopf.

Tripura, Prashanta. 1992. "The Colonial Foundation of Pahari Ethnicity." In *Journal of Social Studies* 58 (October): 1–16. Dhaka: Centre for Social Studies.

Turner, J. Michael. 1991. "Brown into Black: Changing Racial Attitudes of Afro-Brazilian University Students." In *Race, Class, and Power in Brazil,* edited by Pierre-Michel Fontaine. Los Angeles: Center for Afro-American Studies, University of California.

Twine, France Winddance. 1996a. "O Hiato de Gênero Nas Percepções de Racismo: O Caso dos Afro-Brasileiros Socialmente Ascendentes." *Estudos Afros-Asiáticos* 29 (March): 37–54.

———. 1996b. "Brown-Skinned White Girls: Class, Culture and the Construction of White Identity in Suburban Communities." *Gender, Place, and Culture* 3 (2): 205–24.

———. 1997a. "Mapping the Terrain of Brazilian Racism." *Race and Class* 38 (3): 49–61.

———. 1997b. "Brown-Skinned White Girls: Class, Culture, and the Construction of White Identity in Suburban Communities." In *Displacing Whiteness: Essays in Social and Cultural Criticism,* edited by Ruth Frankenberg. Durham: Duke University Press.

———. 1998. *Racism in a Racial Democracy: The Maintenance of White Supremacy in Brazil.* New Brunswick: Rutgers University Press.

———. 1999a. "Bearing Blackness in Britain: The Meaning of Racial Difference for White Birth Mothers of African-Descent Children." *Social Identities: Journal of Race, Nation and Culture* 5, no. 2 (June 1999): 185–210.

———. 1999b. "Transracial Mothering and Anti-Racism: The Case of White Mothers of 'Black' Children in Britain," *Feminist Studies* 25, no. 3 (fall): 729–46.

Twine, France Winddance, Jonathan W. Warren, and Francisco Fernandiz. 1991. *Just Black? Multiracial Identity.* New York: Filmakers Library.

Valentine, Charles A., and Betty Lou Valentine. 1970. "Making the Scene, Digging the Action, and Telling It Like It Is: Anthropologists at Work in a Dark Ghetto." In *Afro-American Anthropology: Contemporary Perspectives,* edited by Norman E. Whitten, Jr., and John F. Szwed. New York: Free Press.

Varenne, Hervé, ed. 1986. *Symbolizing America*. Lincoln: University of Nebraska Press.

Visweswaran, Kamala. 1994. *Fictions of Feminist Ethnography*. Minneapolis: University of Minnesota Press.

Wacquant, Loic. 1993. "Décivilisation et démonisation: la mutation du ghetto noir americain." In *L'Amerique des francais*, edited by Christine Faure and Tom Bishop, pp. 103–25. Paris: Editions Français Bourin.

Wagley, Charles. 1972. *Race and Class in Rural Brazil*. Paris: UNESCO Press. Originally published in 1952.

Waldinger, Roger. 1996. "When the Melting Pot Boils Over: The Irish, Jews, Blacks, and Koreans of New York." In *The Bubbling Cauldron*, edited by Michael Peter Smith and Joe R. Feagin. Minneapolis: University of Minnesota Press.

Wallace, Roderick. 1988. "A Synergism of Plagues: 'Planned Shrinkage,' Contagious Housing Destruction, and 'AIDS in the Bronx.'" *Environmental Research* 47: 1–33.

Ware, Vron. 1992. *Beyond the Pale: White Women, Racism, and History*. London: Verso.

Warren, Carol A. 1988. *Gender Issues in Field Research*. Qualitative Research Methods Series, vol. 9. Newbury Park, Calif.: Sage.

Warren, Jonathan W. 1997. "O Fardo de Não Ser Negro: Uma Análise Comparativa do Desempenho Escolar de Alunos Afro-Brasileiros e Afro-Norte-Americanos." *Estudos Afro-Asiáticos* 31: 103–24.

———. In press. *Contesting White Supremacy: Indian Resurgence in Brazil*. Durham: Duke University Press.

Warren, Jonathan, and France Winddance Twine. 1997. "Whites, the New Minority? Non-Blacks and the Ever-Expanding Boundaries of Whiteness." *Journal of Black Studies* 28 (2): 200–218.

Washington, Mary Helen. 1999. "Prison Studies as Part of American Studies." *American Studies Newsletter* 22, 1 (March).

Waters, Mary C. 1990. *Ethnic Options: Choosing Identities in America*. Berkeley: University of California Press.

Wellman, David T. 1977. *Portraits of White Racism*. Cambridge: Cambridge University Press.

West, Cornel. 1993. "The New Cultural Politics of Difference." In *The Cultural Studies Reader*, edited by Simon During. New York: Routledge.

Whitehead, Tony Larry. 1986. "Breakdown, Resolution, and Coherence: The Fieldwork Experiences of a Big, Brown, Pretty-Talking Man in a West Indian Community." In *Self, Sex, and Gender in Cross-Cultural Fieldwork*, edited by Tony Larry Whitehead and Mary Ellen Conaway. Urbana: University of Illinois Press.

Whitehead, Tony Larry, and Mary Ellen Conaway, eds. 1986. *Self, Sex, and Gender in Cross-Cultural Fieldwork*. Urbana: University of Illinois Press.

Whitten, Jr., Norman E. 1974. *Black Frontiersmen: Afro-Hispanic Culture of Ecuador and Columbia*. Prospect Heights, Ill.: Waveland Press.

Wieviorka, Michel. 1993. *The Making of Terrorism*. Chicago: University of Chicago Press.

Williams, Brackette F. 1995. "Skinfolk, Not Kinfolk: Comparative Reflections on the Identity of Participant-Observation in Two Field Situations." In *Feminist Dilemmas in Field Research*, edited by Diane Wolf. Boulder, Colo.: Westview Press.

Williams, Raymond. 1977. *Marxism and Literature*. New York: Oxford University Press.

Willis, Paul. 1977. *Learning to Labor: How Working Class Kids Get Working Class Jobs*. Aldershot, England: Gower.

Wilson, William Julius. 1974. "The New Black Sociology: Reflections on the 'Insiders' and the 'Outsiders' Controversy." In *Black Sociologists: Historical and Contemporary Perspectives*, edited by James E. Blackwell and Morris Janowitz. Chicago: University of Chicago Press.

———. 1978. *The Declining Significance of Race*. Chicago: University of Chicago Press.

Winant, Howard. 1994. *Racial Conditions: Politics, Theory, Comparisons*. Minneapolis: University of Minnesota Press.

Wittgenstein, Ludwig. 1973. *Philosophical Investigations: The English Text of the Third Edition*. New York: Prentice Hall.

Wolf, Diane L., ed. 1996. *Feminist Dilemmas in Fieldwork*. Boulder, Colo.: Westview Press.

Wolf, Eric. 1990. "Distinguished Lecture: Facing Power—Old Insights, New Questions." *American Anthropologist* 92 (3): 586–96.

Wolin, Sheldon. 1969. "Political Theory as a Vocation." *American Political Science Review* 63 (December): 1062–82.

Wong, Sau-Ling Cynthia. 1993. *Reading Asian American Literature: From Necessity to Extravagance*. Princeton: Princeton University Press.

Wrigley, Julia. 1998. "From Housewives to Activists: Women and the Division of Political Labor in the Boston Antibusing Movement." In *No Middle Ground: Women and Radical Protest*, edited by Kathleen M. Blee, pp. 251–88. New York: New York University Press.

Zavella, Patricia. 1993. "Feminist Insider Dilemmas: Constructing Ethnic Identity with Chicana Informants." *Frontiers: A Journal of Women Studies* 13 (3): 53–76.

Zinn, Maxine Baca. 1979. "Field Research in Minority Communities: Ethical, Methodological and Political Observations by an Insider." *Social Problems* 27 (2): 209–19.

Contributors

Howard S. Becker teaches at the University of California at Santa Barbara. His major books are *Outsiders* (Free Press, 1963), *Art Worlds* (University of California Press, 1982), *Writing for Social Scientists* (University of Chicago Press, 1986), and *Tricks of the Trade* (University of Chicago Press, 1998). In 1998 Becker received the Award for a Career of Distinguished Scholarship from the American Sociological Association.

Kum-Kum Bhavnani is Professor of Sociology and Women Studies at the University of California at Santa Barbara. She is the author of *Talking Politics: A Psychological Framing for Views from Youth in Britain* (Cambridge University Press, 1991) and is coeditor with Kathryn Kent and France Winndance Twine of "Feminisms and Youth Cultures," a special issue of *Signs: Journal of Women in Culture and Society,* vol. 23, no. 3 (spring 1998), and with Ann Phoenix of *Shifting Identities, Shifting Racisms: A Feminism and Psychology Reader* (Sage, 1994). She is a corresponding editor for *Feminist Review,* and a coeditor of the Gender, Racism, Ethnicity series published by Routledge.

Kathleen M. Blee is the Director of Women's Studies and Professor of Sociology at the University of Pittsburgh. She is the author of *Women of the Klan: Racism and Gender in the 1920s* (University of California Press, 1991), and the editor of *No Middle Ground: Women and Radical Protest* (New York University Press, 1998), the coauthor with Dwight B. Billings of *The Road to Poverty: Making Wealth and Poverty in an American Region* (Cambridge University Press, 1999), and the coeditor with France Winndance Twine of *Feminisms and Antiracisms: International Struggles* (forthcoming, New York University Press).

Philippe Bourgois is Chair of the Department of Anthropology, History, and Social Medicine at the University of California, San Francisco. His most recent book, *In Search of Respect: Selling Crack in El Barrio* (Cambridge University Press, 1995) won several awards, including the C. Wright Mills Prize and the Margaret Mead Prize. In addition to *Ethnicity at Work: Divided Labor on a Central American Banana Plantation* (Johns Hopkins Press, 1989) and three coedited volumes, he has also published several dozen academic and popular media articles on political and intimate violence as well as on substance abuse, HIV, inner-city poverty, and ethnic conflict in venues such as *New York Times Magazine, Harper's, Social Problems, Actes de la Recherche en Sciences Sociales, Contemporary Drug Problems, American Anthropologist, British Journal of Criminology, Les Temps Modernes, Cultural Anthropology, Substance Use and Misuse, American Ethnologist,* and *The Nation.*

Angela Y. Davis is Professor of History of Consciousness at the University of California, Santa Cruz. She is the author of *Blues Legacies and Black Feminisms: Gertrude 'Ma' Rainey, Bessie Smith and Billie Holiday* (Pantheon, 1998), *Women, Race, and Class* (Random House, 1981), *Women, Culture and Politics* (Random House, 1984), *Angela Davis: An Autobiography* (Random House, 1974), and the editor of *If They Come in the Morning: Voices of Resistance* (Third Press, 1971).

Mitchell Duneier is an Associate Professor of Sociology at the University of Wisconsin at Madison and the University of California, Santa Barbara. He is the author of *Slim's Table: Race, Respectability, and Masculinity* (University of Chicago Press, 1992) and *Sidewalks* (Farrar, Strauss and Giroux, 1999).

Troy Duster is Professor of Sociology at the University of California at Berkeley and Professor of Sociology and Researcher at the Institute for the History of the Production of Knowledge at New York University. In addition to numerous articles, he is the author of *Backdoor to Eugenics* (1990) and *The Legislation of Morality* (1970) and coeditor of *Cultural Perspectives on Biological Knowledge* (1984) and a member of the National Advisory Council for the Human Genome Research Project.

Charles Gallagher is an Assistant Professor of Sociology at Georgia State University in Atlanta, Georgia. His current research explores the various social meanings whites attach to their race and the political and cultural conditions which give rise to white identity construction. His is currently collecting data for his book, *Beyond Invisibility: The Meaning of Whiteness in Multiracial America.*

Michael G. Hanchard is Associate Professor of Political Science at Northwestern University. He is the author of *Orpheus and Power: The Movimento Negro of Rio de Janeiro and São Paulo, Brazil, 1945–1988* (Princeton University Press, 1994), and the editor of *Racial Politics in Contemporary Brazil* (Duke University Press, 1999).

Naheed Islam is a doctoral candidate in the Sociology Department at the University of California at Berkeley. Her publications include "In the Belly of the Beast I am Named South Asian," in *Our Feet Walk the Sky: Women of the South Asian Diaspora* (Aunt Lute Foundation: San Francisco, 1993); "Naming Desire, Shaping Identity: Tracing the Experiences of Indian Lesbians in America," in *A Patchwork Shawl: Chronicles of South Asian Women in America,* edited by Samita Das Gupta (Rutgers University Press, 1998). She is currently completing her dissertation entitled "The Space between Black and White: Coloring Bangladeshi Immigrants within the Racial Kaleidoscope of Los Angeles."

Lorraine Delia Kenny is the Public Education Coordinator for the American Civil Liberties Union's Reproductive Freedom Project in New York City and is the author of *Daughters of Suburbia: Growing Up White, Middle-Class and Female* (Rutgers University Press, 2000).

France Winddance Twine is an enrolled member of the Muskogee (Creek) Nation of Oklahoma and is Associate Professor of Sociology at the University of California at Santa Barbara and Associate Professor of International Studies at the University of Washington in Seattle. She is the author of *Racism in a Racial Democracy: The Maintenance of White Supremacy in Brazil* (Rutgers University Press, 1998) and the coeditor of three volumes. She has published articles on racism, antiracism, and racial consciousness in interdisciplinary journals including *Estudos Afro-Asiáticos; Journal of Black Studies; Feminist Studies; Gender, Place and Culture; Race and Class; Social Identities: Journal of Race, Nation and Culture;* and *Transition.* She is currently completing *Bearing Blackness in Britain,* an ethnography of racism, reproduction, and nationalism.

Jonathan W. Warren is Assistant Professor of Latin American Studies in the Henry M. Jackson School of International Studies at the University of Washington. He is the author of *Contesting White Supremacy: Indian Resurgence in Brazil* (Duke University, in press), the coproducer of the award-winning documentary *Just Black?* (Filmmaker's Library, 1992), and has published articles on race and education, and whiteness and ethnic cleansing in *Estudos Afro-Asiáticos, Journal of Black Studies,* and *Journal of Historical Sociology.*

Index

Abu-Lughod, 114
activist research, 249
Adler, Patricia, and Peter Adler, 4
affirmative action, 8; and white views in focus groups, 83–84
Africans, conducting fieldwork research in U.S., 11, 15
Aguilar, John, on insider research, 9
American Indians (Native Americans), 106–107, 117, 120
Amerswiel Prison for Women (Netherlands), 234–235
Amityville, Long Island, N.Y., 111
antiblack racism, 18, 48; among Bangladeshi immigrants in U.S., 47–51, 54–55; among Brazilians, 136, 138–141, 152–153, 157; among U.S. whites, 70, 222
Anti Defamation League of B'nai B'rith, 98
antiracism: accountability to racial and ethnic communities, 25–26; antiracist discourses in Britain and the U.S., 23; antiracists, conducting research as, 26, 27, 247–253; antiracist scholars, attacks against, 175–176; and imprisoned women, ability to theorize, 227; measures of, 14; scholarship, 73–74; scholars of color, the risks for, as racial/ethnic insiders, 58–59; transformation of public policy, 227–228; white researchers, risks for, in white communities, 58; white supremacists, deployment of published research by, 26
Anti-Semitism, 93, 106
apartheid, in N.Y. City, 187–190, 204–207, 208
Asian Americans, 40

Asian researchers in U.S., perceptions of, 16
Association of Cuban Women, 229
auto-ethnography, 113; and near-native anthropology, 114

"back talk," 148–150. *See also* white talk
Bangladeshi-Americans, 35–66; and antiblack racism, 25, 47–51, 54–55; in Bangladesh, non-elite experiences, 45–46; and black spouses, 54–55; gender expectations, 42–45; and Hill Peoples in U.S., 52–53; memories of, 54, 57; and Mexican spouses, 54–55; notions of Americanness, racialized, 46; notions of race and racism, 40–41, 54; racist aesthetics, 49; and racism in the U.S., 46, 54
Becker, Howard S., 1, 221
Beoku-Betts, Josephine: on the African researcher as "insider" in cross-national research, 11
Bhavnani, Kum-Kum, 21, 243n. 1
black and brown Brazilians: and antiblack racism 2, 3, 16, 138–139; memories of, 2, 150–151; partner preferences, 157; and racism, perceptions of, 150; and racism, responses to, 153–154; and racism-evasiveness, 16, 151–153; representations of, 136, 181; and U.S. blacks, ambivalent relationship to, 182–183
Black Metropolis: A Study of Negro Life in a Northern City (Drake and Cayton), 225
black researchers, U.S.: in Brazil, 2, 15–16, 18, 19, 165–185; in Cuba, 21; in Jamaica, 17–18; in Latin America, 2;

black researchers, U.S. *(continued)*
in Netherlands, 21, 23; in Thailand, 13;
in the U.S., 11–12, 13; with U.S. black
focus groups, xiv

blacks, U.S.: censorship in presence of non-
blacks, 221; memories (historical knowledge), 123, 150; partner preferences,
158; and racism, perceptions of, 148–
150; and racism, responses to, 148–150;
and whites, perceptions of, 158

blacks, U.S., representations of: as perceived by Brazilians 17–18, 19, 166,
182–183; as perceived by British,
18–19; as perceived by Canadians, 182;
as perceived by Jamaicans, 17–18

Blee, Kathleen: countering uses of her research, 26

Blumer, Herbert, 249

Bonnett, Alastair: on anti-racist discourse
analysis, 23, 74

Bourdieu, Pierre, 201, 208

Bourgois, Philippe, 24–25, 26

Brazil, Bahia, 135–36; Rio de Janeiro,
Zona Norte, 178; Rio de Janeiro, Zona
Sul, 168, 179; São Paulo, 170–173

Brazilian Indians, 150

British communities, racial matching in:
black British researchers on, 13; a white
researcher on, 7, 12

California Department of Corrections
(CDC), 232

California Institution for Women (CIW),
229, 232

Carroll, Rebecca, 148–149

Casa Grande e Senzela (Freyre), 180

Center for Afro-Asiatic Studies, at Candido Mendes University, 168

class and racial blinders, 215–217

Clifford, James, and George Marcus: on
critical ethnography, 21

Collins, Patricia Hill, 41

color-blindness, 111–113, 145

Crenshaw, Kimberlé, et al., 244n. 14

Cuba. *See* incarcerated women, research
among

culture of terror (Taussig), 191

D'Amico-Samuels, Deborah, 22

Davis, Angela Y., 21, 244n. 5

Denzin, Norman, on taking social location for granted, 68

DeVault, Marjorie, 93–94

Devine, John, on culture of violence,
191

discourses, racial, 20–22; in Cuba, 236,
241–42; in Netherlands, 240–41

*Drylongso: A Self-Portrait of Black Amer-
ica* (Gwaltney), 22

Duneier, Mitchell, 23, 26

Dyer, Richard, 74, 114

Ebony, 182

embranquecimento (whitening), 2, 139,
157, 161n. 1; and naming white privilege, 128; promotion of racist ideologies, 100–101

ethnographic representations. *See* representing racial subalterns

ethnoscape (Appadurai), 167

eroticization: of blacks and browns in
Brazil, 19, 179–180; of whites in Brazil,
20, 159; of women researchers in Ban-
glasheshi-American communities, 45

Essed, Philomena, 15, 37, 39, 148

Essence, 182

Facio, Elisa, 12

Fanon, Frantz, 15

Feagin, Joe, and Melvin Sykes, 15, 148

Ferguson, James, 4

Fictions of Feminist Ethnography
(Visweswaran), 113

focus groups: in prison, 234; and white-
on-white researchers, 76, 78

Foley, Douglas, 117

Foucault, Michel, 249

Frankenberg, Ruth, 11, 20, 37, 75, 93,
114, 116, 145–46

Gallagher, Charles A., on white-on-white
insider perspective, 10–11; weaknesses
in survey research on whiteness, 81–82

gender bending, 199–201

Gilmore, Ruth Wilson, 244n. 11

Gilroy, Paul, 183

Giroux, Henry, 74, 75, 83, 84

Goffman, Erving, 44, 249

Gordon, Edmund T., 174

Greenwich Village, N.Y. City, 215

DATE DUE